Making Kitchen Cabinets

Making Kitchen Cabinets

A foolproof system for the home workshop

PAUL LEVINE

The Taunton Press

For my partner in this life—Janet, this one's for you.

Cover photo: Joseph Kugielsky
Text photos: Paul Levine and Taunton Press staff, except where noted

First printing: August 1988
Second printing: August 1989
Third printing: May 1990

International Standard Book Number: 0–918804–94–9

Library of Congress Catalog Card Number: 87-51674

Printed in the United States of America

A FINE HOMEBUILDING Book

FINE HOMEBUILDING® is a trademark of The Taunton Press, Inc.,
registered in the U.S. Patent and Trademark Office.

The Taunton Press
63 South Main Street
Box 5506
Newtown, Connecticut 06470-5506

Contents

Introduction

Why tackle a project as complex as building a kitchen, and why especially should you build the cabinets? There are lots of reasons, really, but two appeal to almost everyone: cost and quality. A new kitchen is an expensive undertaking. By making the cabinets yourself, you can save as much as 75% of what you might otherwise pay for a comparable commercially made kitchen. You can pocket the difference, or use it to buy better-quality materials. Whereas birch might have been all you could afford in manufactured cabinets, maybe you can consider walnut if you do the work yourself. Also, there's no limit to the intriguing design features you can include. Of course, if you enjoy making things with your hands, you won't need any other reason.

The cabinet system described in this book was inspired by the latest developments in European cabinetry. The cabinets themselves are not complicated, and their measurements have been standardized for maximum flexibility of design and ease of construction. The characteristic clean, crisp look of the European-style kitchen is derived mainly from the doors and drawer faces that cover the cabinets. These are sheathed in either high-pressure plastic laminate or wood veneer, and because they are separate from the cases, they are easily switched to effect a kitchen facelift. A new generation of hardware has evolved to facilitate this modular design. If you've never encountered a full-extension drawer slide or a 176° concealed cup hinge you'll be amazed at how pleasant they can be to install in the shop and to use in the kitchen. From the hardware to the machinery used to prepare the carcase stock, the European system is highly engineered and totally integrated.

Until recently, this style of cabinetmaking was practically unknown in North America. But with the growing impact of European design on this continent (along with significant changes in lifestyle), designers, architects and consumers have begun to demand the clean lines and functional advantages of a European-style kitchen. Unfortunately, many North American cabinetmakers and hardware manufacturers haven't caught up with their clients. They still build kitchens the old way—by constructing elaborately joined cases of traditional face-frame cabinets. The primary purpose of the face frames is to stiffen the cases, which are usually built of ½-in. or ⅜-in. sheet material. The European system employs ¾-in. stock, and once the cases have been glued and joined and the components assembled, the cabinets require no further bracing.

Over the last 10 years, I have adapted the European system for my own custom cabinet shop. I work mostly alone, and without the exotic computerized (and costly) machinery that was developed to suit the system—although it's there in force for those who want it, from simple drill-press jigs to fully automated leviathans. In this book, I will show you how I build kitchen cabinets using mainly a table saw, a router and a drill press.

Best of all, there are no compromises in design or quality. My adaptations preserve the system's logic and simplicity, but make it more accessible. The work is organized into a simple progression of tasks that a person with basic skills can accomplish. And I never assume perfection—each step anticipates and corrects any errors made in the previous procedure. By following this system or adapting it to your own needs, you can build first-rate cabinets—even better than the best you can buy. The custom features you include will add a look to your kitchen that is not available anywhere else.

How much will it cost?   Many factors will affect the final cost of your kitchen. Its size and the materials you use are two of the biggest variables, and they can double, triple or even quadruple the price tag. A smart shopper should be able to buy good-quality materials for about $50 per lineal foot, or $2,000 for a medium-sized kitchen (about 40 lin. ft. of cabinets). If you substituted less expensive materials, you could probably whittle the price down to about $1,200, or $30 per lin. ft. Comparable semi-custom cabinets, most likely of cheaper materials, would cost $8,000 to $12,000 (plus installation). Add to this the cost of a new range, refrigerator, dishwasher and sink—from $2,000 to $7,000—and you can appreciate the amount you'll save by doing the work yourself.

Don't despair if you can't afford your dream kitchen right now. You can always build the cabinets first—allowing space for the range, dishwasher or refrigerator of your choice—and put off purchasing the appliances until later. Purchase the sink and install it with the countertop, however, since it must be custom-fit. That exotic faucet can always be hooked up later.

How long will it take?   This depends largely on you. The planning and design phase can stretch out for years, or you can do it in a week. I'll assume you have access to a basic workshop equipped with a table saw, some hand tools, a router and a drill press. I'll assume also that you have basic woodworking skills, like the ability to cut simple joints on the table saw. Given these prerequisites, a medium-sized kitchen should take about three to four 40-hour weeks.

If you're doing the work in your spare time, of course, it will take much longer, but the job can easily be broken down into manageable tasks. From cutting stock to joining cases, making drawers, shelves, a countertop, backsplash and bases, you could probably complete the project in about 12 weekends, plus a week to install it. If you find yourself slipping behind schedule, you might work evenings during the week. When you plan your time, don't be overly optimistic. Most people overestimate their ability and underestimate the job. When it comes to the kitchen, your family (or clients) will be very disappointed if deadlines are not met. And if you want to enjoy the work and create a kitchen you're proud of, you'd be wise to allow yourself a full six months to build the cabinets.

Finally, remember that there are many skills involved in making kitchen cabinets—from designing the floor plan to finishing the cases. It is no loss of face to seek the help of a professional. (This is especially true when it comes to plumbing and electrical work.) There is no limit to how much work you can farm out, but the return will still be proportional to how much you put in. You can walk into a cabinet showroom and write a big check, but you may end up with a kitchen the salesman likes, not one you like.

You can expect to invest a good deal of effort in building your own cabinets, but the task is well within the range of anyone of moderate skill level. I have taught several workshops in which people without much prior training learned to make fine cabinets. For the most part, the work is a long path of small and easy steps, but I don't want to minimize the challenge. However easy a single step is, walking from Boston to Buffalo is a hard job.

PLANNING THE KITCHEN

Chapter 1

W hether you live to eat or eat to live, the space you call a kitchen can and should reflect your lifestyle. The beauty of the European system of cabinetry is that it is so easily adapted to radically different spatial requirements and design tastes. While traditional North American cabinet construction usually results in long runs of plywood cabinets held together with hardwood face frames, the simple carcase structure of the European system lends itself to small components and infinite variation in design.

Elegance needn't be complicated. Basically, my kitchens are aggregations of plywood boxes—many of them as small as 18 in. wide—screwed together in virtually any configuration imaginable. To these boxes are attached the drawer faces and doors that give each kitchen its distinctive look. The process is so rational that, although I usually work on only one kitchen at a time, I could easily build the components for two or more kitchens at once, and save time by ganging similar operations. Even if the two kitchens look completely different, many of their parts would be interchangeable.

By using such a flexible system to build your own kitchen (or to have it built for you), you will truly be able to tailor the space to your needs. Frequently, these needs are understood only on a subconscious level. To make the most of the space, you must take a close look at the way you use a kitchen. This may seem obvious, but it's surprising how many people charge ahead without taking stock. In this chapter, I'll describe the preliminary steps I follow to design the cabinets for a kitchen. The same process can be applied to any other room in the house, but the kitchen presents many more options and challenges. Although these design steps are generally applicable to any kind of cabinetry, the building system I have described in this book is so powerful that I can't imagine making cabinets any other way.

The way you prepare food in your kitchen is the single most important factor in determining its design. For example, elaborate cooking or baking requires much more space for equipment and food preparation than does simple "heat-and-serve" cuisine. The country kitchen that is used to can vegetables and fruits, bake pies and knead bread also calls for lots of work space and storage. The kitchen of a gourmet chef may resemble a workshop, with the craftsman's "hand tools" hung from racks and machine tools stored in nearby cupboards.

At the opposite end of the spectrum is the Spartan space of the single apartment dweller. Pursuing a career and a social life may reduce the demands on kitchen space to a survival level. At work during the day, out in the evening and asleep at night, this cook needs a kitchen in which things can be done quickly. Counter space and storage are minimal, appliances are placed close together,

If space allows, a kitchen table and chairs
can provide a comfortable space for eating
family meals, visiting with friends and other
daily activities.

and solo eating is often done on the fly, or perched on a stool at a counter.
Surely one of these people is the inventor of the microwave oven.

How you entertain family and friends also can affect the design. I am partial
to an eat-in kitchen, and my clients often request it. The table and chairs shown
in the photo above provide adequate space to enjoy family and meals. When
close friends come over, a lot of the visiting can take place around the table so
the cook won't be left out.

If your kitchen space won't allow for a separate table, you might consider a
peninsula (photo, facing page). By doubling as a workspace and eating counter, a peninsula takes up much less floor space than a table, yet serves many of
the same functions. And there is room for lots of storage in the drawers and
cabinets beneath the countertop.

If properly planned, the kitchen will be one of the best-lit rooms in the house.
This cheerful atmosphere, combined with the generous amount of countertop
workspace, makes it an ideal place to conduct activities unrelated to either

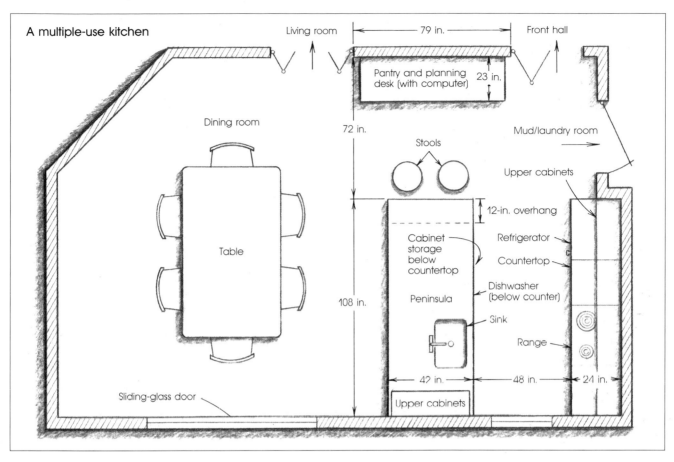

A multiple-use kitchen

Living room

79 in.

Front hall

Pantry and planning desk (with computer)   23 in.

Mud/laundry room

Dining room

72 in.

Stools

Upper cabinets

12-in. overhang

Cabinet storage below countertop

Refrigerator

Countertop

Table

Peninsula

Dishwasher (below counter)

108 in.

Sink

Range

42 in.

48 in.

24 in.

Sliding-glass door

Upper cabinets

If space is tight, a peninsula can serve several functions in a kitchen. This peninsula provides ample workspace, storage areas and an informal eating counter.

cooking or eating. A small dining table provides additional workspace for school projects, everyday accounting and carving pumpkins. But even if your kitchen won't accommodate a separate table, a small planning desk or sit-down work station may still be fashioned. A counter with no cabinets beneath works quite well for this purpose (photos at left and on the facing page).

With all the time spent cooking and cleaning in the kitchen will come the need to answer the telephone and take messages there. This often makes the kitchen the communications center of the home. What refrigerator isn't plastered with notes, lists, recipes and artwork? A corkboard for messages and a drawer to store the phone book, paper and pencils can make life a lot easier. A work light might extend the usefulness of a work station considerably, in which case you'll need an electrical outlet. (The outlet may also be used for small appliances, like an adding machine or a telephone-answering machine.) This is by no means a universal list of needs for such a family center, but it should give you an idea of how much thought goes into the planning. If you eventually decide to include a telephone or a work light, you'll be glad you provided for wiring before, rather than after, installing the cabinets. (For more on wiring and lighting, see pp. 12-13.)

For some of us, the standard kitchen is a handicap. Very tall or short people or those in a wheelchair will find 36-in. high cooktops and counters difficult, if not impossible, to use. The kitchen for a disabled cook must be even more carefully planned than a kitchen designed for normal reach and capacity. Until recently, there wasn't much information available concerning kitchen designs for the disabled. Happily, there are now various resources for such specialized information, a few of which I've listed on p. 186.

It is possible, of course, to build a kitchen without having a particular user in mind. Every builder must provide a kitchen, even if the house hasn't yet been sold, in which case the kitchen is designed for the mythical average family. The standards used by many builders and commercial designers, however, are based on information that is 10 to 30 years old, and some of it is outdated. You can take the safe approach of building the kitchen for some hypothetical user, but you may also have to store your pasta machine in the hall closet.

The extent to which your lifestyle molds your kitchen's design is not without limits. How long you will occupy your home should affect the extent to which you personalize your kitchen. A young couple starting a family will have different needs for space as the family grows, which may even cause them to move with each new child. Before you plunge into designing a highly personalized kitchen, consider how it will fit a prospective owner—or even yourself—several years down the road. While kitchen renovation is a good investment generally, too much customizing usually leads to a diminished value in resale.

Listing your needs   All the best thinking won't make a new kitchen unless there's some way of putting your thoughts to work. I've learned a lot from my wife about how to do that.

Janet is super-organized. She always has a list of things to do, and one by one they get done. Many of these lists find homes on the insides of the kitchen-cabinet doors, like little sentinels guarding Janet's wishes. When she was getting ready to enter the hospital to give birth to our second daughter, Jordana, Janet was on her way out of the house (her suitcase had long since been packed) when she realized in horror that with the cabinets closed, I wouldn't be able to see any of the lists. Soon after, I found the light of my eyes in the kitchen—writing a list of all her lists. This one was posted on the refrigerator, in plain view. I have learned from a great teacher that you can't make a kitchen without a list.

The needs list is the job of whoever uses the kitchen, and the more time spent compiling it, the more useful the kitchen will be. If you're a professional,

A telephone and small wall-mounted desk form a compact kitchen message center.

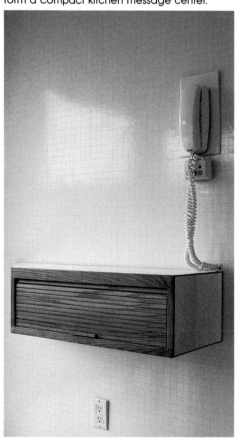

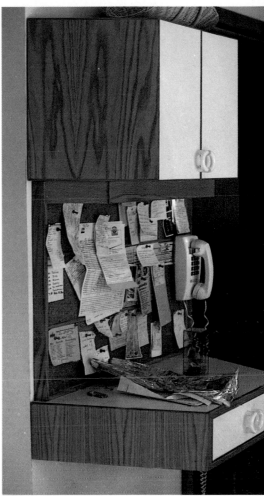

There are many ways to organize the telephone, cookbooks, notes and schedules. Clutter may be tacked on a corkboard or tucked away behind tamboured doors. Space beneath the counter lets you pull up a chair.

have your client make the list; otherwise make it for yourself (and make sure to include your whole family in the process).

The purpose of the needs list is to identify what the cabinets have to hold. Baking sheets, serving trays and cutting boards are best stored in shallow drawers or shelves. Pots, pans and large containers are bulky and will do better in deep drawers or shelves. It's not necessary to list every utensil you own, just the ones that are unusual or have never quite fit into your existing kitchen. Be sure to include the items you plan to get soon. Griddles and popcorn machines must be kept somewhere but aren't needed every day, so note how often they're used. The list will alert you to both workspace and electrical requirements. For example, if you have a professional mixer and the space to store it, do you have the counter space and an outlet to set it up and use it efficiently?

Don't forget to list major appliances: refrigerator, stove (this is sometimes broken down into a cooktop, or range, and separate oven), wall oven, microwave, freezer, sink, dishwasher and trash compactor. If you plan to reuse existing appliances, measure each one to make sure you allow enough space for them. If you're planning to replace one or more of the appliances, you'll want to select the new ones as soon as possible so that you'll be able to design the cabinets to fit. The host of new and improved appliances is endless, and dealers have specification sheets for all the major ones. These will give you not only the gross dimensions but also such information as side clearance, front clearance for door swing, electrical requirements, and plumbing and venting needs.

Also list the activities that will go on in the kitchen. If you eat only breakfast there, you'll need less space than if you eat all your meals in the kitchen. If you use part of the kitchen for an office or another special activity, put it on the list.

Once you make the list, keep it close at hand as the design progresses, and check it regularly to see that all needs are met. If the space available will not allow all that you've written down, the list will give you the items to choose from. You will then have to get out your red pencil and make adjustments.

After you've examined your lifestyle and composed your needs list, mentally place yourself in your dream kitchen and live through a day. Get up and walk around, look in the drawers, in the refrigerator. Pull out some favorite recipes and prepare your favorite dish from scratch. Make notes of the things you need while you "cook." This imaginary exercise will help you assign priorities to the items on your list, which will help you pare them down to meet reality.

Information and inspiration As soon as you have decided to build or remodel your kitchen, you should be looking around for ideas that strike your fancy. Magazines are the greatest source of up-to-date ideas in almost any field. Clip or copy anything that appeals to you. Some may contain a nice door style, others an attractive eating counter. I add to such a file regularly, and when I'm designing a new project I peruse my file for ideas.

Museums are another good source of ideas. Many museums include rooms from old houses, or are restorations of entire homes. Some even display full kitchens to demonstrate the latest in design and technology.

The showrooms of kitchen-cabinet manufacturers are another good place to glean ideas. These are usually advertised in the newspaper, and you can find them listed in your phone book. Showrooms often contain the latest equipment and styles. Most salesmen won't mind your looking around, but it would be unfair to monopolize their time if you've already decided to build your own kitchen. I usually tell them "I've just come to admire your cabinets," and I've found that most are friendly and glad for the chance to try and sell me the accessories. Moreover, in a showroom you'll be able to see design ideas rendered in three dimensions, instead of in a flat photo or drawing. This is invaluable if you have trouble visualizing.

There are a number of good reference materials available from the Department

A well-planned kitchen takes into account the available space, the habits of the cook, the budget, the user's lifestyle and personal taste.

of Housing and Urban Development (HUD), the Small Homes Council/Building Research Council and others. (Check the Resource Guide on p. 186 for their addresses.) Publications from these organizations contain many important ideas for layout and design. I have sifted through much of this material to add to my ideas in this book, but by going straight to the source, you may discover something interesting that I've neglected.

While you are taking advantage of the great fund of ideas that surround you, beware. There are many ill-conceived and poorly executed kitchens, often presented as a model from which to copy. Make sure any design you select satisfies your own criteria.

Principles of design

Shoving a kitchen's worth of cabinets into a room on a floor plan will not get you where you want to go. The process of designing a kitchen begins with setting broad goals and gradually progresses to working out the details of cabinet joinery. Once you've established your needs through the planning exercises described on pp. 8-10, you can further inform and modify them according to a few basic principles. Only then can you tackle the cabinet layout, which in turn must be broken down into cases that will be manageable to build and install. Finally, you'll have to determine and keep track of their dimensions. By proceeding in this fashion, it's possible to develop an efficient kitchen without much difficulty. The rest of this chapter won't turn you into an expert in kitchen design, but it should provide some useful guidelines.

We want to spend as little effort as possible when working in the kitchen so it's important to plan for the efficient use of space and materials. There are several ways to ensure an economical kitchen. One of these is to provide storage for food, dishes and kitchen tools as close as possible to where they will be used. This is sometimes referred to as a "first-use" approach, in which work flows smoothly and efficiently between storage space, appliance and countertop.

To figure out where the best places are for storage, ask yourself a few specific questions. What do you do when you're thirsty? Chances are you reach for a glass, then head either for the sink or the refrigerator. An appropriate place for storing glasses would therefore be somewhere near both, ideally between them. How do you prepare coffee? If you heat water on the range, storage for mugs, coffee and coffee filters should be nearby, along with a drawer for utensils. If you always use a coffee maker, an electrical outlet becomes the center of activity, not the range. Here's another example. When you park your car and grab the groceries, you should be as close to the kitchen door as possible. Once inside, you'll want a surface on which to place the bags. This should be near where most of the groceries will be stored. Keeping related uses close together will require some compromises, however. If you make the distance between the sink and the refrigerator too short, there won't be any countertop between them on which to set the glass when you're pouring the milk.

Another principle to consider is multiple use, which is exemplified by the peninsula shown in the drawing on p. 7. This peninsula provides workspace

Lighting, plumbing and electricity

The kitchen is probably the most complex room in the house—it's much more than just four walls and some cabinets. Besides the woodwork, the kitchen has specific lighting, plumbing and electrical needs. The details of wiring and plumbing are largely beyond the scope of this book (see p. 186 for some basic references on these subjects), but there are a couple of important points

that you should consider when you design your kitchen cabinets.

Lighting Frank Lloyd Wright frequently labeled his kitchen floor plans "Work Space," and that is exactly what a kitchen is. When you're handling hot pots or sharp knives, you must be able to see what you're doing. Sitting in a living-room chair, you can tilt or shift the position of a

Fluorescent lights mounted beneath the upper cabinets cast a soft, shadowless glow over the countertop. The sink is in the center of the run, where the other cabinets and appliances are easily accessible.

and storage, and a place to set incoming groceries. The countertop's slight overhang allows a tired cook to pull up a chair and sit while preparing food, and provides a place for informal family breakfasts. The cabinet below can hold pans for the range area and placemats for the dining area.

Your list of small appliances and other items to be stored will indicate a gross storage capacity. Other items, such as canned goods, will also have to be estimated. If your kitchen space is limited, you may have to provide additional storage elsewhere. The downstairs freezer, the separate pantry, and the cabinet in the dining room for the "good" dishes are a few common solutions. It's best to keep kitchen supplies in the kitchen, but if you've made the most of your available space and still come up short, then secondary storage makes sense.

Before putting pencil to paper, you will have to weigh your needs against a few of the generic functions that apply to most kitchens. Kitchen activity takes place in four major work zones: the sink, the range, the preparation area and the refrigerator. (Other areas, such as a barbecue or a planning desk, may be needed to accommodate individual cooking or work habits.) Each of these areas has its own requirements for work space and storage. The largest, busiest and most important area of the kitchen is the sink (drawing at right and photo on the facing page).

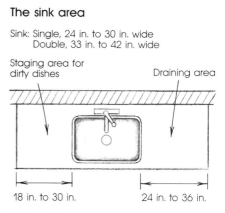

The sink area

Sink: Single, 24 in. to 30 in. wide
 Double, 33 in. to 42 in. wide

Staging area for dirty dishes

Draining area

18 in. to 30 in.

24 in. to 36 in.

This layout is typical for right-handed users. Lefties may want to reverse the staging and draining areas.

lamp so that its light suits the moment. Kitchen lighting isn't quite this versatile, so it has to be well planned.

A lighting engineer or architect can calculate the exact amount of light required for any room, taking into account square footage, ceiling height and the colors of the walls and cabinets. In most residences, however, it's cheaper to overlight than to hire a lighting professional. As a rule, I try to provide enough light for comfortable reading throughout the room, which generally works out to about 5 watts per sq. ft. If, for example, you are illuminating a 12-ft. by 15-ft. kitchen, you'll need about 900 watts. Assuming you could put the lights in the right places, you could get away with six 150-watt fixtures.

The proper distribution of light is at least as important as the quantity, and it's much more difficult to determine. Before locating a lighting fixture on the floor plan, think of where you will be in the room and what you will be doing when you are using that particular light. Make sure it isn't positioned so that your body will cast a shadow on your work. That's why there is usually a light over the sink, and one in the hood over the range. Many people mount fluorescent fixtures to the underside of the upper cabinets — they provide a shadow-free light that washes over the countertops (photo, facing page).

The success of any lighting plan is a function not only of the quantity and distribution of light, but also of its quality. What does this mean for the kitchen? For me, it means the use of incandescent

light and its warm reddish tones instead of the cool green of fluorescents. Although fluorescent tubes are available in warmer tones, these usually cost a lot more, and I still prefer incandescent light. In addition, incandescent lights can be controlled with inexpensive dimmers. Dimmers aren't common in a kitchen, but I think you'll enjoy their effect. After dinner when the coffee is on the table, you can turn down the work light and relax in a softer, more comfortable glow. Dimmers are also available for fluorescent lights, but they are much more expensive and require a motorized transformer.

I particularly like recessed spotlights. Equipped with specular aluminum reflectors, the lights don't glare and you can use ordinary bulbs. They suffuse a work area with soft light, rather than shine harshly on the countertop. They also can be put on dimmers (if the load is 600 watts or less per circuit).

Electricity   Your kitchen runs on electricity — the refrigerator, lights, toaster and dishwasher would all be useless without it. For your own safety and comfort, don't shortchange yourself in this department. Check your local building code and make sure you have enough power in the right places. Modern appliances are particularly dependent on electricity, so the kitchen should have plenty of outlets. The alternative is a countertop choked with snaking extension cords. Some large appliances, like the range, oven and refrigerator, should be on separate

circuits. You must do your homework when it comes to wiring — know the code and know your needs before you dive in.

Plumbing   As you'll no doubt discover about electricity, plumbing requires a grasp of a few basic principles, materials and local building codes. It is not impossible for the novice to learn, just time-consuming. If you're planning to build the cabinets, this may not be the right time to extend your resources. Plumbing mistakes are especially disheartening — water all over the floor, backed-up drains and leaks inside walls. What you will need to know depends on the extent of the changes. If you have to move a sink along with its supply lines, drain and vent, you'll need to know a lot. If you're just replacing the old sink but leaving the rest of the plumbing intact, the job isn't so tough.

The most important thing to remember, whether or not you do the work yourself, is to install a cutoff valve at every appliance and to the kitchen itself. That way, if any fixture springs a leak, you'll be able to stop the water without disrupting the supply to the rest of the house. I've seen houses with only one cutoff valve for the entire house. If anything went wrong, the whole house had to go without water until the problem was fixed. Go without water for two days and cutoff valves will begin to look cheap at twice the price. I prefer gate valves to the common globe valves. Gate valves are more expensive, but they will last many times longer while adding only slightly to the cost of the kitchen.

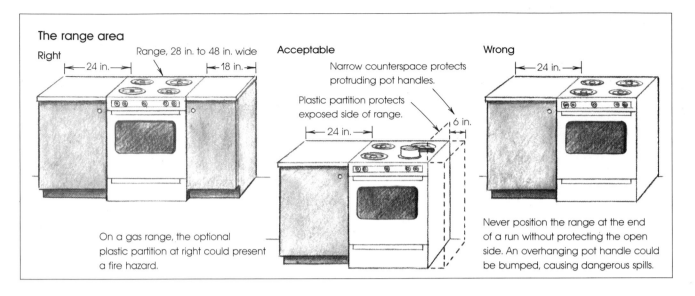

The range area

Right

24 in.

Range, 28 in. to 48 in. wide

18 in.

On a gas range, the optional plastic partition at right could present a fire hazard.

Acceptable

Narrow counterspace protects protruding pot handles.

Plastic partition protects exposed side of range.

24 in.

6 in.

Wrong

24 in.

Never position the range at the end of a run without protecting the open side. An overhanging pot handle could be bumped, causing dangerous spills.

The sink area The sink is used to wash food before preparation, to add water to recipes and to clean up. Nearly everything revolves around the sink, so it should be located as close to the center of your kitchen as possible. Ideally, the sink will have counter surface on both sides. One side is for stacking dirty dishes and utensils, the other drains them after they've been washed and rinsed. I've noticed that right-handed people usually do this work from right to left. If this is the way you operate, the counter to the right of the sink (the staging area) should be 24 in. to 36 in. wide, and the area to the left (the draining area) should be 18 in. to 30 in. wide.

Dishes also may be moved directly from the sink to a dishwasher. Conventional wisdom dictates that, for right-handed users, the dishwasher should be located to the right of the sink below the staging area (to the left for lefties), thus reducing the distance traveled. But my wife and I both prefer the dishwasher on the left with the staging area on the right, even though she's left-handed and I'm right-handed. So much for conventional wisdom.

The range area Safety is the most important consideration around the range, so the design guidelines for this part of the kitchen concern this issue more than they do convenience. The range should not be located near a window, because a sudden breeze might knock things over and pose a fire hazard. In fact, the entire area around the range should be fire resistant. Inevitably, pots of water will be left to boil and be forgotten, causing them to burn or melt. Grease in a pan can catch fire.

There should be at least 24 in. of heat-resistant counter surface on one side of the range for hot pots and pans, and about 18 in. on the other side. If the range is at the end of a run of cabinets, it should be protected so that an overhanging pot handle cannot be bumped. This is usually done with a small counter area or a heat-resistant partition, as shown in the drawing above.

Base cabinets and upper cabinets must be available around the range to hold cooking utensils, pots and pans, as well as foodstuffs that are frequently used at the range (tomato sauce, spices and the like). The upper cabinets should be at least 30 in. above the cooktop, to minimize the effect of heat on their undersides. If you have a range hood, it should be vented as directly as possible to the outdoors. A fire extinguisher should be stored near the stove but not behind it—if stove-top grease catches fire, you don't want to have to reach through the flames to get the extinguisher.

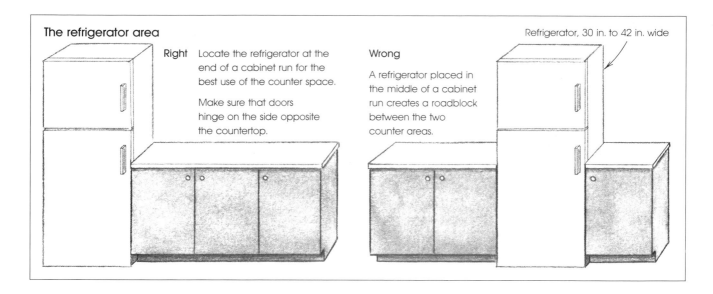

The refrigerator area

Right Locate the refrigerator at the end of a cabinet run for the best use of the counter space.

Make sure that doors hinge on the side opposite the countertop.

Wrong A refrigerator placed in the middle of a cabinet run creates a roadblock between the two counter areas.

Refrigerator, 30 in. to 42 in. wide

The preparation area The preparation area is where most of the action happens: mixing, dicing, slicing, carving. Although you may do these things in more than one location, you will probably have a single spot that you use most. This area should be between the range and the sink for maximum efficiency, and should be at least 36 in. to 42 in. wide. If you place the preparation area between the range and the sink, a total run of 60 in. will allow plenty of room to wash and chop vegetables, add them to a recipe and pop them into the oven. If the preparation area is on the other side of the sink, you'll have to take extra steps to deliver the food to the stove. For real efficiency, store spices and cooking utensils somewhere between the sink and the stove, above or behind the preparation area.

The refrigerator area The refrigerator is usually situated at the end of a line of cabinets simply because of its height. If it were in the middle of a run, it would form a functional roadblock between the two areas, as shown in the drawing above. (The same holds true for any cabinet that extends above the countertop, such as a pantry.) Plan on at least 15 in. to 18 in. of countertop next to the refrigerator, so you can park the pastrami while you're reaching for the rye. The refrigerator door should be hinged on the side opposite the counter so that you won't have to reach around it. Most, but not all, refrigerator doors are reversible.

The work triangle Of the four areas described above, the stove, sink and refrigerator are so closely related that their proper relationship is crucial to the success of the kitchen. This relationship is often referred to as the work triangle, or kitchen triangle, because a line connecting these areas on a floor plan frequently forms that shape. For an efficient plan, the perimeter of the triangle shouldn't measure more than 26 ft.; less than 23 ft. is even better. I'm not sure who first developed this rule of thumb, but it fosters a nice balance between efficiency and spaciousness.

Ideally, no household traffic should cross the work triangle—for safety and convenience, the cook deserves to remain undisturbed. As part of the design process, take a good look at the floor plans of adjacent rooms, as well as that of the kitchen itself, to see how traffic flows, and provide space for this traffic outside of the triangle. In order to achieve these objectives, some common arrangements have proven themselves worthwhile. The corridor, the one-wall

Basic kitchen layouts

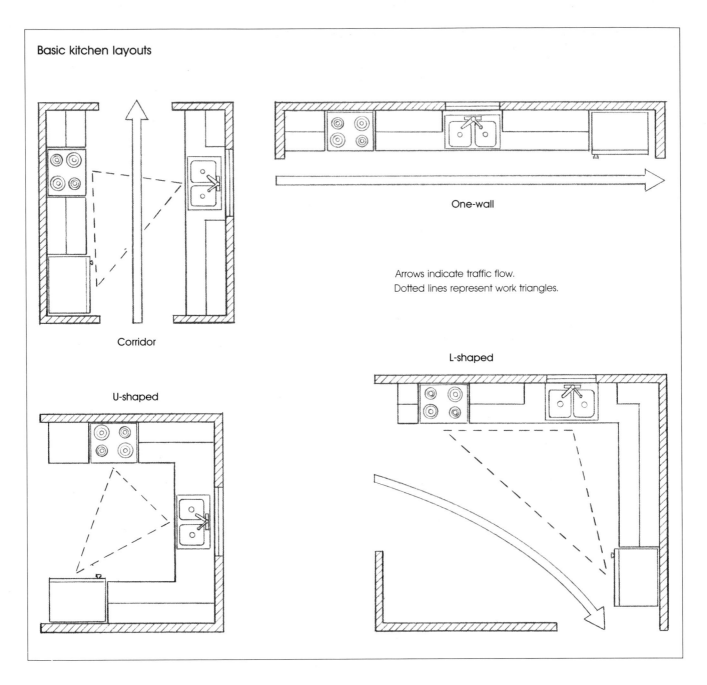

Corridor

One-wall

Arrows indicate traffic flow.
Dotted lines represent work triangles.

U-shaped

L-shaped

and the U-shaped or L-shaped kitchens shown in the drawing above are all viable layouts.

The corridor, or galley, kitchen is usually very small, but it's efficient because the work triangle is compressed. Used primarily in apartments and small houses, its two main drawbacks are the minimal amount of storage and work space, and the flow of traffic through the triangle.

The one-wall kitchen also has to deal with through traffic, but suffers an even greater problem. In order for a reasonable amount of storage and counter space to be provided, the ends of the one-wall kitchen have to be very far apart.

You can solve the problems of the corridor kitchen by closing off one end. Likewise, the one-wall kitchen can be improved by turning the ends of the cabinets into the room. In either case, the result is a U-shaped kitchen, which is one of the most efficient layouts. It effectively forms a dead end, down which nobody but the cook need travel. The L-shaped kitchen, which is a variation on the U, can be used if the shape of the room precludes the U shape.

Bear in mind that U-shaped and L-shaped kitchens are a little more complex to design than the others. In a corridor or one-wall kitchen you can just plot out the adjacent work areas, but wherever a cabinet run turns a corner, additional space must be allowed for clearance. You don't want the cook jammed into a corner, so allow at least 12 in. between the range or sink and a corner.

The floor plan The floor plan used to develop the kitchen design is a scale drawing of the kitchen as seen from above. It shows the location of walls, windows, doors and any other feature that might affect the placement of the cabinets. Use a tape measure to record their location. An easy way to make sure that the drawing contains lines that are straight and perpendicular to each other is to use graph paper.

The floor plan is an information tool, so it should include as much detail as you can bring to it. The swing of all doors should be indicated by an arc, as shown in the drawing on p. 7, which will be a visual reminder not to interfere with their movement. The scale that you use for the floor plan isn't critical, as long as it allows you to get all of the information onto one sheet of paper. I use either ½ in. = 1 ft. or 1 in. = 1 ft. Draw exterior walls to the scale equivalent of 6 in. thick (representing the drywall, studs, sheathing and siding). The interior walls should be 4½ in. thick (the studs plus ½-in. thick drywall on each side).

Once the floor plan is complete, check to see if the walls are straight and plumb, and if they are square to each other, as shown in the drawing on pp. 18-19. A string stretched from one end of a wall to the other can be used to check for straightness. (Use a nail or screw to hold the end of the string in place, and be sure to check at different heights along the wall.) A plumb bob and string (or a 4-ft. spirit level) will help you determine if the walls are plumb. If there is ½ in. or more between the string (or level) and the wall, and you can't correct the wall, record the dimension on your floor plan. The corners of the kitchen should be checked with a carpenter's square to see if they form a 90° angle. Note on the plan any major discrepancies. Later on, you'll have to take these into account when you install the cabinets. (If the walls are seriously out of whack, you should correct the problem before installing the cabinets.)

Beginning to design Once the floor plan is done (make sure to double check all your measurements), you can begin to play with some design ideas on paper. There are several ways to do this. The method you use isn't important, as long as it works. One popular method is essentially designing with an eraser. Simply draw a line on the floor plan, 24 in. inside of the wall, representing the inside edge of the countertop. Then erase the cabinets wherever there is a door or other obstruction and fill in the locations of the various appliances.

You can also place a length of semi-transparent tissue paper over the floor plan and sketch out some placement of appliances and cabinets that makes sense to you. (Architects and designers use a cheap vellum that comes in a roll.) Don't worry about actual dimensions at this point. When one sketch is done, roll out a fresh piece of tissue and sketch another idea. You can keep developing ideas, saving the previous ones, without having to redraw the floor plan. You could photocopy the original floor plan and sketch directly on it, but the impermanence of tissue seems to encourage people to draw freely. Try lots of different arrangements, even ones you think are impossible or too expensive to build. Try wall cabinets, peninsulas and islands. Be as creative as you can, and explore the possible without getting bogged down in reality just yet. Once you spot what looks like a promising design, refine it and trace the entire floor plan onto that tissue, then go ahead and do some more designing. As you're working, critique each sketch against your storage and workspace needs.

Another way to try out your design ideas is to make cardboard cutouts, or templates, of crucial work areas and appliances. These should be made to the same scale as the floor plan so you can slide them around the plan to try different configurations. Again, don't be afraid to experiment. When you find an arrangement that pleases you, trace around the templates to mark their location on the floor plan.

One way of evaluating your designs is to lay them out full size on your kitchen floor, using masking tape to outline the cabinets and appliances. Walk around the tape for a few days as if the cabinets were really there, and then change the tape to test the next design. But don't leave the tape on the floor for more than a few days—it develops an amazing affinity for vinyl flooring.

After you've mulled and sketched for a time, the design process may stall. This is where lots of people get frustrated. But rather than waste time forcing the design, I simply send it back to my subconscious, where it can simmer unattended. Then one day a full-blown idea will pop into my head. This can happen at any time, and if it occurs when I'm sleeping, I usually awaken. If I don't get up and sketch it, I may lose it altogether. The answers don't always come quickly, but they always come. My clipping file serves as a data base, and the more information fed into it, the greater the resources for my subconscious to draw on.

You may find that none of the tissue or template designs is quite right. If doors or other obstacles are in the way, consider moving or eliminating them (on paper, first). If that doesn't help, you may need to revise the floor plan by moving the walls themselves. Moving a wall can be tricky for the novice, so if you're not sure if you can tackle it, turn the work over to a professional.

How far to go? Getting the kitchen you want might involve replacing the cabinets, or it might mean changing the floor plan for the entire house. If you are satisfied with your existing kitchen layout but would like more up-to-date cabinets, you might get away with simply replacing the old doors and drawer faces. On the other hand, if your kitchen doesn't get morning sun, it might be worth moving it to the sunny side of the house. Likewise, a major job like moving the kitchen entry so that it's nearer the driveway may save 40 years of extra steps and is worth a bit of effort. Don't hesitate to consider major work if it will rectify serious problems.

When we remodeled our kitchen we stripped the room to the framing and changed the location of doors and windows. The old kitchen was plenty big

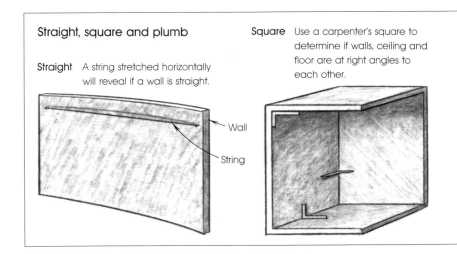

Straight, square and plumb

Straight A string stretched horizontally will reveal if a wall is straight.

Square Use a carpenter's square to determine if walls, ceiling and floor are at right angles to each other.

Wall

String

enough, but the layout left us with insufficient counter space and storage, and traffic circulation was terrible. By changing doors and windows we created a bright, cheerful space and tripled our counter and storage. (The plans for this kitchen are shown on pages 20 and 27.)

We solved some other problems, too. Built as a summer house during the 1940s when oil was very cheap, our house had only the barest of insulation. We tore off the old wallboard and installed new insulation and drywall. While the walls were open we were also able to make changes to the electrical wiring, adding circuits and moving outlets. Our plumbing was old, and was located on an exterior north wall. The pipes had frozen several times in the past, so we moved them to an interior wall, where they were protected from freezing. All this, combined with the new Thermopane windows, made a dramatic difference in the warmth, comfort and utility of the room. The renovation was significant, but we could have gone much further. The next step would have been to move the walls, and beyond that, add a room to the house.

When remodeling is in order, try to consider all the alternatives and ramifications. Adding on to the house may seem drastic, but compared to moving to a new house in order to get what you want, it's not so bad. If the cost of the addition will be high and your house is in a neighborhood of similar old homes, you may be investing poorly. But if your house is on a lovely site in a good neighborhood or is well situated for commuting, you may wish to stay there regardless of the cost. Whatever your circumstances, don't hesitate to attack the really serious problems. Spending money on new cabinets and ending up with an inferior space is a poor investment indeed.

Getting design assistance If you do choose to add to the house (or even to make a significant renovation), careful consideration should be given to getting professional help. There are qualified specialists who can help you, but take care how you choose. The right person can help fulfill your dreams, but the wrong person will make the project a nightmare. Designers may be certified or licensed by their respective professional associations, but the best way to tell if they can do the job you want is to look at kitchens they have designed.

If you want help designing the space, but not the cabinets, a Certified Kitchen Designer (CKD) can translate your needs into a working kitchen. You can also get help from an interior designer or architect who specializes in kitchens. Design fees vary, but you can expect to pay from $500 to $1,000 for a floor plan. If you want a perspective rendering of the space, you will pay another $500 to $1,000. Other sources of design assistance are listed on p. 186

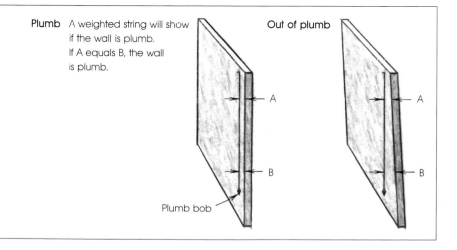

Plumb A weighted string will show if the wall is plumb. If A equals B, the wall is plumb.

Out of plumb

A

B

Plumb bob

A

B

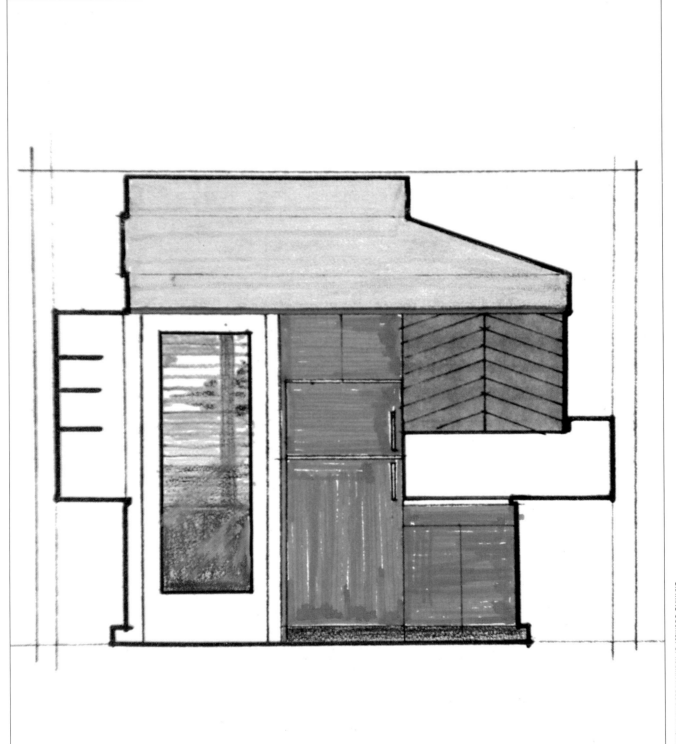

DESIGNING THE CABINETS

Chapter 2

In the home, technology appears in many guises—from microchip amusement centers to synthetic foods. But it's tough to think of any place in the home that has become as thoroughly enmeshed in technology as has the kitchen. When electricity entered the home, it landed with greatest impact in the kitchen. Out with the icebox, in with the fridge. Gone the woodstove, enter the microwave. Likewise, the relatively recent introduction of modern materials, like plastic laminate, has changed not only the way the kitchen looks, but also how well it works and how long it lasts.

For the cabinetmaker, new materials have ushered in another technological revolution. At its heart is the 32mm system, which was developed to rebuild whole cities in post-war Europe. Faced with the extraordinary task of replacing so many kitchens at once, European engineers devised an integrated system of hardware, materials and machinery. Typically, 32mm construction begins with a stack of plastic-laminated plywood panels, which are cut to size and then automatically bored with a grid of 5mm, 10mm and 35mm holes. The holes are placed on 32mm centers, which gives the system its name. These holes provide multiple options for mounting all of the hinges, drawer slides and other hardware required. Other machines apply edge-banding to the panels, and still others install the hardware. The finish is applied by robot arms, and the components are assembled into cabinets.

Sometimes the hardware and panels are shipped knocked-down in flat cartons to the job site, where they will be installed. The hardware is designed so that the "cabinetmaker" need only unpack and assemble the cases using a screwdriver. The system is so cleverly conceived that I am convinced we have not even scratched the surface of its applications. If NASA had to build a kitchen, I bet it would use the 32mm system.

The cornerstone of the system is the concealed hinge, or cup hinge. Instead of fastening to the surface of the door and face of the cabinet like a standard leaf hinge, or flap hinge, the cup portion of the hinge is mortised into the back of the door, and a separate base plate is screwed to the inside wall of the cabinet carcase. Once installed, the hinge is adjusted with two setscrews, in less time than it takes to remove one screw from a conventional leaf hinge. The cup hinges I like to use allow a door to swing open almost 180°, making the contents of the cabinet fully accessible. What's more, the hinge performs its magic hidden completely from view. The first time you see these hinges they may look ugly, but after you've used them for a while you'll appreciate their beauty. (Hardware is described in greater detail in Chapter 3.)

The real strength of the 32mm system lies in its flexibility and utter simplicity. There are no glitzy items for show, just solid details that enhance the function of the cabinets, as well as their looks. Although the drawers and doors vary in width and placement, case parts are standardized, which makes them easy to assemble—a side of one cabinet may be used in another cabinet, or a left side exchanged for a right. Sometimes the components can even be used upside down. The doors and drawer faces are completely independent of the casework they conceal, allowing the designer to change the look of the kitchen with a minimum of fuss—wood doors can be substituted for plastic ones, trimmed ones for untrimmed ones, red ones for white ones. The faces become a platform on which designers can express themselves—in much the same way that artists use canvases. Consider these possibilities as you begin to give shape to the cabinets on your floor plan.

Breaking runs into cabinets   Once you have a layout you like, the long runs of casework must be divided into cabinets. Individual units make the casework flexible. If one case is too small or if you want to change it in some way, it's easy to pull it out of the line. This is impossible when you're restricted to long, continuous cases. Besides, hauling around large cases is likely to damage something—the case at least, and possibly your back. Smaller units can be made, finished, stored, moved and installed much more easily.

I treat each straight run of cabinets separately, usually starting at the sink (or other dominant appliance in the run). To allow space for installation hardware, the inside dimensions of the sink case should be 4 in. to 8 in. wider than the sink. (Apart from the fact that the sink case receives a drawer face but no drawer, it is identical in construction to all of its neighbors.) The dishwasher typically is placed next to the sink for convenient operation and for access to the same drain and water supply. It will take up the full 34½-in. height under the counter, and should fit in a 24-in. wide space. If there are no other appliances in this run, the rest of the cabinets can be figured out quite easily.

Measure the remainder of the run and divide it into equal units, 13 in. to 19 in. wide, making sure to allow for adjacent runs of cabinets (drawing, facing page). This dimension represents the approximate width of doors and drawer faces, and I aim for 15 in. or 16 in. A 12-in. wide case is rather narrow for storage, while a door that is wider than 19 in. will intrude into the kitchen too much when open. Large doors are also heavy, and will eventually wear out their hinges and sag.

The cases themselves can be made to accommodate at least one drawer and one or two doors. For ease of handling, I make my cases no more than

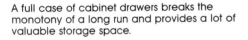
A full case of cabinet drawers breaks the monotony of a long run and provides a lot of valuable storage space.

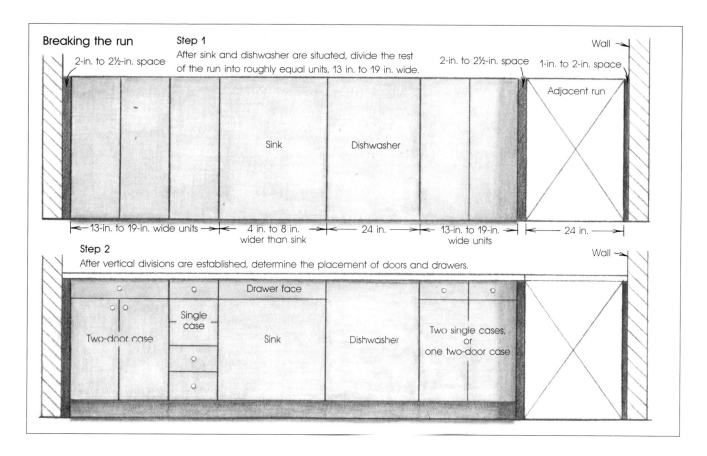

Breaking the run

Step 1

After sink and dishwasher are situated, divide the rest of the run into roughly equal units, 13 in. to 19 in. wide.

2-in. to 2½-in. space

2-in. to 2½-in. space   1-in. to 2-in. space

Wall

Adjacent run

Sink

Dishwasher

|← 13-in. to 19-in. wide units →|← 4 in. to 8 in. wider than sink →|← 24 in. →|← 13-in. to 19-in. wide units →|← 24 in. →|

Step 2

After vertical divisions are established, determine the placement of doors and drawers.

Wall

Drawer face

Two-door case

Single case

Sink

Dishwasher

Two single cases, or one two-door case

38 in. wide. As shown in the drawing on p. 24, cases up to 19 in. wide get a single door. Larger cases—up to 24 in. wide—can have one wide door or two narrow doors of equal width. A very wide case—say 38 in.—either gets two 19-in. doors, or it may be broken into a 25½-in. two-door case and a 12½-in. one-door case, with all the doors slightly over 12 in. wide. In most situations, I prefer one wide case with two doors, because it provides unobstructed access to its contents when both doors are open.

On a single-door case, the door may be hinged from either side. I usually hinge the door on the right side when the case is to the right of the sink, and on the left side when it is to the left of the sink. On a two-door case, one door is hinged from each side. For uniformity, I like to place a drawer at the top of each case. There is only one drawer on a single-door case, while a two-door case may have a small drawer over each door or one wide drawer over both doors, as shown in the drawing on p. 24. (Remember that you can attach any number of faces to a single drawer to correspond with the doors in the case, or with other cases in the run.)

I like my kitchens to be balanced. A very wide cabinet next to a skinny one might look funny, while two of about the same size would go together nicely. Sometimes, however, a kitchen with all drawers on top, all doors below, and all door widths the same is monotonous. Breaking up a run of cabinets with a case of drawers does wonders for the look of the kitchen (photo, facing page), and offers valuable storage for small paraphernalia.

To simplify production and for the sake of consistency, I try to make the upper cabinets the same width as the lower cases, but this can only be done in straight runs. Because I make my lower cases about 11 in. deeper than the uppers, wherever a run turns a corner, the adjacent run of upper and lower

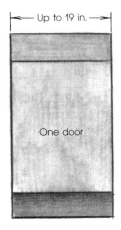

|← Up to 19 in. →|

One door

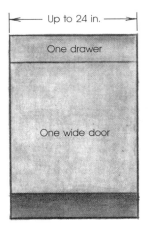

|← Up to 24 in. →|

One drawer

One wide door

One drawer

Two narrow doors

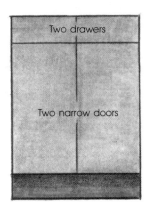

Two drawers

Two narrow doors

Cases up to 19 in. wide
get a single door.

Cases up to 24 in. wide may have
one or two doors and drawers.

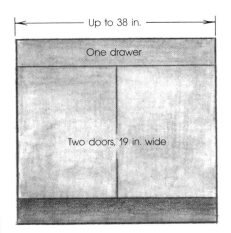

|← Up to 38 in. →|

One drawer

Two doors, 19 in. wide

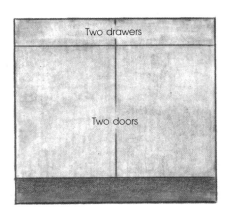

Two drawers

Two doors

Cases up to 38 in. wide may have two large doors and
drawers (above) or may be divided into separate units (below).

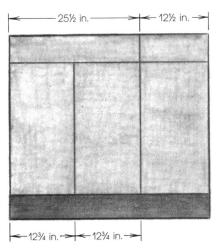

|← 25½ in. →|← 12½ in. →|

|← 12¾ in. →|← 12¾ in. →|

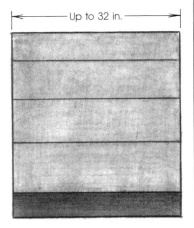

|← Up to 32 in. →|

Multiple drawers or drawer faces

cases will start at different places. This discrepancy can be handled in several ways. You can cut the corner between runs of upper cases with a diagonal cabinet and door, or you can install an 11-in. wide cabinet in the corner, as shown in drawing A at right. If neither of these solutions is appealing, you can always make up the difference by increasing the width of the corner case in the upper run (B) or by distributing the 11-in. difference equally across all the upper cabinets (C).

Which arrangement you select depends on personal preference and the layout of the particular kitchen. If the kitchen is large enough to afford a full view of both upper and lower cabinets, I generally try to match them as shown in solution A. In a narrower kitchen, though, I would probably settle for arrangement B or C.

At the end of a run, where the cases turn a corner, I allow 2 in. to 2½ in. for an L-shaped spacer, as shown at left in the drawing below. Without it, a drawer at the end of one run would skim the surface of the cabinets in the adjacent run, and perhaps even bump into the pulls. The L-shaped spacer is made of the same material as the cabinet doors and is screwed to 1x1 braces attached to the sides of the cases.

If a case does not start at the corner but extends into the dead space, as shown at right in the drawing below, it is called a blind-corner cabinet. In this case, I still use the L-shaped spacer, but one leg of the L is mounted to the face of the blind-corner cabinet. The other leg is mounted, as usual, to the end of the adjacent run of cases.

Likewise, wherever a run of cases fits between two walls, I allow a couple of inches at both ends for a starting and ending spacer, as shown in the drawing on p. 26. If you make the cabinets the exact length of the opening they may not fit, either because the walls are not plumb or because they are not square to one another. Install the cases first, and then make the spacers to fit. If you have a peninsula or a run of cases that starts at one wall and is open at the other end, spacers are usually not necessary.

It's important to remember that the cases are always made square—even if the walls are out of plumb. Any discrepancies are easily accommodated with the spacers. This system saves time both in building the cabinets and in installing them, and results in a neater job. (The construction and installation of spacers is discussed in greater detail in Chapter 11.)

Matching upper and lower cases

A. Cut the corner with a diagonal cabinet, or add an 11-in. wide case.

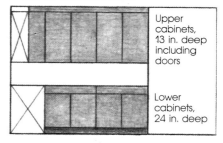

Upper cabinets, 13 in. deep including doors

Lower cabinets, 24 in. deep

B. Increase the width of the corner case.

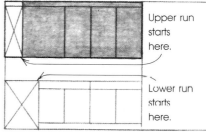

Upper run starts here.

Lower run starts here.

C. Distribute difference across all upper cases.

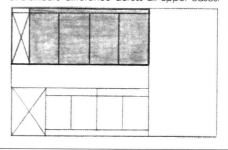

L-shaped spacers (top view)

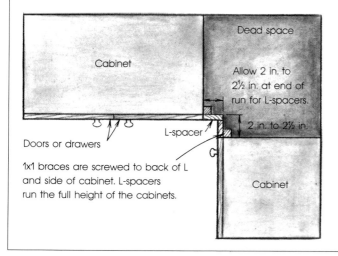

Cabinet

Dead space

Allow 2 in. to 2½ in. at end of run for L-spacers.

2 in. to 2½ in.

L-spacer

Doors or drawers

1x1 braces are screwed to back of L and side of cabinet. L-spacers run the full height of the cabinets.

Cabinet

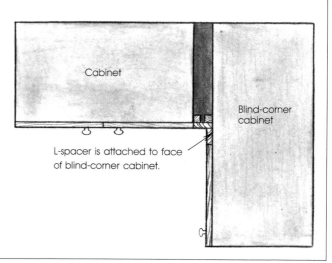

Cabinet

Blind-corner cabinet

L-spacer is attached to face of blind-corner cabinet.

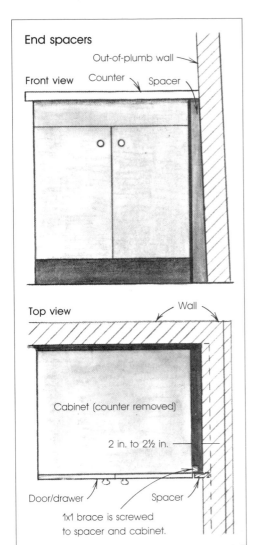

End spacers

Front view

Out-of-plumb wall

Counter

Spacer

Top view

Wall

Cabinet (counter removed)

2 in. to 2½ in.

Door/drawer

Spacer

1x1 brace is screwed
to spacer and cabinet.

The final plan and elevations When you have decided on a floor plan that meets your needs and the cabinets have been divided into individual units, front-view elevations can be drawn to see how the kitchen will look. The drawings shown on the facing page were done by an architect and, although they do an excellent job of conveying the look and feel of the kitchen, yours need not be so elaborate.

An elevation should be drawn for every wall that will contain new cabinets. It takes time to do this, but it's the best way to judge how the kitchen will really look. The elevations should be drawn to the same scale as the floor plan, and should include all wall features, existing and proposed: cabinets, windows, outlets, switches, doors, beams and columns. To aid in drawing the elevations, sketch the outlines of the wall first, then lightly mark horizontal lines to represent the height of the countertop (typically 36 in. from the floor), the bottom of the upper cabinets (typically 54 in. from the floor) and any other major features, like the top and bottom of windows or doorways. When locating windows and doors, be sure to include their moldings. Now all you have to do is mark vertical lines to delineate the cabinets and appliances.

Don't expect to sit down one evening and come up with a good design. Even after you think you have one, live with it for a few days. Designing should be fun, so don't rush it. And making mistakes is part of the process, so why not make them on tissue first? If you need help with the drawing, one of the most useful books I've found is *Architectural Drawing & Light Construction*, by Edward J. Mueller.

Shop drawings Once the widths of the cabinets have been determined and I've decided how to fit them with doors and drawers, I make freehand shop drawings of each case. These needn't be fancy, but they should include the dimensions of the individual carcase pieces and the joints, as shown in the drawings on pp. 28-29. I sketch two front views for each case—one showing doors and drawers and another showing carcase joinery. (I don't generally draw the top view because it conveys only the cabinet depth, which is a constant 23 in. for base cabinets and about 12 in. for uppers (not including doors), but you might find it useful if you're just starting out.) The drawings record in detail how the cabinets will be made, and help me estimate the materials needed to do the job. In this section, I'll describe my basic shop drawings. You may want to familiarize yourself with them now and refer to them later, when you know more about hardware, materials and cabinet construction.

I start by labeling the overall outside dimensions on the front and top views of each case. Then I assign measurements to the individual parts of the cabinet. I make my standard counters 36 in. high—30 in. for the base cases, 4½ in. for the kick plate and 1½ in. for the countertop, as shown in the drawing on p. 29. The plywood sides of the base cases are 30 in. high by 22½ in. wide. (The full depth of the case is 23 in., including a ¼-in. back and ¼-in. facing.) The bottom and top of the case will have the same 22½-in. depth. For the width of the bottom and top, subtract ¾ in. from the overall width of the case to account for the joints (⅜ in. for each joint). For example, on the 24-in. wide case in the drawings on pp. 28-29, the bottom and top will be 23¼ in. wide. The back should be the full 24-in. width of the case by its full 30-in. height. (I label my base cases B1, B2, B3 and so on, proceeding sequentially from one end of the kitchen. Upper cases are labeled U1, U2, U3 and so on. These labels are transferred from the drawing to the cutting list and, later on, may be marked on the case pieces themselves.)

Upper cases are treated in the same way, except that their dimensions are different. I generally make my upper cases between 11½ in. and 13 in. deep (including the trim and back), depending on the client, and between 30 in. and 40 in. high, as shown in the drawings on pp. 29. (I allow a few inches of space

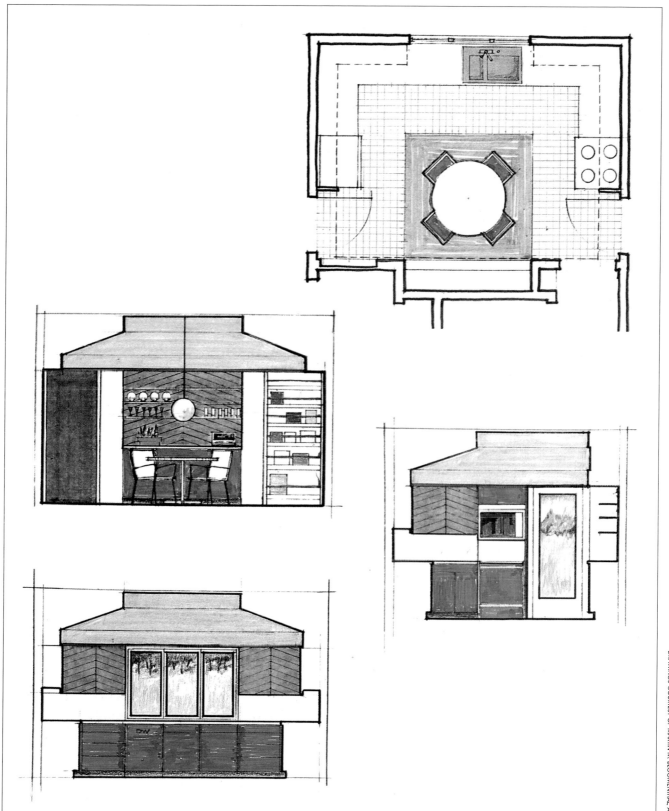

DRAWINGS COURTESY OF MARTIN M. BLOOMENTHAL, AIA

Shop drawing of standard base case

Front view

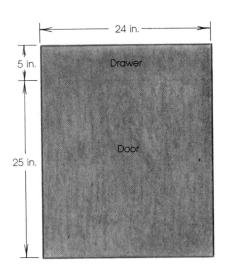

24 in.

5 in.

Drawer

Door

25 in.

Arrows represent grain direction.

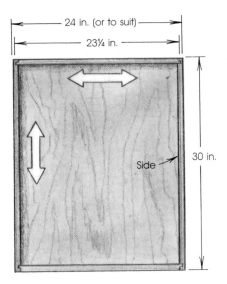

24 in. (or to suit)

23¼ in.

Side

30 in.

All standard base cases are 23 in. deep, 22½ in. without back or edging.

Top view (with back and edging)

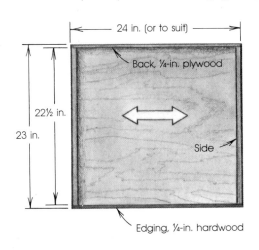

24 in. (or to suit)

Back, ¼-in. plywood

22½ in.

23 in.

Side

Edging, ¼-in. hardwood

Corner-joint detail

¾ in.

⅜ in.

¼ in.

¾ in.

½ in.

Shop drawing of standard upper case

Front view

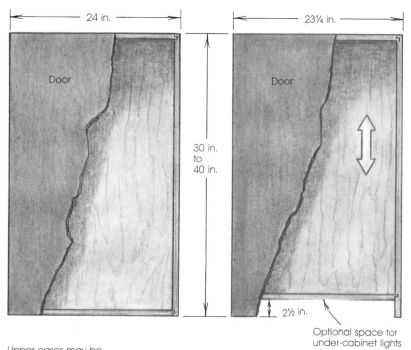

24 in.

Door

30 in. to 40 in.

23¼ in.

Door

2½ in.

Optional space for under-cabinet lights

Upper cases may be 11½ in. to 13 in. deep, depending on the kitchen.

Top view

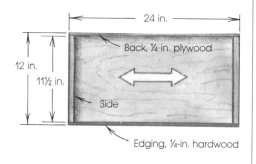

24 in.

12 in.

11½ in.

Back, ¼-in. plywood

Side

Edging, ¼-in. hardwood

Standard cabinet anatomy, section through case

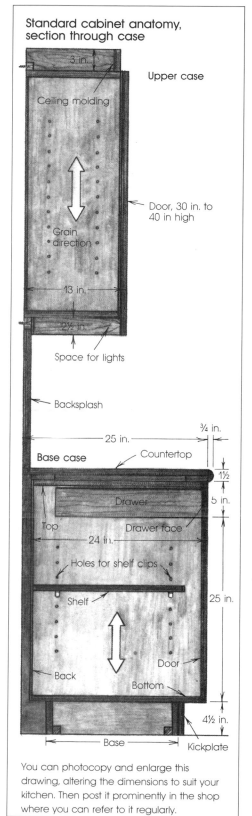

3 in.

Upper case

Ceiling molding

Door, 30 in. to 40 in. high

Grain direction

13 in.

2½ in.

Space for lights

Backsplash

25 in.

¾ in.

Base case

Countertop

1½

Drawer

5 in.

Top

Drawer face

24 in.

Holes for shelf clips

Shelf

25 in.

Door

Back

Bottom

4½ in.

Base

Kickplate

You can photocopy and enlarge this drawing, altering the dimensions to suit your kitchen. Then post it prominently in the shop where you can refer to it regularly.

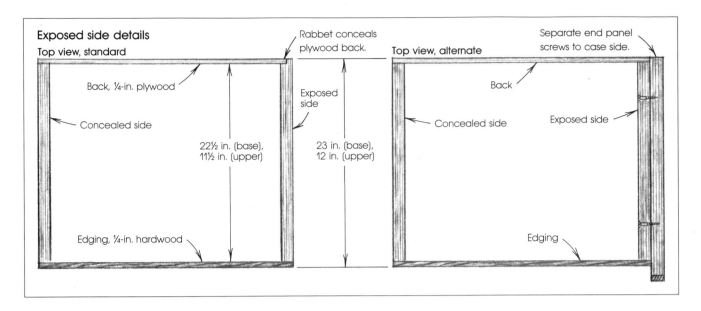

Exposed side details

Top view, standard

Rabbet conceals plywood back.

Separate end panel screws to case side.

Top view, alternate

Back, ¼-in. plywood

Concealed side

Exposed side

22½ in. (base), 11½ in. (upper)

23 in. (base), 12 in. (upper)

Back

Concealed side

Exposed side

Edging, ¼-in. hardwood

Edging

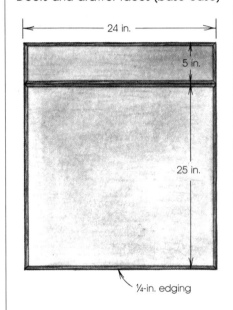

Doors and drawer faces (base case)

24 in.

5 in.

25 in.

¼-in. edging

Drawer face
Nominal dimension: 5 in. by 24 in.
Subtract ³⁄₃₂-in. allowance: $4^{29}/_{32}$ in. by $23^{29}/_{32}$ in.
Subtract ½-in. edging for final plywood
dimension: $4^{13}/_{32}$ in. by $23^{13}/_{32}$ in.

Door
Nominal dimension: 25 in. by 24 in.
Final plywood dimension: $24^{13}/_{32}$ in. by $23^{13}/_{32}$ in.

Hardwood edging
13 lin. ft. or more

for molding between the tops of the cabinets and the ceiling, to match the kick plate at the bottom, and include an optional 2½-in. space beneath the cabinets for lights.) Most commercially made upper cabinets are 30 in. high, a measurement that is derived by default rather than by design. It is determined by subtracting the height of the base cabinets (36 in.) and the backsplash (18 in.) from the height of the top of the trim that surrounds interior doors (84 in.). With houses costing between $50 and $100 per sq. ft., arbitrarily wasting all the space above the door trim is extravagant. I prefer to make use of this space by building taller cabinets. Although this adds somewhat to the cost of the cabinets and the space may be difficult to reach, I consider it much more economical than having to build extra storage elsewhere.

On cases that have one side exposed, like the end cabinet in an L-shaped kitchen, the exposed side can be made deeper to cover the back, as shown at left in the drawing above. Increase the width of the exposed side of the base case to 22¾ in. (11¾ in. for an upper case) to provide room for a rabbet that will conceal the ¼-in. thick back of the cabinet. (The width of the concealed side of the case remains 22½ in.) If both sides of the cabinet will be exposed, as in a peninsula, both sides of the case can be made 22¾ in. deep. Most of the time, however, I prefer to cover the exposed side of the end case with a separate panel, as shown at right in the drawing above. It takes a bit more material, but this method saves time and minimizes errors by allowing me to make all the cases the same—the extra panel is screwed on from the inside after the cases are built.

The next sketch you'll make for each cabinet provides the details of the doors and drawer faces. These must be slightly smaller than the case to leave clearance for opening and closing. I simply make each face ³⁄₃₂ in. less than the full height and width of the case, as shown at left. Thus, the drawer face that is nominally 5 in. high by 24 in. wide will measure $4^{29}/_{32}$ in. high by $23^{29}/_{32}$ in. wide. The door, which is nominally 25 in. high, will measure $24^{29}/_{32}$ in. high by $23^{29}/_{32}$ in. wide. If the same case were to receive two 12-in. wide doors and drawers, I would reduce the width of each face by ³⁄₃₂ in. (resulting in $11^{29}/_{32}$-in. wide doors and drawer faces). This allows enough room to adjust the faces later on, yet doesn't look awkward.

To determine the actual plywood dimensions of a face, you have to deduct the thickness of the edging from the overall dimensions. (Traditional frame-

and-panel doors do not require edging.) I usually use ¼-in. thick hardwood edging around the perimeter of each plywood face, so the actual plywood dimensions are ½ in. less than the dimensions that were determined for clearance. Taking this into account, the plywood drawer face will measure 4¹³⁄₃₂ in. by 23¹³⁄₃₂ in., and the door will be 24¹³⁄₃₂ in. high by 23¹³⁄₃₂ in. wide. The size of the edging may be increased if you incorporate a molded pull into the face, and this is described in greater detail in Chapter 8. If you edge your faces with plastic laminate instead of solid wood, allow about ¹⁄₁₆ in. for each edge.

Once I've completed the sketches for each set of faces, I add the approximate dimensions of the drawers and shelves. I make all top drawers 3½ in. high by 20 in. deep, with an overall width 1¹⁄₁₆ in. less than the inside width of the case to allow for the slides. For interior shelves, I allow ⅛ in. overall for the supporting clips. (See Chapter 3 for more on drawer and shelf hardware and Chapter 7 for drawer construction.)

Bases, kick plates and ceiling moldings are drawn last. They can be laid out on a copy of the floor plan, and are frequently cut from leftover material. Spacers are cut oversize and trimmed to fit after the cases have been installed. Likewise, I never cut the stock for shelves, doors, drawers and drawer faces until after the cases have been built. That way, I can accommodate any errors that may have resulted from variations in the materials or mistakes in construction.

After all dimensions have been logged, I identify each plywood part with a grain-direction arrow. When I cut the plywood, the arrows will remind me how to orient the case parts within each sheet. When a job is done and I'm finished with the drawings, I check the actual measurements of each cabinet and add them to the file I keep for each job under my client's name. Later on, if I have to add a shelf to one of the cases, I won't have to go to the site to measure it.

Cutting list   When you've made a drawing for each case (you need only one drawing if two or more cases are the same), you're ready to make the cutting list. A sample is shown at top right. I use ¾-in. plywood for all case parts except for the backs, which are ¼ in. thick. Since my standard base-case sides, top and bottom are all 22½ in. wide (standard upper-case pieces are 11½ in. wide), I simply record their lengths, and then figure out how best to cut them out of the sheets of plywood.

At this point, you must decide if you will use plywood for the tops of the base cabinets or construct solid-wood frames. I do both. The main advantage of using a frame is that the case will be lighter and easier to handle. You can just reach down into the top of the open case and grab the frame to carry or move it. You'll also save money on materials if you build frames—I use poplar because it is cheap and I can get clear stock. The drawback to using frames is that they take longer to make. But if you have a plate-joining tool such as the Lamello, or if you are good with dowel joints, the work goes quickly. If you decide to build frames, make them slightly oversize. You can trim them to their final dimension at the same time that you cut up your plywood (using the same saw setting). Once the frames have been made, they are treated just like plywood. If you elect to make plywood tops, just figure them into your cutting list.

To determine the actual amount of plywood I'll need, I block out the dimensions of each case part on a drawing of a 4x8 sheet, as shown at right, making sure to observe all grain-direction arrows on my earlier sketches. I always order a bit more plywood than I think I'll need—maybe 11 or 12 sheets, if the drawings call for 10—in case I make a mistake, or the customer wants an extra cabinet. (I can always use the leftover plywood on the next job.) Even after the cabinets are made and installed, I've sometimes had to lower or raise them several times to get the height just right, so it's handy to have some extra stock around. Remember that kitchen design is an organic process that goes on until you walk out the door for the last time—or maybe even after.

Cutting list

TOP AND BOTTOM (2 PIECES, ¾ IN. STOCK):
  22½ IN. WIDE BY 23¼ IN. LONG

SIDES (2 PIECES, ¾ IN. STOCK):
  22½ IN. WIDE BY 30 IN. LONG

BACK (1 PIECE, ¼ IN. STOCK):
  24 IN. WIDE BY 30 IN. LONG

EDGING (¼ IN. BY ¹³⁄₁₆ IN. STOCK):
  9 LIN. FT. OR MORE

NOTE: IF THE BOTTOM OR THE SIDES OF THE CASE ARE LAMINATED, MAKE THE EDGING ABOUT 1 IN. WIDE TO ACCOMMODATE THE EXTRA THICKNESS.

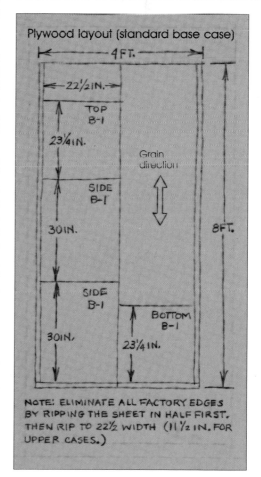

Plywood layout (standard base case)

4 FT.

22½ IN.

TOP
B-1

23¼ IN.

Grain direction

SIDE
B-1

30 IN.

8 FT.

SIDE
B-1

30 IN.

BOTTOM
B-1

23¼ IN.

NOTE: ELIMINATE ALL FACTORY EDGES BY RIPPING THE SHEET IN HALF FIRST, THEN RIP TO 22½ WIDTH (11½ IN. FOR UPPER CASES.)

HARDWARE

Chapter 3

f the case and face of a European-style cabinet are its skeleton and skin, the hardware is its heart. Seldom seen and less frequently adjusted, well-engineered hardware is what makes the system tick. Despite the fact that this hardware was developed hand in hand with the 32mm system of production, it is readily available to North American cabinet-makers—professionals and amateurs alike. Whether or not you use the machinery and design of the 32mm system, the hardware will be most useful.

The hardware I use is manufactured by several different companies (see the Resource Guide on p. 185 for their names and addresses), but they all share one critical feature—quality. Wherever it comes from, top-quality hardware will make your cabinets a pleasure to use, and will add greatly to their value. If you make cabinets for a living, fine hardware is like a good partner. If you are making your own kitchen, use the best hardware you can afford. Whatever you save by buying cheap hardware will be more than offset by having to replace it, adjust it or simply live with it.

If you're still inclined to skimp here and there and figure that cut-rate hinges or drawer slides won't make that big a difference, consider the experience I had with one of my customers. Robert put off building his cabinets until he needed them so badly that he couldn't wait for my order of drawer slides to arrive. "Build them with anything," he said, so I substituted a less substantial product. He got his cabinets alright, but when he saw the difference in the quality of the slides, he wanted the cheaper ones removed, and paid me to install the ones I'd ordered. The first set of slides is now stashed in a closet.

While this lesson appears to have been lost on most North American manufacturers, others around the world—notably the Japanese and Europeans—have been quick to pick it up. "Made in Japan," which was once synonymous with "cheap," now implies quality, whether it's from Honda, Nikon or Sony. Likewise, in the field of high-quality kitchen hardware, Europeans have effectively captured the market. Most of the hinges I use are of Austrian or German manufacture. Grass and Blum have become to the world of cabinet hardware what BMW and Mercedes are to the automobile.

With a few important exceptions, which I'll discuss later, American hardware manufacturers are still cranking out cheap three-quarter-extension drawer slides and stamped hinges instead of high-quality full-extension slides and fully adjustable case hinges. They apparently feel they can't afford to use the best hardware, but the truth is they can't afford *not* to. Across the country American consumers are buying more European-made cabinets than ever before.

The array of available hardware seems endless. There are dozens of hinge manufacturers, and each one produces several different varieties. Selecting from this huge assortment can be an overwhelming task, especially for the

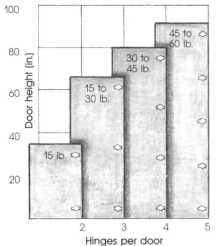

Hinge layout, standard 24-in. wide door

Door height (in.)

100			45 to 60 lb.
80		30 to 45 lb.	
60	15 to 30 lb.		
40	15 lb.		
20			

Hinges per door: 2 3 4 5

The larger the door, the more hinges you'll need. Use two hinges for a standard 25-in. high door, three hinges (or more) for doors over 38 in. high.

The concealed cup hinge (in this case, a Grass #1200 full-overlay hinge) moves smoothly and strongly on a series of pivots and is adjustable in three planes.

novice, but you can make it easier by focusing on the three essential elements: hinges, drawer slides and pulls. Later on, you can consider some of the accessories that will make your kitchen a more pleasant place to be in.

Hinges

The concealed cup hinge, shown below, is the key to the European-style cabinet. The hinges themselves are not much to look at, but their forte is function. They are very strong and fully adjustable, and they stay out of sight. No hinge knuckles poke out between doors.

If you recall that these hinges were designed for the mass production of the 32mm system, you will appreciate their rationale. The automated machinery that builds the cabinets may place a hinge mortise too high or too deep in the case. By simply adjusting the hinge (up, down or sideways about ⅛ in., and in or out as much as ¼ in.), such errors can be corrected. The custom cabinetmaker can work more carefully, but adjustability is still important. When I'm working on a project, I always anticipate the worst. If the cases aren't perfect, will the doors line up? If the walls aren't plumb, will the cases rack out of square? The concealed cup hinge accommodates these inaccuracies, and adjustment is so easy that I can show my customers how to do it in a few minutes.

Compare this to mounting a door with a traditional leaf or butt hinge. Because the hinge is not adjustable, you must place it exactly or you'll have to move it. And moving the hinge is a real chore. All the screws must be removed from one leaf of the hinge while you hold the door. If the adjustment is slight, the screws or drill bit will wander into the old holes, unless you fill them. And

many of these traditional hinges must be mortised into the door, in which case you'll also have to plug the old mortise.

All this means a lot of work and frustration. Frequently, it also means that the cabinetmaker allows minor (and sometimes not so minor) defects to go uncorrected. Look closely at any face-frame kitchen and you'll see drooping doors.

With the unique adjustability of the cup hinge, you can mount all the doors at once and line them up perfectly in about 15 minutes—without removing any screws. If you have to make a gross adjustment that is beyond the capacity of the hinge, simply loosen one screw to remove the door. When you move the hinge you'll discover that the base plates on many hinges have two sets of mounting holes, so you needn't worry about wandering screws or drill bits.

If somebody claims he can mount a traditional hinge right the first time (don't embarrass him by asking how long it takes), ask him what he does when four-year-old Johnny swings on the door two years later and it starts to droop. Those non-adjustable hinges won't look so good then, and may be beyond repair. With your cup hinges, you can pull out a screwdriver and be a hero.

Another advantage is that the cup hinge distributes the door's weight over the entire rim of the cup, a bearing surface of more than 4 sq. in. Standard hinges put all the weight on two or three small screws. Although it's tough to get exact weight ratings for cup hinges, the manufacturers offer some rules of thumb (drawing, facing page). The standard cabinet door (7/8 in. thick and up to 24 in. wide by 25 in. high) requires two hinges. Doors larger than about 39 in. high by 24 in. wide need a third hinge, centered between the first two.

The chart below shows the array of cup hinges available from various manufacturers. The Grass #1200 full-overlay hinge (photo, facing page) is the one I

Concealed cup hinges

Manufacturer	Full opening (about 180°) 3-way adjustability	Full opening minimal protrusion	Glass door	Cross corner
Blum:	90A610	90.750	98M410	98M350
Grass:	1200	1203 (full overlay)	1603	1106
Häfele:	345.47.665	345.56.619	345.49.614	332.95.500
Hettich:	Euromat Plus 3955	Euromat Plus 3944	Euromat Plus 3901	Euromat Plus W45
Mepla	SSP65	SSP65 (full overlay)	SSP17	SSP05/45

Manufacturer	Blind corner	Face frame	Thick door
Blum:	98M950	33.360	90M950
Grass:	1103	TEC 830	1806
Häfele:	332.95.519	343.84.604	332.59.602
Hettich:	Euromat Plus W90	ET 2045	Euromat Plus 3735
Mepla:	SSP 05/90	ACC 150 Series	SSP 25

Note: This chart has been greatly simplified for ease of comprehension. Many manufacturers offer an assortment of hinges in each category. These may be purchased with a metal or nylon cup, a screw-on or press-in mount, an adjustable or non-adjustable base and may be self-closing or free-swinging. And most cup hinges are available in full-overlay, half-overlay and inset models. Full catalogs are available from the manufacturers.

Base plates and mounting screws must be purchased separately.

The Grass #1203 hinge swings the door out of the way, so that it will not obstruct interior drawers or shelves pulled out of the cabinet.

rely on the most. With a 176° swing, the #1200 is twice as expensive as most of the hinges on the chart, but the money is well spent. Standard cup hinges that open only 90° or 110° can actually be dangerous in the kitchen. If you walk into an open cabinet door mounted on such hinges, the door may be ripped from the case—and it won't be good for you, either.

An articulated hinge like the Grass #1200 moves on a sophisticated series of pivots. These allow the cabinet door to swing clear of the sides of the case, opening almost flat against the cabinet, as shown in the photo on p. 32. If a cabinet door mounted on these hinges happens to obstruct your path, the collision will simply bump the door out of the way.

Specialty hinges   The Grass #1200 is my workhorse, but I also occasionally use several kinds of special-purpose hinges. Lots of my customers want their cabinets to include drawers or pull-out trays concealed behind a door, like those shown at left. While most hinges leave the door obstructing the trays or drawers, the Grass #1203 moves the door out of the way when opened only 90° to the face of the cabinet. This means that the trays can be made with little or no allowance for the door. In a situation like this you can get by with a hinge like the Grass #1200, but you'll have to shim the slides out ⅛ in. to ¼ in., and reduce the width of the drawers or trays accordingly.

When you have to install hinges on an ordinary corner cabinet, you can save money by using a hinge that opens 90° to 110°. Moreover, a complex hinge like the #1203 may be difficult to adjust if it cannot be opened more than 90° (at 90°, the adjustment screws are partially obscured).

There are also hinges designed to be mounted on a surface parallel to the door, a useful feature for blind-corner cabinets. In the typical configuration (drawing, below), the cabinet that starts in the blind corner has no right-angle surface on which to mount the hinges. Julius Blum Inc. makes a blind-corner hinge that opens only 95°, more than enough for a corner cabinet. Blum also makes a hinge for cross-corner cabinets (top drawing, facing page). The hinge can be mounted to a surface that lies at 135° to the face. Neither of these hinges requires any special provisions for mounting.

Special hinges are also available for unusually thick doors. Any door that is thicker than ⅞ in., for example, will bind against the adjacent doors unless the hinge pivots slightly away from the case. There are also hinges for thin doors,

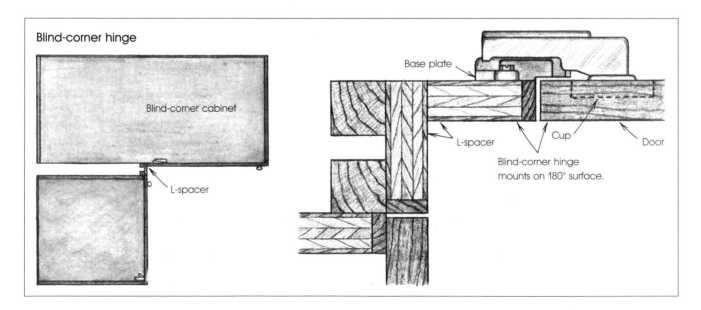

Blind-corner hinge

Blind-corner cabinet

L-spacer

Base plate

L-spacer

Cup

Door

Blind-corner hinge mounts on 180° surface.

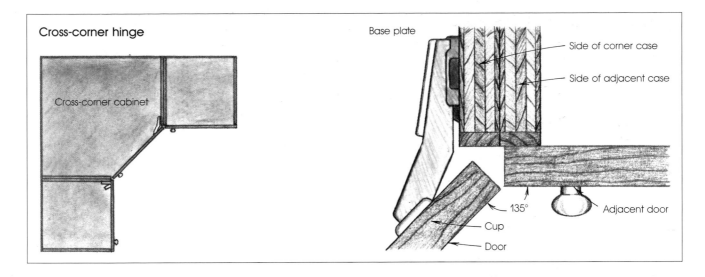

Cross-corner hinge

Cross-corner cabinet

Base plate

Side of corner case

Side of adjacent case

135°

Cup

Door

Adjacent door

solid-glass doors and other special situations, some of which are listed in the chart on p. 35.

All concealed cup hinges are available in models to accommodate the three different installations shown below. These are generally referred to as full over lay, half overlay and inset. I use only the standard full-overlay hinge, which is designed so that the door covers most of the exposed edge of the case. The half-overlay hinge is used where two doors are mounted to opposite sides of the same partition, a situation I never encounter because I assemble my cabinet runs of individual cases. (The sides of adjacent cases are simply screwed together.) Inset hinges permit a door to fit inside the case, but for a number of reasons, I never use them. In the first place, I prefer not to interrupt the continuity of a run of well-matched doors with visible case sides. This would introduce a new design element that would somehow have to be treated. Because inset doors are confined within the established rectangle of the cabinet, they are also much more limited in their adjustability than overlay doors.

You'll note from the drawing that the three types of hinges are identical, ex-

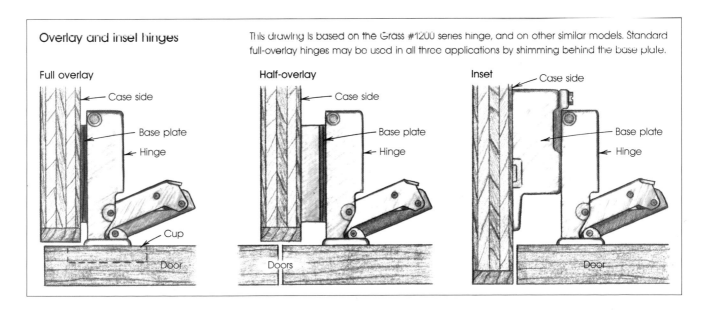

Overlay and inset hinges

This drawing is based on the Grass #1200 series hinge, and on other similar models. Standard full-overlay hinges may be used in all three applications by shimming behind the base plate.

Full overlay

Case side

Base plate

Hinge

Cup

Door

Half-overlay

Case side

Base plate

Hinge

Doors

Inset

Case side

Base plate

Hinge

Door

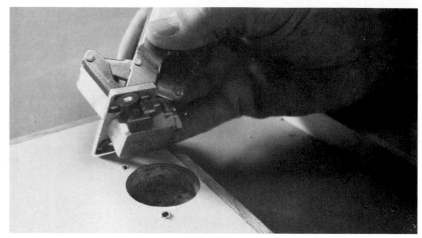

The European hinge consists of a base plate (above), an arm and a cup. The cup fits tightly in a mortise bored in the inside of the door (right). The arm slides over a base plate screwed to the inside wall of the case (facing page, top left). The hinge is adjusted by turning one or two screws that secure the arm on the base plate (facing page, top right).

cept for the thickness of the base plate. (This is the case for the Grass #1200 series hinges I use, and is increasingly true for other types as well.) This means that if you decide to use either half-overlay or inset doors, there's no need to order a different hinge—you can still use the standard full-overlay hinge. Simply glue a wooden shim behind the standard base plate and proceed as usual. (If your case is built of ¾-in. plywood, use a ⅜-in. thick shim for half-overlay doors and a ¾-in. shim for inset doors.)

The great success of cup hinges has led to a curious phenomenon—they are now being made for face-frame mounting. The hinges are completely concealed, yet the cabinets retain the look (and all the construction features) of traditional face-frame cabinets. This is a mixed blessing. Cup hinges certainly facilitate installation and adjustment, but they can't correct the most serious flaw of the face-frame cabinet: The frames themselves still obstruct full access to the interior of the case. Another drawback is that the frame must be made even wider than usual to mount the cup hinge, which makes the cabinets that much less accessible.

Mounting cup hinges All cup hinges mount in a similar fashion, though each has its idiosyncrasies. I will outline the process briefly here, but for more detailed information on mounting cup hinges, see Chapter 8.

First, a 35mm-dia. hole is bored in the inside of the cabinet door. The hinge cup is pressed into this tight-fitting mortise (photo, above right), which holds it in place until the hinge is fastened with two small screws. Next, a base plate (photo, above left) is screwed to the inside of the case. Then the hinge slides over the base plate (top left photo, facing page), and a single screw locks it in place.

Adjusting the hinge is just as quick. Once the hinge has been screwed to the base plate, the door is aligned by eye. Its height is adjusted by one screw (top right photo, facing page), its sideways orientation by another. This is where the Grass #1200 really shines, because the setscrews provide direct adjustment. (Some other cup hinges have an additional screw that locks the setscrews in place.) If the door binds, just loosen the appropriate setscrew and adjust the hinge along its track, then retighten the screw. It may take a little practice at first to know exactly which way and how much to adjust the setscrews, but after several doors you should get the hang of it.

If this process sounds simple, that's because it *is* simple. Once you see how easily and solidly cup hinges are mounted, I'll bet you won't go back to whatever hinge you're using now.

Drawer slides

The second critical piece of hardware is the drawer slide, and, once again, quality is what you're after. The best slides roll on nylon wheels or polymer or steel ball bearings (steel bearings probably last longer, polymer bearings are quieter), and they have no sharp edges on any metal parts. The finest slides also have built-in bumpers to cushion the impact of the drawer front closing against the cabinet.

You can tell a good-quality slide just by picking up several different ones—the good ones are much heavier. Once the slide is in place, you'll recognize quality by the fact that when you pull out the drawer, you won't hear a blessed thing. Cheap slides rattle like skeletons on a tin roof. A drawer mounted on good slides will not droop—it will pull straight out and stay even.

Types of slides I prefer full-extension slides because they are easy to install and they grant access to the entire contents of a drawer. But lots of other slides are available. Three-quarter-extension slides are cheaper and lighter, and I use them occasionally. You can also get slides that will permit greater than full extension. These are useful if a drawer has to be installed under a table or countertop with a wide lip. There are even pull-through slides that permit a drawer to be opened from either side, a great feature for a peninsula or island cabinet.

All slides are either corner mounted, side mounted or bottom mounted (drawings, p. 40). These alternatives permit considerable flexibility in cabinet design and in mounting. I like the corner mounting best because the slides cradle the drawer, just as you would if someone handed it to you. But alas, the brand of slides I like best doesn't mount this way. So I use side-mounted slides (photo, right). These may be positioned anywhere on the side of the drawer, but the closer to the bottom the better. If mounted too near the top, there won't be enough drawer stock above the slide to support the weight of the drawer and its contents, and the drawer side might split. If you make your drawers out of oak, allow at least ½ in. of wood above the screws that attach the slide to the drawer side. In a softwood like pine or a soft hardwood like poplar, allow ¾ in.

The bottom-mounted slide serves as a center rail beneath the drawer. Only one slide is needed for each drawer, which saves money, but this type of slide can be used only on a face-frame cabinet. At the front, a pair of rollers must be mounted to the face frame to keep the drawer from tipping, while the other end of the slide is attached to the back of the case. My cabinets don't have face frames, so I can't use bottom-mounted slides. It's no sacrifice, though, as they are not usually adjustable, and tend to be among the shabbiest on the market.

I opened this chapter by maligning U. S. manufacturers for their tendency to

There are all kinds of drawers—and as many different slides with which to hang them. These Grant full-extension drawer slides run smoothly on ball bearings, and each one supports a load of 150 lb.

make low-quality hardware. The finest slides I've found, however, are made by Accuride and Grant. They run on ball bearings and are the quietest on the market. The Grant full-extension slide, shown in the bottom photo on p. 39, has a load-bearing capacity of 150 lb. The sliding mechanism is attached to the case wall, and a mounting rail is attached to the side of the drawer. With the slide and rail installed, all you do is drop the drawer in place (photo, facing page). A small steel catch holds the slide to the rail at the rear, and a flexible plastic tab grabs the rail in the front. By releasing the tab, the rail (and drawer) may be lifted off the slide.

This installation feature is important. Some slides mount in an odd way that requires clearance above the drawer. For these, you must first tip the front of the drawer up slightly to engage two sets of wheels—one on the drawer, and the other on the case. Only when the drawer has been pushed about one-quarter of the way into the case will it drop down and sit level. If the drawer is mounted near the top of the case, as it is in most kitchen cabinets, this means that the drawer sides must be made about ¾ in. narrower than the opening, or

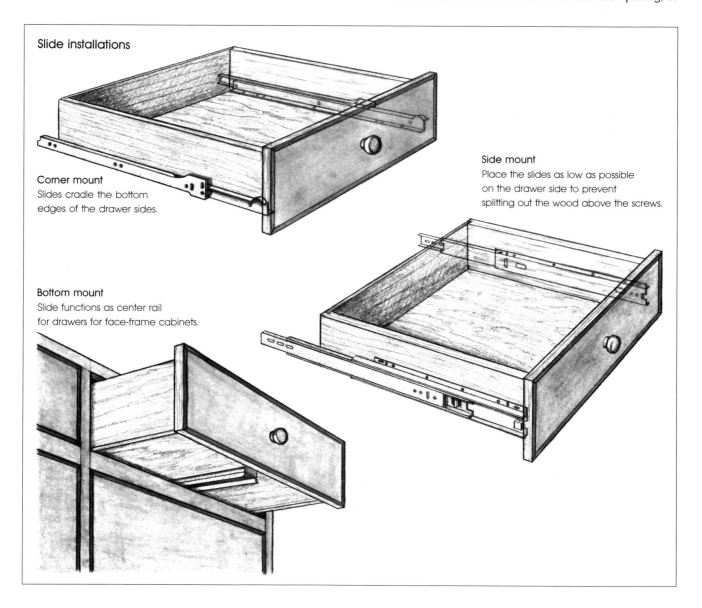

Slide installations

Corner mount
Slides cradle the bottom
edges of the drawer sides.

Side mount
Place the slides as low as possible
on the drawer side to prevent
splitting out the wood above the screws.

Bottom mount
Slide functions as center rail
for drawers for face-frame cabinets.

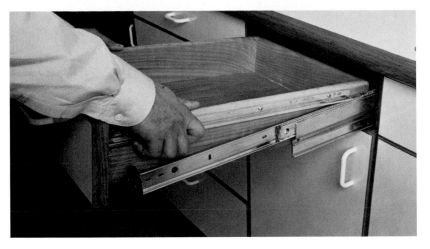

A full-extension sliding mechanism is attached to the case wall, and a mounting rail to the side of the drawer. The drawer simply drops into place outside of the cabinet.

the drawer can't be installed. And you may not discover this until after you've mounted the slide and rail and are ready to install the drawer. Because the parts of the full-extension slides are engaged outside the case, no extra clearance is necessary.

Accuride slides come with a detent (a curved nub in the metal stamping), which keeps the drawer from rolling open on its own, and built-in felt bumpers to eliminate the thud when the drawer is closed. They cost at least twice as much as the best European slides and four times as much as the cheaper American slides, but I think they're worth it. Once my customers have tried the slides, they always agree.

Accuride also offers a variety of specialty slides. There is an under-counter slide for computer keyboards and a TV slide that can be used in conjunction with a swivel. Accuride also makes a hinged slide, which is used to mount a door that swings out on the hinge and then pushes back into the case on the slide. The company's heavy-duty lateral-file slide has a load rating of 250 lb. All of these souped-up slides look neat in the catalog, but I rarely use them. I find that the Accuride #C3017 does almost everything I need it to do, with only occasional shimming or modification required.

Grant makes two fine full-extension, ball-bearing slides (#555 and #527). I've used both models and like them a lot. Whenever I can't get the Accurides, I use the Grants.

Slide finishes Drawer slides are made of stamped metal and most have no added finish, but many, such as the Accurides I use, are now available in black or dark brown. I much prefer a painted finish to the Spartan, industrial look of the metal slides. The black finish makes a particularly nice contrast with oak drawer sides, too. Painted slides cost as much as 20% more, however, and since a lot of people don't look at the slides once they're installed, you may be willing to put up with a bit of glare.

The slides that are made by European companies like Grass and Blum come from the factory with a white or almond epoxy-coated finish, which I think surpasses the unfinished slides. (The almond slides blend better with wood than anything else I've found.) Both full-extension and three-quarter-extension slides are available with an epoxy finish and, while they cost as much as 30% more than the cheaper American slides (they're still half the price of the Accurides), I think it's only a matter of time before they completely replace them. Not only do they look better, but they're quieter and sturdier to operate because of their large rollers.

Mounting drawer slides   The European slides, like the hinges described earlier, are designed for the 32mm system, but they can be mounted with ordinary No. 6 flat-head wood screws, or they can be purchased with dowel mounts. (The latter are simply pressed into pre-bored holes in the drawer sides and case—no screws or adhesives are necessary. Templates are also available to facilitate boring the holes for the European slides and hinges. Of course, these are used only when the case sides have not been prepared with the line-boring pattern of the 32mm system. You can make your own templates, or use none at all, which is what I usually do.

I begin by placing the finished drawer (without its face) on a flat surface. Holding the complete drawer-slide assembly against the side and flush with the front of the drawer, I pre-bore the holes for the screws. Then I separate the slide from the rail and screw one rail to each side of the drawer. Finally, I mark the positon of the drawer on the inside of the case, and, with the bottom of the slide aligned with the mark for the bottom of the drawer, I install the slides.

It's easy to mount Accuride slides—and I do it with a minimum of measuring and marking. Even though the slides cannot be adjusted like the concealed cup hinges, flexibility is provided by the separate drawer face, which is attached after the drawer is installed. I can make up for slight errors in a drawer's location simply by adjusting the position of its face.

Each brand of drawer slide mounts in its own peculiar way, so it's a good idea to obtain specific information from the manufacturer. (See Chapter 7 for a more detailed description of how to mount Accuride slides.) But whichever slide you select, consider the orientation of the case before you mount the slide. I used to hunch over to install the slides in the upright case, dropping screws in dark corners. Now I lay the case on its side on my workbench to mount the slides (photo, below). With gravity on my side, the job is much easier, and my back thanks me every night. This may seem obvious, but it took me many years of hunching and a simple coincidence to figure it out. I was installing the slides in a case that was too tall for my low shop ceiling, so I had to lay it down. It's easier, of course, to bore the flat panel with holes before assembling the case, but I prefer to keep my options open for as long as possible.

Place the case on its side to install the slides. It's much easier to work with gravity than against it.

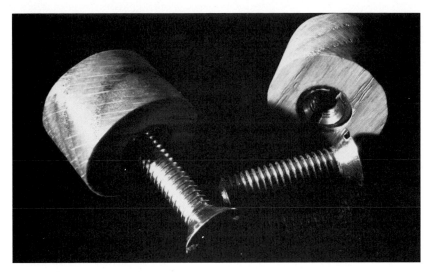

These simple button pulls are made of red oak, cut with a plug cutter on the drill press. A machine screw is inserted from the inside of the door to engage a threaded insert in the back of the pull.

Door and drawer pulls

The last critical item of cabinet hardware is the pull. It can be mounted separately on the face, like a knob or handle, or it can be an integral part of the door or drawer, as when it forms a cove in the edge of the face.

Traditional pulls   You're probably familiar with the pulls commonly found on face-frame cabinets. Knobs and handles of porcelain or brass come in a great variety of shapes, sizes and colors, but the selection and quality to be found in your local hardware store or retail lumberyard are usually mediocre. You'll do better (and probably pay more) at one of the specialized hardware stores that deal in brass, or the mail-order suppliers listed in the Resource Guide, p. 185.

Sometimes I make my own hardwood button pulls, shown in the photos above. These are made quickly with a plug cutter on the drill press and receive a threaded insert in the back of the pull. They are easily installed by inserting a machine screw from the inside of the drawer face or door. You can also buy similar pulls made of hard, black rubber, which have a nice feel and are an interesting alternative to the traditional button pulls. Like the wooden button pulls, they have a threaded insert cast into the body of the pull.

Perhaps you'll be lucky and find that really old-time, boxes-to-the-ceiling hardware store, the kind with squeaky floor boards and a cash register to match. Behind the counter, you may also find a truly knowledgeable salesman who carries in his head an inventory that would strain a computer. Not only will he know what you're looking for, but he will also remember that the peculiar bolt you need to install it with is in the drawer labeled "clothespins." One wall of the store will be filled with little drawers, and he'll head directly to the correct one to locate the pull you thought you'd never find. I just hope he has enough of them for you.

Contemporary pulls   Wire pulls like those shown in the top photo on p. 44 have become one of the hallmarks of European-style cabinets. They are highly functional and unadorned, reflecting the nature of the modern kitchen. Wire pulls may be made of polished steel, brushed chrome, aluminum, plastic or brass, and are named not for the material they're made from, but for their uniform cylindrical shape.

The most popular wire pulls are made of high-quality cast resin. The best among them have threaded inserts cast into the body of the pull, which provide a strong anchor for the machine screws that fasten them to the face of the

Cast-resin wire pulls on drawers and doors suit the sleek lines of the European-style kitchen.

People will notice and remember your kitchen by its details, and custom-made wooden pulls are an excellent way to leave a distinctive 'signature' on your work.

cabinet. The cheaper ones are made from inexpensive plastic, and have no inserts. When the screws that hold them to the cabinet eventually strip the plastic threads, the pull will loosen, and either the screws or the entire pull will have to be replaced. (I also think these cheap plastic pulls have a rather dull, lifeless look compared to the resin pulls, but many people seem to like them.)

Wooden pulls made in the style of the cast-resin wire pulls have become more common in recent years, and are sold through hardware stores, lumberyards and mail-order firms. They usually come unfinished, but can be painted, stained or oiled to match the cabinets. A nicely oiled wooden pull can provide a welcome contrast to sleek laminate cabinets. Oak is the wood most frequently used for these pulls.

No matter how hard you look, you may find that the perfect pull continues to elude you. If so, consider making your own. Handcrafted wooden pulls can be a unique trademark for the custom cabinetmaker. One style of pulls I make, shown in the photo at left, is molded into the edge of the door and has a silky, organic appearance. The pulls are finish-sanded with 220-grit paper and are inviting to the touch. Although elegant in appearance, they are made by following a simple progression of machine woodworking operations. The extra value created by the pulls more than offsets the effort required to make them. (See Chapter 8 for more on how to make them.)

Shelf supports

Hinges, slides and pulls aren't the only hardware items you'll need for your cabinets. You'll also want some way to support and adjust the shelves inside. The easiest way is to rest the shelves on wooden cleats fastened to the inside of

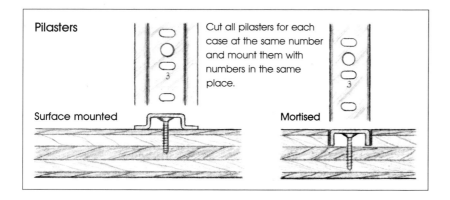

Pilasters

Cut all pilasters for each case at the same number and mount them with numbers in the same place.

Surface mounted

Mortised

the case walls. This doesn't let you move the shelves, however, and the technique is rather crude. Instead, I recommend the use of manufactured shelf supports, which permit much greater flexibility.

Pilasters   The pilaster is the mainstay of shelf-support systems. A slender metal channel, the pilaster is attached vertically to each inside cabinet wall (two of them on each side), and small metal clips are snapped into slots in the pilaster to support a shelf. Although pilasters are not particularly attractive, they have been popular for quite a while, and with good reason: They carry a lot of weight and are easily adjusted.

There are two kinds of pilaster—those that mount on the inside surface of the cabinet, and those that fit in a groove, routed (or dadoed) in the inside of the case. Surface-mounted pilasters have a small flange on either side for greater bearing surface; mortised pilasters are shaped like a long strip of staples (drawing, above).

It's not difficult to install pilasters, but they must be carefully aligned so that the shelves won't rock when they're slipped into place. I usually place them about 3 in. from the front and the back of the case (the exact distance isn't crucial), and run them the full height of the case. (Upper-case shelves are only 11 in. to 12 in. deep, so you may wish to locate the pilasters 2 in. from the front and back.) Be sure that they're plumb, and that the notches in the pilasters line up—there are few things more frustrating than finding out after they've been cut that the support notches are at different heights. Preventing this problem is easy, though, once you know what to look for. Each strip is marked along its length with a row of incised numbers (1 to 6). Cut all four pilasters for one case at the same number, and mount them with the numbers in the same orientation. When it comes time to install the metal clips, you can use the numbers again to establish relative heights for each shelf.

Both types of pilaster are fastened to the cabinet with slender, ring-shank nails (called pilaster nails) about $5/8$ in. long. They are usually included when you buy the pilasters and are sometimes colored to match them. No. 4 flathead wood screws can be used in place of the nails, but they're mighty small and difficult to handle.

To fit shelves to either type of pilaster, subtract $3/32$ in. from the distance between pilasters, and cut the shelves to that length. This will provide enough clearance to lift the shelves in and out without binding. If you use surface-mounted pilasters, the shelves must either be notched around the pilaster or cut shorter to fit between them.

Most pilasters are available only in black, gold, brown or the silver color of stamped metal. Some come with a nickel finish that can be painted, but you probably won't find these in your local hardware store and will have to hunt around in specialty shops.

Holes bored in each side of the case provide a full range of adjustment for small shelf clips. This plastic clip is molded around a steel pin.

Shelf clips Although my customers frequently request pilasters, I prefer to bore two lines of holes in each side of the case to hold any of a host of shelf clips. The shelf clips are a lot easier to install than the pilasters, and I find them much less obtrusive. The most common ones are made to fit ¼-in. dia. holes. Another type includes brass sleeves, or tubes, that slip into each hole before the clip is inserted, ostensibly to strengthen the hole and make it resistant to wear. (I think these are a waste of time, though. There's not much movement in a shelf clip installed in hardwood plywood, and consequently not much wear.) Whichever you choose, drill the holes every 1½ in. vertically, and center the rows about 2 in. to 3 in. from the front and back of the case, like the pilasters. You can mark and bore each hole by hand, but it's much faster to use a jig. (For more on installing shelf clips, see Chapter 6.)

There are several support clips intended specifically for the 32mm system, the most popular being either entirely plastic, or plastic with a steel pin for the holes. I like the latter clips because the steel pin says "strong" to me. They are available in white, tan, brown and clear. All the European-made clips require 5mm-dia. holes, but a standard No. 8 drill bit will do the job perfectly.

There is also a type of forked shelf support that pivots in the hole and has two "fingers," one above and one below the shelf. These compensate for small errors in hole alignment, and grip the shelf securely.

Accessories

You'll find lots of other goodies that will allow you to customize your cabinets. Most of these are a matter of refinement more than functional necessity, but many will help you make better use of the space inside your cabinets. You can include these features in your initial design, or leave them to add later. For the most part, they don't require a lot of advance planning.

Bumpers I like to include bumpers on my cabinets because they help cushion the shock of closing a door or drawer. They might also contribute to making the drawers last longer, but I use them because the dull thud of a bumpered door is a lot more pleasant than the sharp smack of an unbumpered door. (If you have young children, you will immediately appreciate the difference this makes over the course of a typical day of banged doors.) Most bumpers are inexpensive, stick-on dots made of plastic, felt or cork, and they are mounted on the inside of the door or drawer face or on the front edge of the case. Some drawer slides, like the Accurides, have built-in bumpers, but most don't. The 32mm system provides for special bumpers that mount in the grid of holes bored in the sides of the case. Other bumpers can be mounted with a small brad or screw.

Lazy Susans The lazy Susan is used primarily in corner cabinets, though it can be installed in any lower cabinet to increase access (drawing, right). The semicircular shelves are attached to the door and a vertical stile that is mounted in the corner so they pivot out when you open the door, exposing only half of the shelves.

Another type of lazy Susan has shelves shaped as three-quarters of a circle, and also fits in a corner cabinet. The L-shaped door for this cabinet fits into the missing quarter of the circle and disappears into the cabinet when the shelves are opened. This type of lazy Susan pivots at its center on a post screwed to the top and bottom of the case.

A third type of lazy Susan has full circular shelves. The door is not attached to the shelves, but rather is hinged on the cabinet like any standard door. The pivot is installed independently at the desired location inside the cabinet.

Now that you know what's available, I should tell you that I rarely put lazy Susans in my cabinets. To understand why, just look at all the space wasted in the corners between the round shelves and the square case. A unit with three-quarter shelves and 12-in. wide, L-shaped doors makes use of only about half of the available space. For some cooks, the convenience of having the contents of a cabinet pivot into view is worth the sacrifice, but I prefer to build a blind-corner case, like the one shown in the bottom drawing on p. 25. There's no loss of space, only a loss of convenient access—a compromise I'm willing to make. I don't believe the average kitchen can afford to waste any storage space.

Drawer liners Several companies make drawer liners—removable plastic trays divided into compartments for cutlery. The molded flange on the tray is trimmed on a table saw to fit the exact inside dimension of the drawer. My clients love them.

Wire accessories All kinds of sleek and useful items are made of coated wire. There are shelves, trays, baskets, bins, drawers, towel bars and even panels from which odd-sized utensils can be hung. These accessories are also washable—a great feature for any kitchen. Many of them mount on slides, allowing them to be stored conveniently inside the cases. If you want to include wire products in your cabinets, make sure you know their space requirements before you begin your design work—there is not enough variety available to fit every size of case.

New wire accessories are coming out all the time, but one that I particularly like is a wire form over which a plastic garbage bag is suspended. Mounted to the inside of a cabinet door, this nifty device also provides space to store a continuous roll of garbage bags. When the bag is full, you just tear it off the roll and pull a new one over the form.

Lazy Susans

Semicircular
Blind-corner version exposes only half the shelf when open.

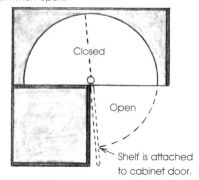

Three-quarter
Three-quarter version pivots 360° and door disappears into the cabinet.

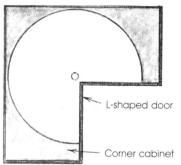

Full circle
Circular version is independent of door and may be installed in any standard cabinet.

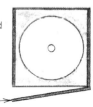

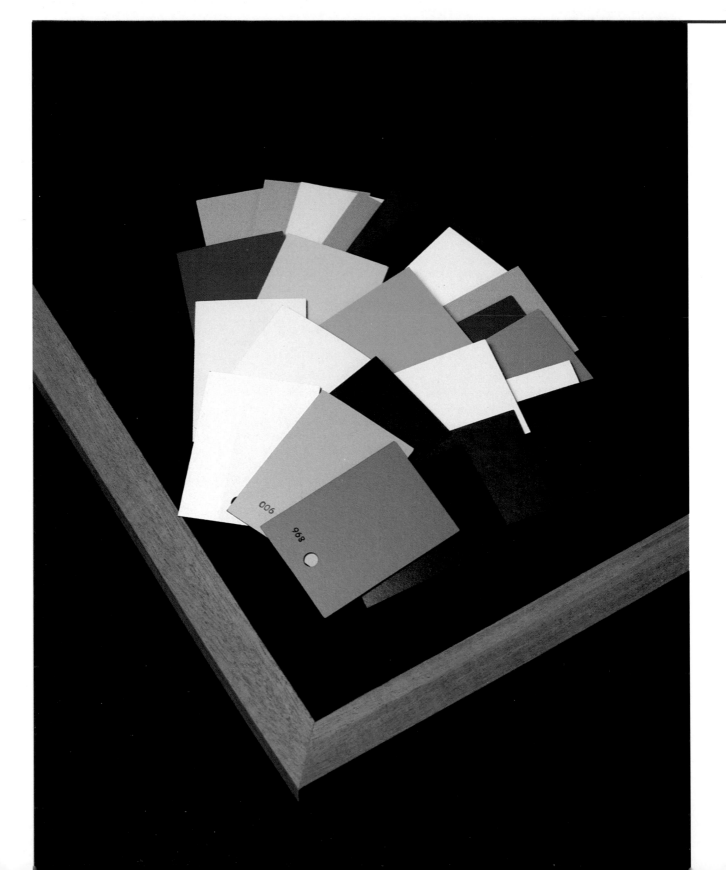

ext to hardware, modern sheet-laminated and composite materials have done more than anything else to influence both the style and the construction of kitchen cabinets. Plywood, in particular, is very stable, and I use it for almost all of my casework, which I cover with either plastic laminate or hardwood veneer. I use hardwood for trim and drawers, and sometimes to build the top frames for the base cases. While I don't recommend particleboard or medium-density fiberboard for custom casework, they are commonly used in manufactured cabinets.

Whichever materials you choose, they must be selected and applied with care, and used appropriately. Each of the above materials has certain characteristics that make it more or less desirable in different applications. In this chapter, I'll discuss the features of each material, where to use it and how to select it.

As always, use the best material you can afford. Whether you're building a single cabinet or an entire kitchen, high-quality materials will ensure not only that the job progresses smoothly, but also that the results are worth the time spent obtaining them.

Plywood

Wood veneer is the essential component of all plywood. Plain, unattractive or even slightly flawed veneer is used in the core, and the best wood is used for the exposed faces. Because it is comprised of thin sheets of veneer that are laminated in alternating directions, plywood has several advantages over solid wood. To start with, it is inherently more stable and is available in much wider sheets. Inch for inch, plywood is also much stronger than solid wood, and it is available dry and ready to use.

Plywood comes in a seemingly endless variety: aircraft plywood is made of core veneers laminated at a 45° angle to the faces; marine plywood can be boiled in water without delaminating; furniture-grade plywood is often faced with beautiful veneers. While I generally avoid the more exotic varieties in my work, I always use a good grade of hardwood plywood for its light weight, strength and good looks. Softwood, or construction-grade, plywood is less expensive than hardwood plywood, but it should never be used for fine cabinetwork. The fir face veneers are generally unattractive (photo, p. 50), and voids in the core are common.

Even more troublesome, the wide bands of earlywood (spring growth) in fir are so much softer than the narrow bands of latewood that sanding creates hills and valleys in the face veneer. If you look closely at a piece of fir plywood, you

The rotary-cut faces of softwood plywood (top) are uneven and unattractive, and there are frequent voids in the core. Hardwood plywood (bottom) is the material of choice for quality cabinetmaking because of its smooth grain and lack of voids in the core.

can often see places where the low spots in the face veneer have been sanded right through. Even if you plan to cover the fir plywood with plastic laminate or hardwood veneer, the face material will telegraph any irregularities in the substrate. Also, the wavy surface and wild grain patterns of most softwood plywood won't accept paint or stain evenly. I wouldn't waste my time (or precious veneer) on fir plywood.

Cores and faces   Hardwood plywood is a two-part material, with a hardwood face veneer and a core made up of five, seven or more layers of ⅛-in. (or thicker) hardwood veneer or blocks of solid hardwood, as shown in the drawing below. Plywood with a solid hardwood core is called lumbercore plywood, and its core is typically made of lauan, a stable, even-grained hardwood, sometimes sold as Philippine mahogany.

Lumbercore plywood is very well made, and is excellent to use where a panel must have extra strength in one direction to span a long distance. It's the next best thing to solid wood—without the instability. But it is expensive, and in most situations veneer-core plywood is more versatile.

Hardwood plywood may be purchased with faces of birch, cherry, oak, walnut or almost any other hardwood you desire (and are willing to pay for). Several different hardwoods may be used for the core, including birch, poplar and

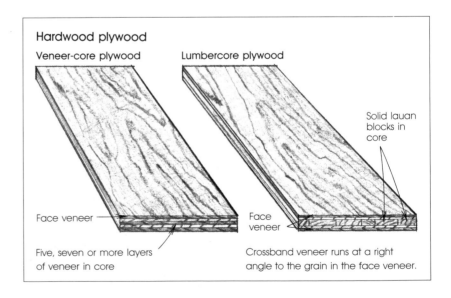

Hardwood plywood

Veneer-core plywood

Lumbercore plywood

Solid lauan blocks in core

Face veneer

Five, seven or more layers of veneer in core

Face veneer

Crossband veneer runs at a right angle to the grain in the face veneer.

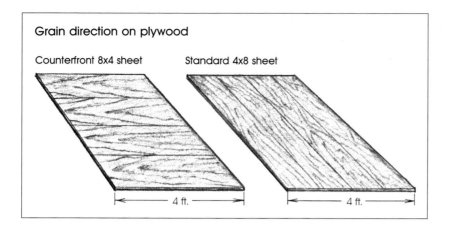

Grain direction on plywood

Counterfront 8x4 sheet   Standard 4x8 sheet

|← 4 ft. →| |← 4 ft. →|

lauan. I have used them all with good results, but lauan is my favorite core material because of its workability.

Never assume that a hardwood face veneer will be covering a hardwood core. If you don't specify a hardwood core, it will almost always be fir. While I find this unacceptable for exposed portions of cabinets (for the reasons I mentioned earlier), it's okay for the interior of a case.

Grades   A sheet of plywood is specified by noting its short-grain dimension, followed by its long-grain dimension. In the standard 4-ft. by 8-ft. sheet (drawing, above left), the grain runs along the 8-ft. length of the panel. If the grain runs across the width of the sheet (drawing, above right), it is called counterfront plywood and specified as an 8-ft. by 4-ft. panel.

The front and back faces of a sheet of plywood can be specified not only by the direction of the grain, but also by the kind of wood they're made from, the quality of the material, and how it is produced. The two faces are not necessarily of the same type or quality of veneer, so they must be specified when you purchase hardwood plywood.

An A face has no knots, splits or defects. It is the best readily available plywood face in the industry, although higher-quality faces can be custom ordered from specialty plywood manufacturers. Lesser-quality plywoods are identified as having a B or C face, and "shop-grade" plywood usually contains an otherwise A-quality face that has been marred in spots by a sand-through, dent or other similar accident.

The designation A2 means that both faces on the sheet are of A quality; AB or AC indicates one A face and one B or C face. Hardwood-veneer grading is totally different from softwood-veneer grading, so you won't find the hardwood equivalent of low-grade CDX plywood, which is used in construction. I often use plywood with only one A face for the back or sides of a cabinet, where the other face won't show. I always use an A2 grade for doors, unless they will be covered with another laminate (in which case I use a shop-grade plywood). If the plywood is to be used under plastic laminate, the veneer should be smooth, and any gaps or holes should be plugged.

Rotary-cut vs. flat-cut veneers   All cabinet plywoods are faced either with rotary-cut or flat-cut (also called flitch-sliced) veneer (drawing and photos, p. 52). Rotary-cut veneer is peeled from a spinning log in a long, continuous sheet—like paper towels pulled off a roll. Flat-cut veneer is produced by passing the log across a stationary knife, resulting in narrow, individual sheets. Rotary-cut veneer is generally not as good as flat-cut veneer, although it is commonly used on softwood plywood. It includes some structural defects—the predictable

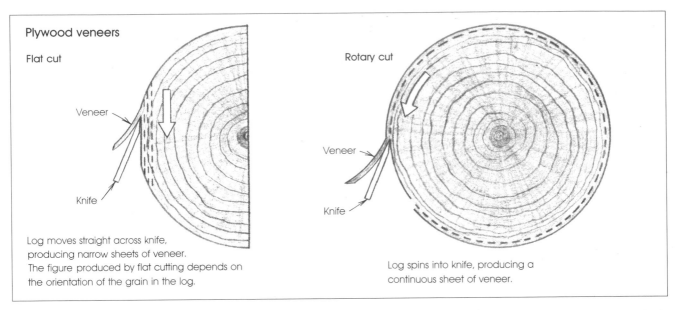

Plywood veneers

Flat cut

Veneer

Knife

Log moves straight across knife, producing narrow sheets of veneer. The figure produced by flat cutting depends on the orientation of the grain in the log.

Rotary cut

Veneer

Knife

Log spins into knife, producing a continuous sheet of veneer.

The rotary-cut surface at right reveals an unnatural and unsettling grain pattern, while the flat-cut face at bottom right resembles a hardwood board cut at a sawmill.

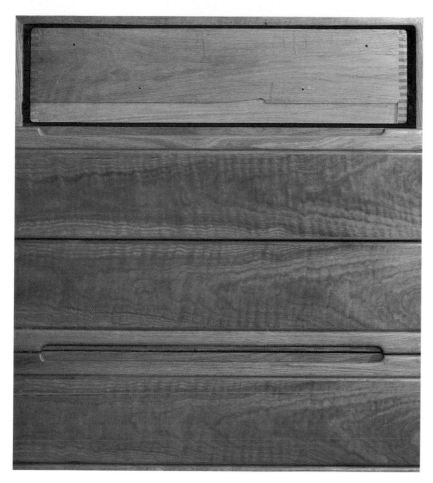

Wood veneer may not be as practical as plastic laminate for kitchen cabinets but it makes a warm and attractive addition to any room.

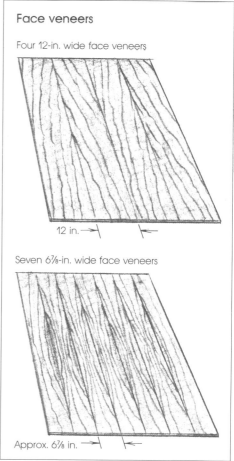

Face veneers

Four 12-in. wide face veneers

12 in.

Seven 6⅞-in. wide face veneers

Approx. 6⅞ in.

result of straightening out the curved surface of the log—and its pronounced grain patterns are not particularly appealing.

Flat-cut veneer makes the finest cabinet faces because it resembles solid wood. The sheets are stacked consecutively as they come off the knife, just like boards at a sawmill. But to make up the width of a piece of plywood from the narrow sheets, the manufacturer must glue a number of pieces of flat-cut veneer to a core (unless, of course, he happens to have a 4-ft. dia. log). This process makes flat-cut veneer more expensive than rotary-cut veneer, but its grain pattern tends to be less wild. I prefer it for doors and drawer faces, or wherever it will be exposed. (Of course, if the plywood will receive a laminate, you may as well use a cheaper, rotary-cut plywood.)

Matching veneers The pieces of sliced veneer that make up the face of a sheet of plywood vary in size from sheet to sheet and face to face. For example, it's not unusual to find some faces made up of four 12-in. wide pieces, while others have seven pieces, each about 6⅞ in. wide, as shown in the drawing at right. (The width of these pieces of veneer may even vary slightly within a single sheet of plywood—the pieces that were sliced from the center of the log are wider than those cut from the outside edge.) The width and number of veneers used will affect the appearance of the smaller panels that you cut from the full sheet, so you'll have to select your plywood carefully to minimize waste.

Sheets of plywood that have been faced with veneer sliced from the same log are usually kept together, or flitch matched. You can buy up to 12 sheets of

To lay out a bookmatched door on a sheet of plywood, measure from the seam of the bookmatch in both directions, half the width of the door, as shown at center. Align two matched doors on either side of the seam, and lay out three doors by flanking the single matched door, as shown at bottom.

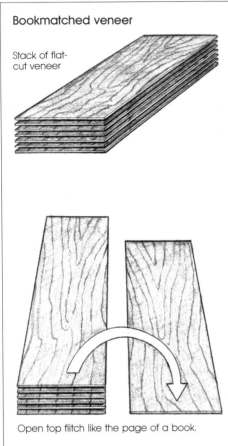

Bookmatched veneer

Stack of flat-cut veneer

Open top flitch like the page of a book.

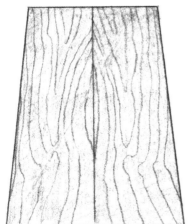

Put adjoining sheets together for a bookmatch.

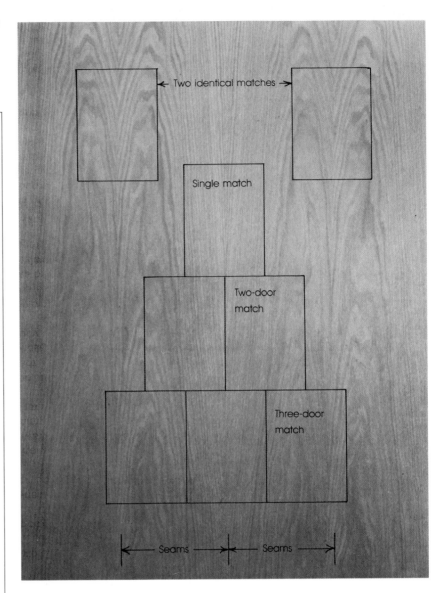

Two identical matches

Single match

Two-door match

Three-door match

Seams   Seams

flitch-matched plywood, and these will be consecutively marked: 1/12, 2/12, 3/12, etc. If you want to build uniform door and drawer fronts, you should always use flitch-matched plywood.

There are several ways for the veneer manufacturer to arrange the individual pieces of veneer into 4-ft. by 8-ft. sheets. The method I prefer is called "bookmatching." To create bookmatched veneer, two adjacent pieces of sliced veneer are opened like the pages of a book so that one surface is the mirror image of the other, as shown in the drawing above left. With the matches paired across a sheet of plywood, each pair will look practically identical. Plywood with bookmatched veneer can thus be selected so that each door in an entire kitchen will appear the same.

I have heard that Louis Tiffany, the great glass artist, would cut up a whole sheet of glass just to get a small piece of the right color. Sometimes a cabinetmaker has to take the same approach. If you're not able to veneer the plywood yourself or to pay someone else to do it to your specifications, you can approximate bookmatched faces by carefully selecting and cutting your stock from

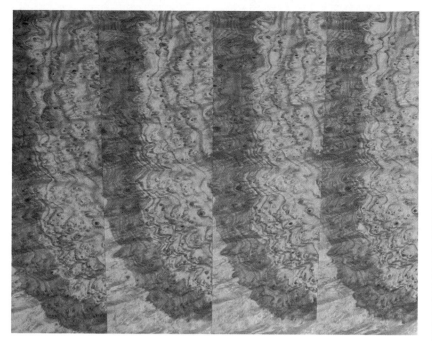

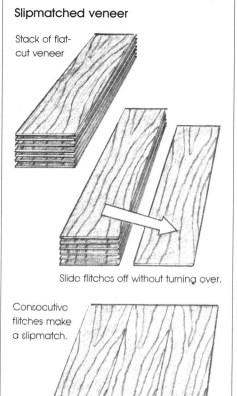

The consecutive orientation of slipmatched veneer on these panels has a much different impact from a bookmatched pattern.

Slipmatched veneer

Stack of flat-cut veneer

Slide flitches off without turning over.

Consecutive flitches make a slipmatch.

flitch-matched plywood. While this is sometimes wasteful, you can also achieve striking results.

Cutting a bookmatched door from a sheet of bookmatched plywood is not difficult. Locate the seam of the bookmatch, as shown in the photo on the facing page, and measure from it in both directions to half the width of the door to capture the bookmatch.

To match two doors, simply lay out one to the left of the seam and the other to the right. For three doors, orient the center door as though it were a single door, and then place the second and third doors directly to the left and right of this. If you're lucky and the bookmatched face is centered on the plywood panel, the entire width of the sheet can be used. Many times, however, the pattern is not centered exactly, and you'll have a lot more waste.

Sometimes flat-cut veneers are "slipmatched" by pulling each piece of veneer off the one beneath it without turning it over, as you might count a deck of cards. When multiplied in a series of adjoining faces slipmatched veneer reminds me of the consecutive frames of a movie, as shown in the photo above. Each piece looks almost the same, but I find the difference can be unsettling. I think that bookmatched veneer makes a better-looking cabinet. Most of the flat-cut plywood you're likely to find will be bookmatched.

Whatever you use for the faces, rotary-cut birch and lauan plywood are much less expensive than flat-cut plywood, and they're fine for interior casework or anyplace where they will be covered by plastic laminate. The grain pattern of birch is less distinct than that of fir, which gives the panel an innocuous, creamy appearance, while the homogeneous color of lauan makes the rotary surface even less obtrusive. Also, lauan makes one of the best substrate materials for veneering. In fact, there is a grade of lauan plywood specifically intended for this purpose, sometimes called "core stock." Its surface is roughened slightly to improve the adhesion of the glue.

Purchasing plywood The average kitchen requires about 10 to 15 sheets of hardwood plywood for cases, faces and shelves. The typical commercially made cabinet case is made of ⅜-in. or ½-in. plywood or ¾-in. particleboard. I use ¾-in. plywood for all casework except the back. (Another five or six sheets of ¼-in. plywood take care of case backs, drawer bottoms and patterns.) The added thickness and quality of the ¾-in. material offers superior strength and makes a more attractive case. By the time you add everything up, there's a fair amount of material in the average kitchen, so it's worth the extra time to do some careful shopping.

The price of plywood varies considerably, depending on the type and species of the core and the species and grade of the face veneers. Whether the faces are rotary cut or flat cut will also have an effect. Although lauan and birch are fairly close in price, lauan has a wider range. At the time of this writing, you could pay anywhere from $30 to $60 for a 4-ft. by 8-ft. sheet of A2, rotary-cut lauan plywood. Birch plywood is slightly less expensive, but you can expect to pay much more for cherry, oak or walnut plywood.

It's a good idea to buy all your plywood at once, for reasons of cost and consistency. If your supplier has a price break, it will probably come at ten sheets. The next break will be for a unit, which is somewhere around 30 sheets. If you order a unit, it will be shipped directly to you from the mill, and because the distributor does not have to handle it, you can save quite a bit.

If you're trying to match the doors and drawer faces in the kitchen, be sure to get enough plywood before you begin. If you overestimate your needs and end up with any extra sheets, you can always find a use for them in another project. But if you come up short, chances are you won't be able to match the plywood.

Composites

As I mentioned before, plywood isn't the only sheet material that's used to build cabinet cases. The two principal composite sheet materials for cabinet work are particleboard and medium-density fiberboard (MDF), examples of which are shown in the photo below. Both are made from wood by-products that have been reconstituted with urea-formaldehyde glue and pressed into large sheets. Both have become well established in all types of commercial cabinetwork— from the bottom end to the highest quality.

Particleboard The size of the chips that make up a sheet of particleboard varies, with larger chips in the core and finer chips on the surface. Because of this variable density, the larger chips won't work their way through the face when it is veneered. You can buy particleboard that has been pre-veneered with many woods, including oak and birch.

Particleboard is commonly available in thicknesses from ⅛ in. to 1⅛ in., in widths of 4 ft. and 5 ft. and in lengths of up to 12 ft. (A standard 4-ft. by

Particleboard (top) and medium-density fiberboard (MDF) are the two most common composite materials in cabinetry. The relatively dense and uniform chip pattern of the MDF (bottom) makes it a better choice for joinery and lamination.

8-ft. sheet of particleboard may be 49 in. wide by 97 in. long, to leave extra material for trimming.) The glue-saturated wood chips result in a product that is dense, uniform and more than twice as heavy as plywood. Its weight makes it difficult to handle if you're working alone.

The weight of particleboard is not the thing that should most concern you. One of the most controversial issues in the world of industrial cabinetmaking is the formaldehyde emissions from composite sheet material. Unless every exposed surface of a sheet is covered with paint or laminate, the material will release a low level of formaldehyde into the atmosphere. Although this occurs in the kitchen as well as in the shop, the formaldehyde is most readily absorbed by inhaling the fine dust produced by the belt sander and table saw. The same glue used to make particleboard is also used to make plywood, but much more of it goes into particleboard, so the emissions problem is more severe. Manufacturers are attempting to lower these irritating—and possibly carcinogenic— fumes by using low-fuming resins in place of urea-formaldehyde glue (these products are labeled accordingly).

Apart from its weight and potential health hazard, particleboard has some other properties that make it difficult to work. It is relatively weak, and joinery can be difficult because particleboard lacks the long-grain structure of solid wood. Its screw-holding capacity is also poor, and once a screw has been withdrawn it should not be reused in the same hole. For all of these reasons, I try to avoid using particleboard for my cabinets. Its only virtues are its low price and its use of waste wood.

Medium-density fiberboard Although their basic ingredients are essentially the same, medium-density fiberboard (MDF) differs significantly from particleboard in its composition and working characteristics. Because MDF is made of very fine wood fibers that are compressed under great pressure, its surface is very smooth, making it ideal for veneer and paint. And the size of these fibers is consistent throughout the sheet, so it cuts and glues beautifully. MDF is about the same weight as particleboard (a 4-ft. by 8-ft. sheet of ¾-in. MDF weighs about 100 lb.) and about 50% more expensive.

Medium-density fiberboard is also available as a plywood look-alike, with veneer covering both faces. But beware—its super-smooth surface makes it possible for industry to use very thin veneers (¹⁄₆₄ in. thick or less). You'll find it much easier to sand through these veneers than the more robust veneers found on plywood. (This is not to be confused with medium-density overlay, or MDO, which is plywood covered on both sides with a resin-treated fiber. MDO has a very smooth surface that is particulary suited to painting.)

Like particleboard, medium-density fiberboard has no grain, so the kerf created by cutting it on a table saw will not open or close behind the blade. Thus the material is not prone to kickback. But its lack of grain means that MDF shares the poor strength and screw-holding ability of particleboard. Formaldehyde emissions are also a problem. All things considered, I usually avoid using MDF, too.

Plastic laminate

Plastic laminate has caused two revolutions in this country. The first occurred when it was introduced in the early 1920s. Laminate was like penicillin—indispensable. It was also inexpensive, easily cleaned, scratch-resistant and wear-resistant. The material was quickly adopted by designers, who used it for everything from office furniture to interiors. Unfortunately, the rather tacky patterns of some early laminates gave them a lingering association with poor taste.

The second revolution is still going on. With the advent of the European-style case and new kinds of laminates, it has emerged as the material of choice for

The range of available colors and the practicality of plastic laminate have made it ubiquitous in the modern kitchen.

Plastic laminate

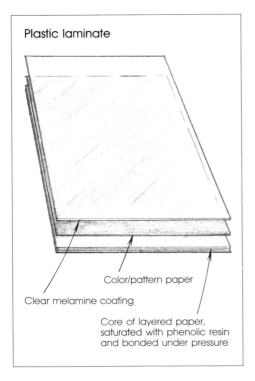

Clear melamine coating

Color/pattern paper

Core of layered paper, saturated with phenolic resin and bonded under pressure

the finest kitchen cabinets. Even though wood can be almost entirely encased within a protective polyester finish, nothing beats plastic laminate—for all the reasons that made it popular in the first place.

Plastic laminate is basically paper saturated with phenolic resin and layered and bonded under high pressure (drawing, left). The core is covered with a sheet of paper to provide color and pattern, and the whole is then covered with a protective shield of melamine resin. Its surface may be embossed with a design or texture, and there are metallic and laboratory-grade laminates to suit just about any taste or need. If you don't see it, ask. (Address your questions directly to the manufacturers, who are most likely to know what's available.)

Many people think plastic laminate is impervious to water, but it isn't. Like wood, it is hygroscopic—that is, it takes on and gives off moisture, and will swell or shrink accordingly. The back of the laminate is particularly susceptible to moisture—indeed, its porous quality is what permits it to bond well to a substrate. For this reason, it is important that both the laminate and the plywood substrate be allowed to acclimatize for a day or two before being used. If they've been stored in areas of different humidity (maybe the laminate was in a damp basement while the plywood was in a heated shop), they should both be brought into the same area. The job site is ideal, but you'll probably have to settle for the workshop. In any case, if either material has been stored in an unheated area, it won't be ready to use until brought to room temperature.

A large sheet of plastic laminate can be rolled into a tube for easy handling when moving it, but don't roll it too tightly. A 4-ft. by 8-ft. sheet should be rolled into a 4-ft. long tube about 2 ft. in diameter, with the good surface facing in. Tie the tube securely with string, but make sure to protect the edge of the laminate beneath the string with a piece of cardboard.

Grades and dimensions Like plywood, plastic laminate comes in different grades. The most common one—horizontal grade—is about 1/16 in. thick, and I use it for nearly everything, horizontal and vertical surfaces alike. Vertical and postforming grades are about half the thickness of horizontal grade (or less, depending on the manufacturer) and much less expensive. They're intended mainly for easy bending. Postforming laminate, as its name suggests, can be heated to 325°F and bent to a 3/8-in. radius to wrap the rounded edges of a countertop or door. Because of their delicacy, however, vertical-grade and postforming laminates are much more susceptible to damage both before and after laminating than is horizontal-grade material.

Plastic laminate is available in sheets of different sizes. Glossy and textured laminates usually come in 4-ft. by 8-ft., 10-ft. or 12-ft. sheets. (Like some particleboards, the actual measurements of the sheets are larger than these nominal dimensions by about 1 in. in both directions, which provides extra material for trimming.) Some new countertop laminates come in 30-in. wide sheets, commonly available in 8-ft., 10-ft. and 12-ft. lengths. Whatever pattern or color you ultimately choose, check to see what sizes it comes in *before* you make up your materials list.

Finishes Many plastic laminates are available with a glossy, matte or embossed surface. When the glossy finish first came out, it was less resistant to scratching than it is now. Glossy and embossed surfaces can be an interesting design element, but I don't use them for countertops because they are hard to clean.

Laminates also come in a variety of imitative designs. To achieve this effect, wood, marble, leather, and all sorts of fabric designs are photographically reproduced on the top sheet of the laminate. With some patterns, like slate and leather, texture is even added. I prefer to use real wood or marble if I want that look, but many people find these patterns pleasant.

The plastic-laminate industry seems to grow by the minute. The variety of colors and patterns now available in plastic laminate is absolutely mind-boggling, and I know of no dealer who stocks a full selection from all the major manufacturers. Even if one did, it would be quickly out of date, as new laminates are coming out all the time. (See the Resource Guide on p. 185 for the addresses of the major manufacturers.)

New developments One of the most interesting new products is a plastic laminate that is the same color all the way through (photo below), called Colorcore by Formica and Solicor by Wilsonart. This type of laminate eliminates the dark brown line of the phenolic-resin core that is visible wherever the edge of a standard plastic laminate is exposed. This line isn't a problem in dark lami-

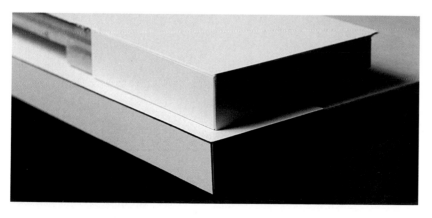

The continuous color of a solid-color laminate (top) eliminates the unsightly brown line of the resin core that is found on conventional laminates (bottom).

nates, but it is clearly visible in light-colored laminates, so I usually try to cover the edge with hardwood.

These solid-color materials can be used in all sorts of creative ways. For example, sheets of different colors can be stacked and laminated, and then machined with V-grooves or a chamfered edge to produce a variegated effect. And because the color is homogeneous throughout the surface laminate, a scratch is less noticeable. The colors of the solid laminates match many of those in the standard laminate lines, and can be successfully mixed. You can, for example, use regular, horizontal-grade, matte-finish laminate for doors and drawer faces, and the solid-color stuff for countertops.

These laminates do have a couple of drawbacks, though. They are more brittle and quite a bit more expensive than standard laminates—about three times the price of horizontal-grade material. And they're available only in 4-ft. by 10-ft. sheets. Switching to all solid-color material throughout the kitchen will raise the cost of the job substantially, so I don't do it very often.

Wood veneer

Although the colorful and wear-resistant surface of plastic laminate is most desirable in the modern kitchen, wood veneers offer a rich alternative. Sometimes plastic can appear bland or even monotonous, but wood is wood. It is always interesting. If your family has young children and a busy lifestyle, you would be wise to stick with the more durable plastics. But for a sense of drama, wood veneer can't be beat.

Veneer (photo, below) provides access to the finest wood and the most unusual figure at a reasonable price. When a very fine board is used in its solid form, most of its beauty lies hidden forever within it. Slice this same board into thin sheets of veneer and use them to cover other less perfect boards or plywood, and you can spread its beauty around.

There's a great variety of highly figured wood available, much of it in veneer; with careful selection, you can use it to great effect. I'm always on the lookout for dramatic wood to use in my cabinets. This unusual figure may be the result of decay, as in the spalted wood in the top photo on the facing page, or of the

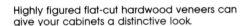
Highly figured flat-cut hardwood veneers can give your cabinets a distinctive look.

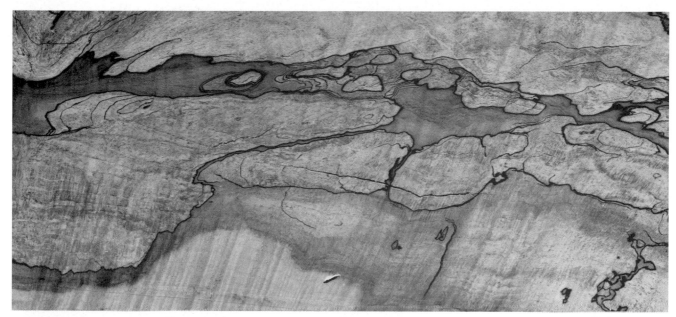

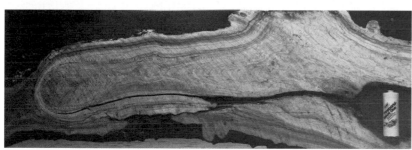

Spalted wood (top) or crotch wood (left) can add a dramatic touch when applied as a veneer to cabinet doors or drawer faces.

peculiar growth patterns that can be found in veneer cut from burls, crotches and stumpwood.

Burls are abnormal lumps that grow like cancers on the trunk or branches of a tree. Their fantastic figure makes some of the most beautiful veneers. Burls are usually small—a growth capable of producing a 2-ft. by 3-ft. sheet of veneer is extremely rare. Even if a burl grew large enough to produce a long, solid board, it would probably twist and warp beyond use. Also, its convoluted grain structure would be weak, difficult to machine and virtually impossible to match.

Crotch wood, shown in the photo above, is cut just below the point where the main trunk of a tree divides into two secondary trunks. Its figure is sometimes described as flame or feather. Both walnut-crotch and mahogany-crotch veneers have been used in furniture for centuries. Like burl wood, crotch wood is highly unstable and difficult to use in board form.

Stumpwood comes from the base, or butt, of the tree and is similarly unpredictable in its figure. Because of its ground-level origin, stumpwood often contains rocks and other debris, which make cutting the wood tough on sawblades. Consequently, you won't find it as easily as you will crotch or burl veneer.

Matching veneers Like plywood veneers, the most common hardwood veneers are either rotary cut or flat cut. As I mentioned before, I much prefer the flat-cut variety for its natural grain and color patterns. Although selecting and using these patterns in veneer can be exciting, flattening and laying the $\frac{1}{28}$-in. thick sheets of veneer can also be intimidating. But don't let this stop you from using it. Start with very small projects and gradually work your way up to larger, more complex ones.

If you feel that handling standard veneer is beyond your capability, two-ply veneer is available to make the job more manageable. This veneer is pre-flattened and bookmatched by the manufacturer before a stabilizing backing of poplar or cloth is attached. This glued-on backing adds another $1/16$ in. or so to the thickness of the veneer, making it much less fragile. Hundreds of kinds of two-ply veneer may be special ordered in sizes up to 4 ft. by 8 ft. And don't despair if you simply don't want to tackle veneering yourself. For a handsome price, a few specialty outlets will lay veneer for you on a core material of your choosing.

Of course, you can always just buy the stuff in sheets of $3/4$-in. flitch-matched plywood and cut out the parts you want. You may waste a bit more material, but you'll save a lot of time and money.

Hardwood

Although my cabinets are built mainly of plywood and plastic laminate or veneer, I cannot conclude my discussion of materials without mentioning hardwood. From the beauty and warmth of a wood-paneled home to the exquisite sounds of a well-made violin, there are few materials that affect our existence as profoundly as wood. Every wood has its own idiosyncrasies and, even used in small quantities, it will have a profound effect on your work. Each time you work wood, you will be introduced to a new personality, with a unique taste, smell, appearance and working characteristics.

Hardwood edge trim, particularly when used in European-style cabinets, minimizes the sometimes antiseptic appearance of plastic laminate and protects its fragile edges (photo, facing page). Because softwoods don't stand up to the abuse a cabinet typically receives, I stick with hardwood.

Grades of hardwood Like plywood, hardwood is graded according to quality, and there's a maze of designations to confuse the first-time buyer. But if you stick to a few basic grades, you can find what you need for most cabinet work. The highest grade commonly sold is FAS, which stands for "Firsts and Seconds." This will be mostly clear of knots, splits, shakes and the like. No. 2 common and No. 3 common are lower grades, and include more defects, but this may not matter if your lumber will be cut into short lengths and narrow widths. And you'll save some money by buying the lower-grade wood.

Moisture content The single most important factor in the preparation and use of wood in cabinet work is the amount of moisture it contains. Green wood is a joy to work, but it can shrink considerably and unpredictably, while overly dry wood will expand after exposure to more humid air. Even a finished cabinet is not immune to changes in humidity, and you'll note the way cabinet doors that won't shut in the summer can be closed with ease in the winter.

Bringing wood to a uniform moisture content is critical. But if this happens too quickly or if too much moisture is removed, the wood may be damaged. The wood must be brought into equilibrium with the environment in which it will end up, either by air-drying or kiln-drying, or a combination of the two.

Air-dried wood is stacked and stickered outdoors and under cover until ready to use. This is the technique I use if I discover freshly cut wood in my neighborhood. Air-drying removes most of the moisture, but not enough for cabinet work. So after the moisture content of the wood has reached equilibrium with the outside humidity—about 15% to 20% where I live in Connecticut—I bring it indoors. (The best way to check air-dried wood for moisture content is with a moisture meter.) Here, too, the boards are stickered so that all surfaces are exposed and the wood can continue to dry evenly. When it has reached about

Solid hardwood protects the fragile edges of the plastic laminate and adds to the warmth of the finished kitchen.

6% to 8% moisture content, the stickers are removed to prevent more humid air from infiltrating the wood.

This process takes a long time, so many people buy kiln-dried wood instead. The heat of a lumber kiln (up to 180°F) will also kill pests or fungus in the wood.

If you purchase hardwood, whether air or kiln dried, I recommend that you get it from a reputable dealer. This will increase the chances that the wood has been dried correctly. But be alert—although the wood may have been correctly dried, if it has been sitting in a damp warehouse, it will still be too wet.

Purchasing hardwood Whether you buy this marvelous material from a sawmill or a lumberyard, it is typically sold in the rough, by the board foot. One board foot equals one square foot of 1-in. thick wood. What you actually get, however, is sometimes less than a full measure. That's because wood that's sawn to a particular thickness at the mill will shrink by the time it gets to you, but you'll be charged for the full dimension. When you're cruising through the lumber stacks, remember that the so-called 1-in. material may be only $\frac{7}{8}$ in. or $\frac{15}{16}$ in. thick. But when you're figuring up the cost of a particular board, use the full, pre-shrinkage dimension in your calculations. To figure out how many board feet are in a piece of wood, use the following formula:

thickness (in.) × width (in.) × length (ft.) ÷ 12 = board feet.

Lumberyards

The key to success in obtaining the right materials is connecting with the right source. If you walk into the wrong place, you won't find much of a selection, and you'll probably pay too much for what you get. Most of the materials I use in building kitchen cabinets can be ordered from one specialty supplier or another, but since you'll likely head to your nearby lumberyard first, you should know what to expect.

There are two types of lumberyards—softwood and hardwood—though you won't find them listed this way in the phone book. In spite of the fact that they are both called lumberyards, they are really in different businesses, with different products.

Softwood yards Most softwood lumberyards are retail outlets that sell dimensioned lumber (1x4s, 2x4s, etc.), softwood plywood and construction materials. In addition, they carry a large variety of other products, including paint, hardware, tools and plumbing and electrical supplies for the general public. (Sometimes they even sell kitchen cabinets.) They may also sell wholesale to building contractors and other professionals.

Red oak, birch and mahogany are the only hardwoods you're likely to find at a softwood yard, if you find any at all. And these will be planed to a finished thickness and width, which naturally costs more. Although softwood lumberyards may carry birch, oak and lauan plywood for cabinet construction, their variety of sizes and grades is usually very limited.

The sad fact is that many softwood-yard salesmen don't know the products they sell. I once suggested that a friend buy a sheet of flat-cut, red oak veneer-core plywood for a project he was building. When he showed me the sheet, I was astonished to see rotary-faced material. He returned it to the yard and they checked to see if it was flat cut—not by looking at the plywood, but by looking at the invoice!

Hardwood yards   You're likely to have better luck at a hardwood lumberyard than at a softwood yard. Hardwood yards are more often wholesale businesses, and they rarely sell anything but lumber, and sometimes hardwood plywood, so they usually have a good selection. (They may also carry softwood lumber, especially those species used in boatbuilding or furnituremaking.) This is important if you want wood of a particular color, width or length. You may also discover other woods that will suit your project better than the one you came for—salesmen at these yards are generally knowledgeable, and can offer some good advice.

Hardwood yards sell rough lumber that has not been surfaced. For an extra milling charge, the yard will plane, rip and joint the boards for you, but you will be charged for the full width and length of the rough board. Don't expect a hardwood yard to be as predictable as a retail yard. Some close for lunch and vacations, and most will not mill stock within a half-hour of closing time, which is usually 4:00 p.m. If you rummage through the stock, you may be charged for the time spent putting it straight again. You may also be charged for selecting stock rather than taking it off the top of the pile. And many hardwood yards are not willing to handle the small quantities sold to retail customers. Check first to avoid disappointment.

Besides hardwood and retail lumberyards, there are sheet-material distributors, who handle all types of plywood, particleboard, medium-density fiberboard and plastic laminate. They also carry laminating adhesives and the rollers and other tools used to spread adhesive, and cut and score laminate. For price and selection, they're your best bet. And since these outfits supply the kitchen market, they may also carry kitchen hardware.

APPLYING LAMINATE
Chapter 5

The crisp, contemporary look of European-style cabinets comes from the broad, uncluttered expanses of plastic laminate. The laminate is applied to a substrate of either plywood or particleboard (as I mentioned in Chapter 4, I generally use hardwood plywood because of its superior strength). The substrate supplies the mechanical strength that the plastic lacks, while the surface material makes the cabinets easy to clean and adds color, texture, pattern, water resistance and wear resistance.

Since most kitchen cabinets are sheathed with plastic laminate, this chapter deals with its application. You can use veneer in many of the same places you would use laminate, and I often use it on doors and drawer faces. But the process of veneering is another subject entirely, and beyond the scope of this book. You can avoid veneering entirely by purchasing a good grade of hardwood-veneer plywood.

The clean lines and homogeneous texture of plastic laminate will not tolerate ragged or nicked edges, scratches or sloppy seams. Imperfections that might go unnoticed in an all-wood kitchen will stick out like a sore thumb against a sea of laminate. Laying the laminate can be a time-consuming activity—even for someone who has done a lot of it—and it's not much fun, either. The glue is messy, the flimsy sheets are difficult to maneuver and the laminate produces an irritating dust when it is trimmed. And while the substrate is covered with contact cement, no other work can be done in the shop that will create dust or chips. But don't worry—professional results can be obtained by using ordinary shop tools and a few specialized items for cutting the plastic, along with a simplified system of production.

The no-fault method

I take a straightforward, streamlined approach to cutting and applying laminate, which I call the "no-fault" method. Like the component system of cabinet construction I use, no-fault lamination assumes that mistakes will be made in the process and that each subsequent step can correct any previous errors.

To understand the advantages of the no-fault approach, let me briefly describe the way laminate is usually applied. The typical process involves several steps. First, the plywood substrate is cut to finished dimension. Next, the laminate is cut oversize and then glued to the substrate. Finally, the edge of the laminate is trimmed flush with the finished edge of the substrate. Later on, the exposed edges are covered with a plastic or wood edging.

The repetition involved in this approach is unnecessarily wasteful—you have to work precisely at almost every step. Following the no-fault approach, I attach the plastic to the substrate before cutting the panels to their final dimensions. Several operations are thus combined, and careful measurements and cutting are done only once—when the finished panels are cut out of the pre-laminated sheets. I use this method whenever I can to laminate all the material for shelves, doors, drawer faces, straight countertops, case bottoms and so on. It saves a lot of time and money, and the results are superior to what I could accomplish the old way.

A cutting diagram Whichever method you use, good planning is essential. I make a cutting diagram of every panel to be laminated, as shown on p. 31, before ordering the plywood and plastic laminate for the job. As I mentioned earlier, I wait until the cases are built to take final measurements for the doors and drawer faces.

The cutting diagram indicates whether each piece will be laminated on one or two sides. Any panel that will not be fixed rigidly in place with screws—such as a door or shelf—must receive laminate on the back side. (Case bottoms and the countertop and backsplash are laminated on one side only.) Without this balancing laminate, the glue joint would shrink on one side of the panel, causing it to warp.

The balancing laminate can be the same grade as the face material or, if it will not be visible, a less expensive backing sheet can be used instead. The backing sheet is a laminated panel without the color surface overlay. If I'm running short of laminate and have no backing material on hand, I'll sometimes use pieces of plastic laminate that are left over from other jobs to cover the underside of the base-case shelves—especially fixed ones that cannot be removed from the case or be seen from above.

Cutting the laminate Plastic laminate comes in panels up to 5 ft. wide by 12 ft. long (several different standard sizes are available), and these have to be cut down to manageable size before they can be laminated to the plywood substrate. If I'm really in a hurry, I'll have the material delivered to a countertop fabricator, who lays the plastic laminate for me in full sheets, half sheets or one-third sheets, according to my diagrams. This service costs me $1.00 per sq. ft.—not bad, considering the unpleasant nature of the materials. But whether I laminate the partial sheets or pay to have it done, I always cut out the finished pieces myself.

There are several ways to cut plastic laminate. You can use a table saw, a special laminate-cutting shears, a scoring tool or a laminate-trimming router bit. Cutting large sheets of plastic on a table saw is a real chore. The sheets are flimsy and hard to maneuver, and they tend to buckle and creep under the

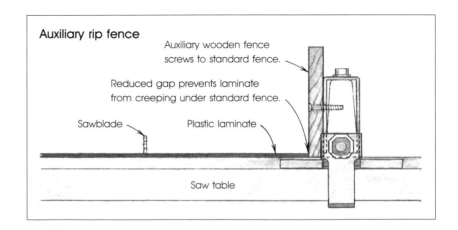

Auxiliary rip fence

Auxiliary wooden fence screws to standard fence.

Reduced gap prevents laminate from creeping under standard fence.

Sawblade

Plastic laminate

Saw table

The scoring tool cuts laminate quickly and easily. Use a straightedge to guide the tool, and make two or three passes (above left). Then lift one edge of the laminate to snap the sheet in two (above right).

fence. You can reduce this gap by attaching an auxiliary fence to the regular fence, as shown in the drawing on the facing page, but full-size sheets are still difficult to handle unless you have access to a panel saw. Likewise, the shears, which work like a large tin snips, are tedious to use on large sheets of laminate. Laminate-cutting shears are expensive, and not a practical investment for the person who is doing only one job.

The quickest and easiest method for cutting plastic laminate is to use a scoring tool with a carbide tooth. This inexpensive tool requires almost no setup, and there are no power cords or clamps to get in the way. Place the laminate face up on a solid, flat surface, and use a straightedge to guide the tool, as shown in the photo above left. Repeat the scoring cut two or three times, and then lift one side of the plastic toward the scored face to snap the sheet apart, as shown in the photo above right. If you fold the plastic away from the scoring cut, it may not break cleanly. Before you begin to cut a good piece of laminate, try the scoring tool on a piece of scrap. You'll find that it can cut all the way through the laminate with repeated passes, a helpful technique if you have to cut a small corner from a larger sheet.

The scoring tool can be used to cut a plastic-laminate sheet of any size, but it can be tricky to hand-hold the sheet and the straightedge while you score a 4-ft. wide piece of plastic. You can clamp the straightedge to the laminate, and I often do, or you can use a router fitted with a laminate-trimming bit, as shown

A roller bearing on the end of the laminate-trimming bit guides the bit along the straightedge to make a flush cut.

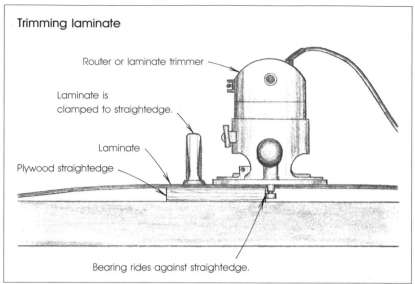

Trimming laminate

Router or laminate trimmer

Laminate is clamped to straightedge.

Laminate

Plywood straightedge

Bearing rides against straightedge.

in the photo and drawing above. To use a trimming bit, draw the line of cut on the back of the plastic and clamp a straightedge to the line. (A long, straight piece of plywood makes a fine straightedge.) Make sure that the clamps will not interfere with the router base, and be sure to protect the laminate with a clamping pad if you don't use wooden handscrews. Flip the plastic over and run the router across the laminate, with the bearing on the bit guided by the straightedge. This is a hefty cut, so use a 1-hp (or larger) router with a ⅜-in. or ½-in. laminate-trimming bit or a two-flute straight bit. (If you use the straight bit, which has no bearing, you will have to set up the straightedge to guide the router base.)

Whichever method you choose (and I use several different ones, depending on the size of the sheet, the quantity of work I have to do and the tool I have on hand), always leave one edge of the plywood exposed. This provides a good edge to run against the table-saw fence when you cut the finished pieces.

Adhesives Many different adhesives can be used to bond plastic laminate to a substrate—including white glue, yellow glue and plastic-resin glue—but I prefer contact cement. Laminate coated with contact cement will bond instantly to the plywood without having to be clamped in place. The other glues are plenty strong (plastic-resin glue and a hot press give the best results), but they must be clamped, and only commercial fabricators have the equipment to clamp large panels. What's more, laminate expands and contracts just like wood, and the plastic can crack if the bond is too rigid. Contact cement is a rubbery substance, so it is more forgiving of movement in the laminate or substrate. I buy my cement in 5-gal. cans with convenient pop-up pouring spouts. Two cans will get me through a small to medium-sized kitchen.

Use a solvent-based cement, rather than a latex-based cement. (Whenever I've used a latex-based cement, the plastic has delaminated from the plywood during subsequent sawing operations.) There are two types of solvent-based cements—one flammable, the other nonflammable. Both emit noxious vapors, but any sparks from a nearby motor (even a refrigerator compressor) can cause the flammable cement to explode. I prefer not to bring explosive materials into the shop, but if you must use flammable cement, do so with great care and turn off all motors. In any case, work in a well-ventilated room and use a respirator intended for protection against vapors—a particle mask won't do the job.

Applying contact cement   Contact cement is a gooey substance, and it has to be applied to both surfaces being bonded. It's usually applied with a brush or roller. Professionals save time by spraying a specially formulated cement. I like rollers best. They coat more evenly and much faster than brushing, and cost a lot less than spray equipment. A short-nap roller is made for this purpose, but any good paint roller will do. (Don't use a cheap roller, or the cement will dissolve the adhesive that holds the roller together, leaving you with a real mess.)

I pour the cement into a paint tray, which I reuse many times until it is thickly encrusted with glue. The glue is very difficult to remove, and the thinner needed for cleanup would cost more than a new tray does. If the roller won't be used again for several days I throw it out. Otherwise, I wrap it tightly in plastic to keep the glue from drying. After a few rolls, it softens up and is as good as new.

Before you start laminating, make sure that the surfaces of the plywood and plastic are thoroughly clean. Use compressed air, if you have it, to blow off the sheets. Then completely cover both surfaces with a thin coat of contact cement. When contact cement is first spread it looks wet and very glossy, but it isn't ready for laminating until the gloss dulls somewhat and the material is dry to the touch (nothing should come away on your fingers). This usually takes between 10 and 20 minutes, depending on the brand of cement and the humidity. Higher humidity means slower drying.

When you apply contact cement to a thirsty material like plywood (particleboard is even thirstier), it will dry to a matte finish. This indicates that too much of the cement has been absorbed and not enough remains on the surface to create a good bond with the laminate. If this happens, apply a second coat of contact cement, and let it dry to the touch. If the surface of the substrate looks slightly glossy after it dries, you're in business. If not, try a third coat. There's

Apply two or more thin coats of contact cement to both of the surfaces that will be laminated.

Laminate large sheets while they're standing on edge. With contact cement on both surfaces, slide the laminate into position, and then press it home.

some tolerance for overcoating, but too little contact cement will cause the plastic to delaminate later on.

Although most manufacturers recommend one coat for surfaces and two for edges, I double-coat everything—even when the first coat has the proper gloss. Because the Wilhold cement I use is thin compared to other cements, and because the coverage I get with rollers is thinner than what I would get with brushes, I feel safer with two coats. You'll use more rollers, but the results will be worth it. One coat of a thicker adhesive will do, but it's hard to put down an even coat.

Applying the laminate   When the contact cement is dry on both surfaces, they can be brought together. Once the laminate touches the plywood, however, it cannot be shifted. It can be removed with great difficulty by lifting a corner and spraying lacquer thinner or a special contact-cement solvent to dissolve the adhesive. But this is time-consuming, and if the plastic is flexed too much it will crack. The solvents won't harm the substrate, but they may harm a finished surface nearby, so you'd better assume that once you bring the surfaces together, that's where they'll stay.

The main trick to laying laminate is to place the plastic exactly where you want it the first time. I find it much easier to apply large sheets of plastic laminate vertically rather than horizontally. Not only is it difficult to position a floppy 4-ft. by 8-ft. sheet of laminate on a horizontal surface, but gravity is always pulling the plastic into the contact cement. Instead, stand the plywood on edge with the contact-cement side out. Place two scrap blocks under the panel to keep it off the floor and away from dust. Then rest one edge of the plastic on the blocks, with its cemented side facing the plywood (photo, facing page). Slide the sheet back and forth until it's where you want it, then press it home.

To ensure a uniform bond over the entire panel, use a clean rubber roller to press the laminate into the cement, as shown in the photo below. The roller can be purchased from most laminate dealers, who also sell special J-rollers for working the edges. These have two rollers—one for each side of the panel—and you apply pressure by using the handle as a lever. If you don't have a roller,

Apply firm pressure with a rubber roller to get a good bond between the laminate and the plywood substrate. Roll the entire surface, paying special attention to the edges.

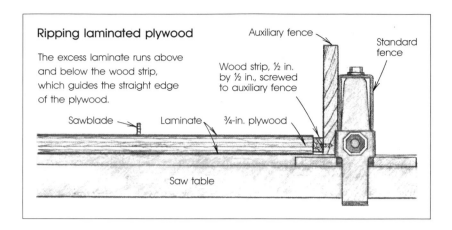

Ripping laminated plywood

The excess laminate runs above and below the wood strip, which guides the straight edge of the plywood.

Auxiliary fence

Standard fence

Wood strip, ½ in. by ½ in., screwed to auxiliary fence

Sawblade

Laminate

¾-in. plywood

Saw table

a 4-in. sq. pine block will do. Use a mallet or a hammer to tap the block frequently as you move it around the surface of the laminate. As soon as the laminate has been thoroughly beaten or rolled, it's ready to be cut.

If a panel is to be completely covered with plastic, the back side should be done first, the edges next and then the face. By proceeding in this order, each laminate will cover the exposed edges of the piece previously applied. The face is installed last so that no edges will be visible from the front. (Any excess glue can be cleaned with lacquer thinner or a special solvent made for this purpose.) Of course, if you plan to laminate the edges, the panel will have to be trimmed to size first. I usually laminate my doors and shelves on two sides and apply hardwood edging, so there's no need to trim the panel until after all the laminate has been applied.

If, despite all your care and cleanliness, a chip of wood or other foreign material gets pressed between the plastic and the plywood, it will reveal itself as a small bubble in the laminate. Such bubbles can sometimes be remedied with a pine block and a hammer. Place the block over the bubble and tap it smartly with the hammer. The offending debris may be crushed or driven into the core, or if it is harder than the plastic, it may come through the surface. If the bubble is on the back of a door, leave it be. But if it's on the face of a door at eye level, go for broke—you'd have to replace the door anyway.

Don't worry if in attaching the laminate you accidently overlap the edge of the plywood that will run against the saw fence—this is the no-fault method. Later on, you can use a trimmer bit to make the laminate flush. And, if you've figured your cutting diagram correctly, the trimmed edge will be removed (along with the other edges) when you saw your panels to size. You can also cut the laminated panel on a table saw equipped with an auxiliary wooden fence, as shown in the drawing above.

Laminating small sheets   While the vertical lamination method works well for large sheets, smaller pieces can be done horizontally. You can use dowels to separate the two surfaces while they're being positioned (photo, p. 66, and drawing, facing page). Lay the panel face up on the workbench, and place the dowels lightly on top of the dried cement. Then place the cement-coated laminate on the dowels and position it over the substrate. Remove one dowel and carefully press the plastic down to lock the sheet in position. Then pull out the remaining dowels, working outward from the center or from one edge to the other to avoid trapping a bubble, and press the plastic into place with your hand as each dowel is removed. I use ⅜-in. or ½-in. dia. dowels. The round dowels make less contact with the cement than square sticks would, and even if one does get stuck, a quick twist will release it.

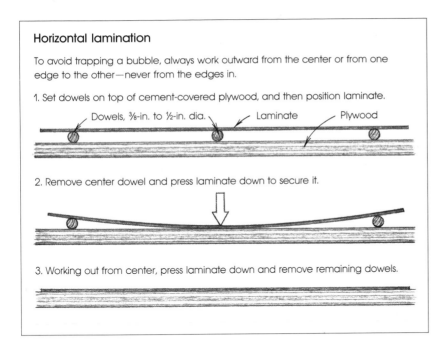

Horizontal lamination

To avoid trapping a bubble, always work outward from the center or from one edge to the other—never from the edges in.

1. Set dowels on top of cement-covered plywood, and then position laminate.

Dowels, ⅜-in. to ½-in. dia.   Laminate   Plywood

2. Remove center dowel and press laminate down to secure it.

3. Working out from center, press laminate down and remove remaining dowels.

Cutting panels to size After all the panels are laminated, cut them on the table saw according to your cutting diagrams. I use an 80-tooth crosscut blade with a triple-chip design, as shown at left in the photo below. This leaves a smooth, finished edge on both sides of the laminated panel. Although I prefer this blade, I have also used other blades (I feed the material more slowly) with excellent results. (Olsen Saw Blade Co. makes 55 and 60-tooth blades that work well.) The success of this operation depends on a good blade, so make sure that your blade is sharp and clean, and that it does not vibrate or wobble. Wobbling can be caused by a number of problems—an out-of-true blade, misaligned pulleys, frayed belts or a bent arbor. Correct any of these problems before starting, and remember to cut slowly.

Cutting the laminate and plywood simultaneously on the table saw has several distinct advantages over the traditional method. If the saw is well tuned and fitted with the right blade, it will cut square edges on the laminate that are perfectly flush with the edges of the plywood and much cleaner than you could produce with a trimmer bit. Also, the cuts will be dead straight, with no nicks in the laminate—even if there are voids in the plywood. These factors add up to superior results in much less time.

The 80-tooth crosscut blade at left leaves an excellent finished edge on both laminate and plywood. The 55-tooth alternate-tooth-bevel (ATB) combination blade at right works well if you don't push the stock too fast. The 24-tooth ATB rip blade at center is used only for solid wood, not plywood or laminate.

The traditional method

Once you see the finished edges of the no-fault panels, you'll never want to go back to the old method again. But don't kiss your laminate trimmer good-bye. In a few situations—such as laminating the outside of a finished case, making a cutout opening in a laminated counter and installing a curved laminate—you'll have to cut the substrate to size before attaching the laminate. Apart from the sequence of operations, the main difference between the two methods is in trimming the laminate. The other steps—rough-cutting the laminate and cementing it to the substrate—are exactly the same.

Trimming laminate   To ensure complete coverage of a plywood panel that has been precut to its final dimension, the plastic should be about ¼ in. larger than the plywood on all sides. This gives you some room for error when you lay the laminate—it's a lot easier to trim the overhang than to position the laminate perfectly on the plywood. You'll have to use the horizontal method, described on pp. 74-75, to position the laminate so it overhangs the substrate.

Once the laminate is attached, use a router or laminate trimmer to trim its edges flush with the plywood substrate, as shown in the photo below. The Porter-Cable laminate trimmer shown is a small, underpowered router designed to be

Use a laminate trimmer and a bearing-guided bit to cut a protruding edge of plastic laminate flush with a finished plywood edge.

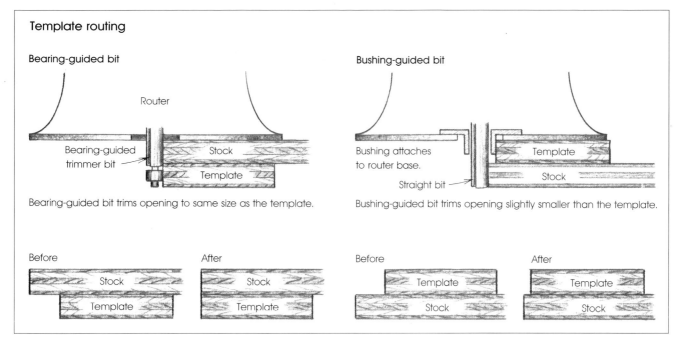

Template routing

Bearing-guided bit

Router

Bearing-guided
trimmer bit

Stock

Template

Bearing-guided bit trims opening to same size as the template.

Bushing-guided bit

Bushing attaches
to router base.

Straight bit

Template

Stock

Bushing-guided bit trims opening slightly smaller than the template.

Before

Stock

Template

After

Stock

Template

Before

Template

Stock

After

Template

Stock

much faster, and keeps you from having to hog through a lot of material with the low-powered trimmer.

Another option is to cut the template slightly larger, to allow for a guide bushing mounted on a straight bit (drawing, above and photo, right). In this case, the template is clamped to the top side of the material. Any of these methods—the trimmer bit or the bushing-guided straight bit with a template or the pilot bit without a template—will produce a neat cutout.

The least elegant but by far the fastest way to cut out the holes for sinks and outlets is to bore a ⅝-in. dia. hole at each corner and then connect the outer edges of the holes with a jigsaw. It's not very neat, but it gets the job done, and no one will notice once the edge is covered by the lip of the sink.

Stress cracks   Although plastic laminate is quite durable, it can crack if subjected to expansion or vibration, or if you fail to predrill holes for screws. Stress cracks are especially prevalent at inside corners and around the countertop cutouts for sinks or electrical boxes. To minimize cracking, it's a good idea to round all laminated corners. A smoothly curved corner is much less likely to crack than an abrupt right angle.

Where a rounded corner cannot be used (if, for example, a countertop must make a right-angle turn), you can minimize stress cracks with the judicious use of yellow glue during lamination. Cover both surfaces with contact cement, as usual, except for the area within about 6 in. of the corner. When the cement has dried, spread a thin coat of yellow glue at the corner and lay the laminate in place. After pressing down the plastic with a roller or block, clamp the corner until the yellow glue dries. Put a scrap of wood under the clamp to protect the laminate.

There's always a risk of breaking a countertop that has been weakened by the removal of a large cutout. It's safer to rout the four corners of the cutout in the shop and use a jigsaw to connect them after the counter has been installed. In this case, do not cut the opening in the plywood before attaching the laminate; the opening will be cut in both the plywood and the laminate at the same time. To ensure that the jigsaw will not crack the surface of the plastic outside the lip of the sink, scribe a line beforehand with the scoring tool, just outside of

This two-part bushing is attached to the router base with a threaded collar.

the line to be cut. Whenever possible, the jigsaw should be used from the back side of the material. That way, the saw cut won't crack the surface, and the shoe of the jigsaw won't scuff it. If it's impossible to work from the back, place a piece of cardboard beneath the shoe of the saw.

If you do chip or crack a finished surface, it can be repaired. I use a product called Kampel SeamFil, which is specifically made for repairing plastic laminate, and is color-matched to Wilsonart and Formica laminates (although other colors can be mixed with special pigments). The filler comes in a small tube and is expensive. It is applied with a putty knife and dries quickly to a hard consistency, so any excess can be trimmed with a razor blade.

Bending laminate   Another situation when you'll have to apply plastic laminate to a precut substrate is in making a bent form. Most standard laminates can be bent to a gentle radius of about 6 in. You can reduce the radius of a bend in postforming laminate to as little as ⅜ in. by heating the laminate with a commercial heater strip. At around 325°F, the laminate will soften enough to take the bend. In general, however, I do not recommend bending laminates yourself. It is a difficult process, and the commercial machinery designed to do the job is very expensive.

Seaming laminate   It's not always possible to laminate a surface with a single sheet of plastic, and so a seam is sometimes unavoidable. The exposed edges of a case of fixed shelving is a good example. To laminate plastic to the edges of the shelves and the case, you could lay a large sheet across the front of the cabinet and then rout out the spaces, but this would be extremely wasteful. It

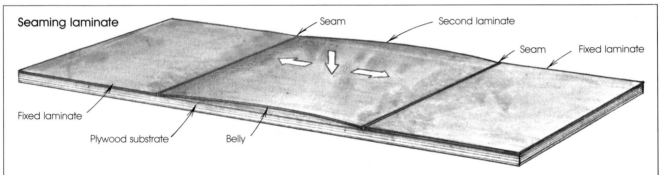

Seaming laminate

Seam   Second laminate

Seam   Fixed laminate

Fixed laminate

Plywood substrate   Belly

To get tight seams, cut the center laminate slightly long. Then butt the ends of the center piece against the ends of the fixed laminates on both sides. Working outward from the center, press the belly down.

makes better sense to cover the edges with individual strips of plastic, but the many seams that are formed where the strips meet can be difficult to match. There are two things that you can do to ensure a first-rate seam.

First, make sure that all laminate edges are straight and square. The factory edge is almost never perfect. The table saw is an excellent tool for producing a crisp edge on plywood, but it often has the opposite effect on plastic. Instead, I use a laminate-trimmer bit in a router. Cut each narrow strip of plastic slightly oversize, and clamp it to a straightedge (drawing, p. 70). The trimmer bit will cut the laminate flush with the straightedge, so make sure that the guiding edge of the straightedge is clean and smooth and at least ½ in. thick to guide the bit. Trim both edges of the strip this way. You can saw the ends of the strips cleanly on a radial-arm saw or a chopsaw (power miter box), with a fine carbide cutoff blade.

In the example of the case of fixed shelves, lay the outside (vertical) strips first, and cut and fit the inside (horizontal) strips that will cover the edges of the shelves. Begin by cutting each strip long and bow it slightly to fit it in place. If the strip can be pressed down tightly along its full length, it fits. If it won't seat properly, slice off a bit more on the saw and try it again. (If you don't have a radial-arm saw, you can use a table saw or a router for this.) When the fit is right, apply the contact cement, set the ends of the strip in place and press down the center. Work from the center toward both ends to press the strip smooth and keep the seams tight.

The same approach can be used to achieve a tight counter seam. Trim the matching ends of three sheets of laminate straight and clean, then cement the two outside pieces of laminate to the counter. Butt the matching ends of the center piece tightly against the ends of the fixed laminates, so that a slight belly is created in the unglued laminate (drawing, facing page). When this sheet is cemented and pressed down, the seams will be forced closed, making a tight fit.

Another way to deal with a seam is to inlay it as a decorative element (photo, right). After the seam has been laminated, run it over the table saw, with the blade set at a depth of ⅛ in. This will replace the seam with a shallow kerf, which can be filled with a strip of hardwood. Plane the wood to fit snugly, apply yellow glue to the kerf and tap the strip into place. When the glue is dry, use a sharp hand plane to trim the strip flush with the surface of the plastic.

This method can be used to extend materials, to decorate a surface with pinstripes or to create a windowpane effect. Choose woods with straight grain for inlaid strips, and they will plane down nicely to match the door edgings that will be applied later. Inlay can be used almost anywhere, but I wouldn't try it on a kitchen counter. Frequent exposure to water might cause the wood to swell, cracking the plastic laminate. You can create some interesting effects with inlaid strips of all different materials, or even with Kampel SeamFil. But inlaying takes time, and as far as I'm concerned, there's no substitute for a tight seam.

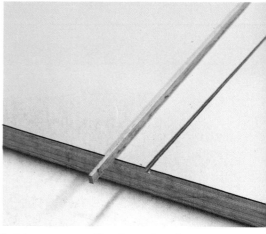

To inlay a narrow strip of wood, make a shallow cut on the table saw and glue the wood in the kerf. Then plane the wood flush with the surface of the laminate.

Chapter 6

fter the hardware and materials have been selected and prepared and the working drawings are done, it's time to start building. Though the sheer volume of materials and joinery may be intimidating, building the cases is not as time-consuming as it appears. This is especially true if you use the simple joinery and the component system I employ. You may move slowly at first, but I know of no faster way to make cases than the process I am about to describe. Considering the setup time involved, not even the 32mm system employed in a large production shop will enable you to make cases faster. With adequate tools, basic woodworking skills and some preparation, you ought to be able to make all the cases for an average kitchen in two weekends. Whether you're making one case or twenty, the techniques are the same.

Making kitchen cabinets is a lot of work, but you'll save a pile of money if you do it yourself. If you invest even a small portion of those savings in upgrading your tools, you may speed your work and improve its quality at the same time. And you'll continue to benefit from the tools long after the job is done. There are many hand tools and a few stationary tools that you'll find useful for the various operations involved in making cabinets. On pp. 84-87 is an introduction to the primary tools and accessories I use to build cases.

As you consider adding to your tool collection, remember to protect the most important tools you have: your ears, lungs and eyes. These cannot be replaced at any price. Buy and wear ear protectors, a respirator, and goggles or shatterproof glasses.

Before you run off to sharpen your tools and get down to work, there is one last item to consider. Where are you going to put the kitchen while you are building it? If your shop is too small to accommodate an entire kitchen of cases, substantial storage space must be provided until you are ready to install the finished cases. After all, this isn't a Windsor chair you're building—you've got a whole room to pack away.

Cutting the plywood   Plywood is never of consistent thickness, so be sure to check your materials before you start cutting. A nominal ¾-in. thick sheet may be as much as ¹⁄₁₆ in. shy. Make all the case parts at once (and using the same saw settings) so you'll be able to assemble them at different times and still maintain consistency. This ensures that the cabinets will be the same height and the countertop won't rest on a bumpy, uneven support system. What's more, if you gang the work, you can usually enlist some help in handling the full-size sheets. If you're reasonably well organized, it should take only two to four hours to unload all the plywood, rip it to width and crosscut it to length. Take

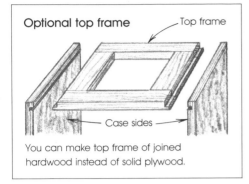

Optional top frame

Top frame

Case sides

You can make top frame of joined hardwood instead of solid plywood.

the time to set up your saw properly—it will pay off in speed and accuracy. And be sure to ventilate your space well when cutting a lot of plywood.

Begin by ripping the plywood lengthwise for all the cases. I use ¾-in. stock for all case parts except the backs, which are made of ¼-in. plywood. The sides, top and bottom of my base cases are 22½ in. wide, and upper-case members are 11½ in. wide. These dimensions allow me to work conveniently from sheets of plywood ripped in halves and quarters. The sides of my base cases are generally 30 in. high, and the length of the tops and bottoms is ¾ in. less than the full width of each case. To determine how many sheets you'll need for a run of cabinets, simply add up the number and length of cabinet sides, tops and bottoms in feet. Divide your total by 16 to arrive at the approximate number of sheets needed for base cases, by 32 for upper cases.

To make the most efficient use of your material, always work from a cutting diagram, like the one shown on p. 31, and remember to eliminate all factory edges when you rip your stock, as described in the drawing. At this point, you must also decide whether to use plywood or to make hardwood frames for the tops (drawing, left). If you use plywood, just figure it into your cutting diagrams. If you build hardwood frames instead, remember to make them slightly oversize. Then, using the same saw setting, cut the frames to size when you rip your plywood, and treat them as though they were plywood from then on.

After all the case sides, tops and bottoms have been cut to width, crosscut them to length. A sliding-table panel saw is by far the best tool for this job, but

Tools for casework

You might be tempted to cut your plywood with a hand-held circular saw, guided by a straightedge, but I don't recommend it. A circular saw tears the wood around the cut, which will make it difficult to fit the wood edging. If you don't have a table saw, you can pay a lumberyard to rip it for you. But before you do, consider investing in a good table saw.

Table saw   The table saw is the most important tool for cutting sheet stock. You can do all the work described in this chapter with a basic saw in good condition. I started out with a Sears saw, which is now 15 years old and still going strong. Its biggest problem is its fence, which has a nasty habit of clamping itself out of line, resulting in burned cuts and wandering stock. To get around this

problem, I bolted a stationary maple fence to the edge of the table, as shown at left in the drawing below.

The stationary fence is set up for a standard 24-in. cut—narrower cuts are made using fixed spacers inside the fence. The spacers are held in place by a hook on one end, which slips over the edge of the saw table.

The spacers also eliminate the need to measure off the blade every time I want to reset the fence. I use the same spacers to cut wider pieces of plywood, too—for example, a 48-in. wide sheet of plywood ripped with a 1-in. spacer will

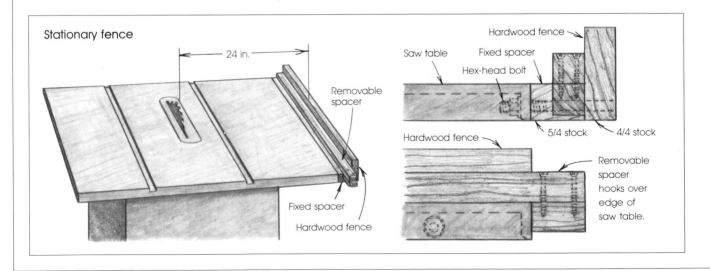

Stationary fence

24 in.

Removable spacer

Fixed spacer

Hardwood fence

Hardwood fence

Saw table

Fixed spacer

Hex-head bolt

5/4 stock

4/4 stock

Hardwood fence

Removable spacer hooks over edge of saw table.

you can use a radial-arm or table saw. Sliding tables are available for some table saws, or you can build your own. If you use a radial-arm saw, you'll have to make the crosscuts in two passes, because the saw won't reach a full 22½ in. This is cumbersome for the first cut in an 8-ft. sheet, but all subsequent cross-cuts should be easier and more reliable. No radial-arm saw I have ever used was true all the time, so do not rely on the accuracy of the saw—cut to layout lines on the plywood instead. Of course, to make it easier to handle, the plywood can be cut to approximate length with a saber saw, and then trimmed to final length on either the radial-arm saw or table saw.

Upper-case parts that are only about 11½ in. wide can be crosscut using a slightly modified miter gauge. Screw or bolt a 3-in. by 36-in. wood fence to the miter gauge to stabilize the long pieces. This extension can be removed after all the upper-case pieces have been cut.

Before you start cutting joints, make separate piles for all the base-case sides, the upper-case sides and their respective tops and bottoms. It may be obvious which plywood face should show on the inside of the cases, but it never hurts to mark the back of each piece. If both sides of your plywood are equally acceptable, check each piece for flatness and place any bow to the inside of the case. If the bow faces out, it will take extra effort to install the cabinets later on.

I use the tongue-and-groove joint shown in the drawing at right to hold both my upper and lower cases together. To make this joint, two horizontal grooves

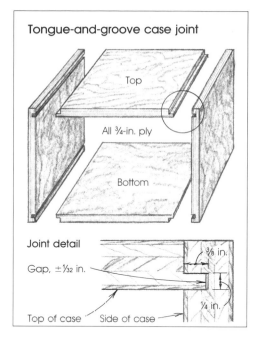

Tongue-and-groove case joint

Top

All ¾-in. ply

Bottom

Joint detail

Gap, ±1/32 in.

3/8 in.

1/4 in.

Top of case   Side of case

A good outfeed table (foreground) and a side-table extension on your saw will enable you to rip large plywood panels with accuracy and safety.

produce two panels, one 23 in. and one 25 in. wide (less the thickness of the saw cut).

I still have the Sears saw, but these days I prefer to use my Rockwell (now Delta) Unisaw. Its 3-hp motor runs with less vibration than the much smaller Sears, and it won't bog down in a cut. It is equipped with a Delta Unifence, which is easy to use and very accurate.

Outfeed tables You'll be ripping a lot of large panels so you'll need to support the work alongside and at the outfeed

end of the saw. I used to use rollers mounted on stands for this purpose, but never liked them. If the rollers aren't perfectly aligned with the cut, they'll cause the work to walk into or away from the fence, spoiling the accuracy of the cut. Even worse, the stock can slide off the end of the saw table and hit the outfeed rollers instead of riding over them, which creates a real problem when you're in the middle of a cut.

I finally upgraded my table-saw setup with a bed of six rollers that I salvaged from an industrial conveyor system. It

worked, sort of, but I now prefer an outfeed table.

Two outfeed tables aid in handling large plywood sheets (photo, above). One table bolted to the side of the saw (an option available for most saws) provides a 50-in. wide surface to the right of the sawblade and at the same height as the table. A second, freestanding table on the outfeed side of the saw supports an 8-ft. long sheet throughout the cut, and doubles as an extra work surface. I've applied plastic laminate to the top of both tables for a smooth-sliding work

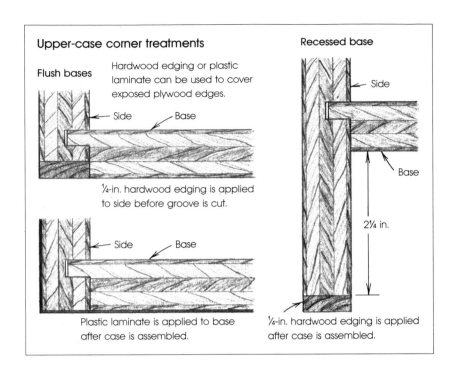

Upper-case corner treatments

Flush bases

Hardwood edging or plastic laminate can be used to cover exposed plywood edges.

← Side — Base

¼-in. hardwood edging is applied to side before groove is cut.

← Side — Base

Plastic laminate is applied to base after case is assembled.

Recessed base

Side

Base

2¼ in.

¼-in. hardwood edging is applied after case is assembled.

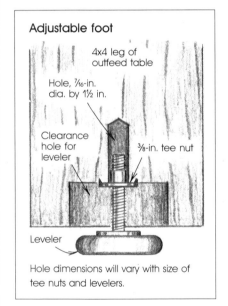

Adjustable foot

4x4 leg of outfeed table

Hole, ⁷⁄₁₆-in. dia. by 1½ in.

Clearance hole for leveler

⅜-in. tee nut

Leveler

Hole dimensions will vary with size of tee nuts and levelers.

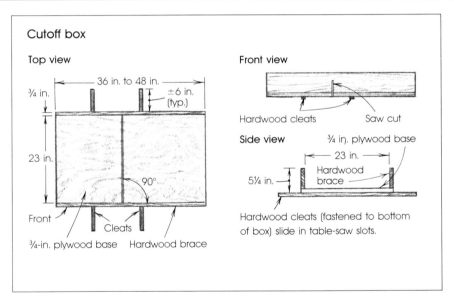

Cutoff box

Top view

36 in. to 48 in.

¾ in.

±6 in. (typ.)

23 in.

90°

Front

Cleats

¾-in. plywood base   Hardwood brace

Front view

Hardwood cleats   Saw cut

Side view

¾ in. plywood base

23 in.

5¼ in.

Hardwood brace

Hardwood cleats (fastened to bottom of box) slide in table-saw slots.

surface. A light sprinkling of sawdust or a coat of wax on the laminate makes for easier sliding.

If the outfeed table isn't level with the saw table, it will be as much trouble as a roller, so mine is equipped with the adjustable feet shown in the drawing at left. (I find that it's easier to slide a sheet of plywood if the top of the outfeed table is a tad lower than the top of the saw table.) The two slots in the top of my

outfeed table allow the miter gauge to travel freely to the end of the saw table without running into the outfeed table.

Cutoff box Another useful table-saw accessory is the cutoff box, which helps in crosscutting plywood (drawing, above). The box is about 23 in. deep by 3 ft. to 4 ft. wide, and works like a giant miter gauge. Two ¾-in. by 5¼-in. hardwood braces hold the ¾-in. plywood base

are cut in the sides of each case, and a corresponding tongue is cut on both ends of the top and bottom pieces.

The tongue-and-groove joint is quick and easy to make, and it forms a strong connection in plywood construction. Even the speedy Lamello plate joinery will take longer to do. Made properly, the tongue-and-groove guarantees a uniform joint, regardless of the plywood thickness. The tongue-and-groove joint is not particularly handsome, I'll admit, but it is always concealed in my cases. In base cases, the exposed ends of the plywood sides will either face the floor or be covered by the countertop. Any exposed plywood edges that would be visible on the underside of upper cases are covered either with a hardwood edging or with plastic laminate, as shown in the top drawing on the facing page. I prefer the tongue-and-groove to any of the others shown in the drawing at right, although they will cover most or all of the exposed plywood edges.

The half-blind tongue-and-groove joint covers the ends of the plywood sides with a narrow tongue, which is very delicate until the joint is assembled. Either the splined miter or the lock miter can be used on any case that will be exposed on all four sides, although you will need a shaper in order to cut the lock miter.

To make room for recessed countertop lighting, I place the bottoms of the upper cases 2½ in. above the bottom edge of the side—2¼ in. from the end of the plywood, plus ¼ in. of hardwood edging (top drawing, facing page). Make sure to obtain the recessed fixtures before you build the cabinets. If the light you choose requires more than 2½ in. of clearance, you might want to recon-

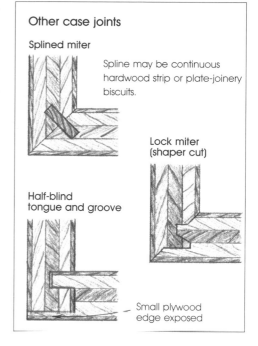

Other case joints

Splined miter

Spline may be continuous hardwood strip or plate-joinery biscuits.

Lock miter (shaper cut)

Half-blind tongue and groove

Small plywood edge exposed

together and provide a reference edge for the 90° cuts. Two slim cleats are attached to the underside of the box to guide it in the saw-table slots. To position the cleats, lower the saw blade completely, set the cleats in the slots and shim them up slightly above the table surface (they must protrude to provide solid contact with the bottom of the box). Run a bead of glue on each cleat and place the box over them so that its edge is parallel to the front of the table. (If the front of the table isn't perfectly perpendicular to the blade, shift the box accordingly.) I use hot glue for this because it dries quickly. Make sure that the cleats extend about 6 in. beyond the box at front and back to make them easier to locate in the slots, and to keep the box running true at the end of a cut.

After the glue sets, turn the box over and screw or staple the cleats to the bottom. With the cleats attached, replace the box on the table, turn on the saw and slowly raise the blade. Bring the blade about 1 in. above the plywood surface of the box to enable you to crosscut ¾-in. material with ¼ in. to spare. Double-check the saw cut to make sure that it's perpendicular to the front brace. To use the box, simply hold a length of plywood firmly against the brace (as you would use a miter gauge) and slide the box across the table. Keep the saw slot in the box free of dust to avoid clogging.

Screw gun A sheetrocking tool, the screw gun can be used to drive case fasteners quickly and efficiently. It is closely related to the woodworker's clutch drill, which can also be adjusted to drive screws. Now that I use pneumatic staples, my clutch drill and screw gun sit on the shelf, but I still love them.

Routers I'd never heard of a router until I was 27, and when I finally saw one I thought it was an odd bit of work. I now own six of them, and as soon as my budget allows, I will have two more. The router is a versatile tool that will permit you to add all sorts of details to your edging and pulls, including roundovers, chamfers, dovetails, coves and rabbets. Standard routers (⅞ hp to 1½ hp) can be used for trimming and most shaping and cutting. Larger routers (2½ hp and up) are used for heavy cutting and can be mounted upside down in a router table. Smaller specialized routers are designed to trim laminates and veneers.

Plate joiners The Lamello plate-joining machine cuts semicircular slots in two pieces of wood to be joined, into which a wooden plate, or biscuit, is glued. The plate soaks up the glue and expands in the slot to form a tight, reliable joint. Plate joints can be made quickly with little or no setup, and are ideal for the top frames of base cases. (The pieces can

be butted or mitered.) Without this machine I wouldn't bother making frames and would use only plywood for case tops.

There are several comparable plate-joining machines, and they range in price from about $175 to $600. These tools will find many applications around a small cabinet shop and are worth their price in time saved.

Pneumatic tools Pneumatic tools are among the few items I could no longer live without, now that I've gotten used to them. Driven by an air compressor, pneumatic tools can be used to drive screws, loosen frozen bolts, shoot fasteners, and sand and spray finishes. In fact, there are pneumatic counterparts to almost every electric hand tool. You can also use compressed air to clean the chips out of your case joints before gluing and to keep the other tools in the shop running cool and clean.

Air-powered staples and brads are driven so fast that the wood has no time to shift or split. This saves aggravation and valuable time at almost every stage of case assembly. Spraying can give you a truly professional finish on your cabinets, and it's faster and less tiring than brushing. If you make kitchens professionally, an air compressor, spray gun and staple gun will pay for themselves in two or three jobs.

sider using it. The more you raise the bottom shelf, the farther out of reach your upper-case storage will be. Those upper-case sides that extend below the bottoms of the cabinets can be edged at the same time that the face edging is done. Just remember to allow for the extra ¼ in. for the edging when you are designing the cabinets.

Many people line the insides of their cabinets with shelf paper to protect the wood and facilitate cleanup, but I don't like the stuff. Instead, I prefer to laminate the bottoms of my cases (and all the shelves) with the same plastic that's used on the faces. (If the faces are glossy or textured, however, I use a matte laminate of the same color inside because it wears better.) Laminate eliminates the need for shelf paper and gives the cases a rich appearance. The laminate must be installed before the joints are cut and the cases are assembled. If you want to laminate the case bottom, the bottom grooves will have to be moved away from the edge of the plywood side by the thickness of the laminate. (The groove and tongue remain a constant ¼ in. wide.)

Cutting the joints I cut the groove in the case sides first. With a ¼-in. dado blade in the table saw, I begin by adjusting the blade height to one-half the thickness of the plywood. Wherever possible, I avoid using a tape measure for these adjustments, because it's slow and introduces the possibility of error. Instead, I use a piece of scrap plywood of the same stock I'll be using in the cases. I place the scrap flat on the saw table next to the blade, as shown in the drawing below left, and raise the blade until it's the right height. This dimension is not critical. Any inaccuracy will be less than the thickness of the center laminate of the plywood, or about $\frac{1}{16}$ in., and this small discrepancy should not alter the overall dimensions of the case. (Whatever slight irregularities might be

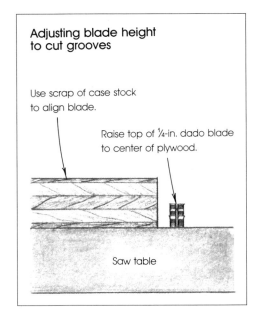

Adjusting blade height to cut grooves

Use scrap of case stock to align blade.

Raise top of ¼-in. dado blade to center of plywood.

Saw table

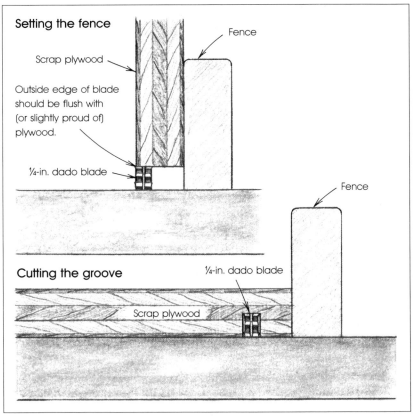

Setting the fence

Fence

Scrap plywood

Outside edge of blade should be flush with (or slightly proud of) plywood.

¼-in. dado blade

Fence

Cutting the groove

¼-in. dado blade

Scrap plywood

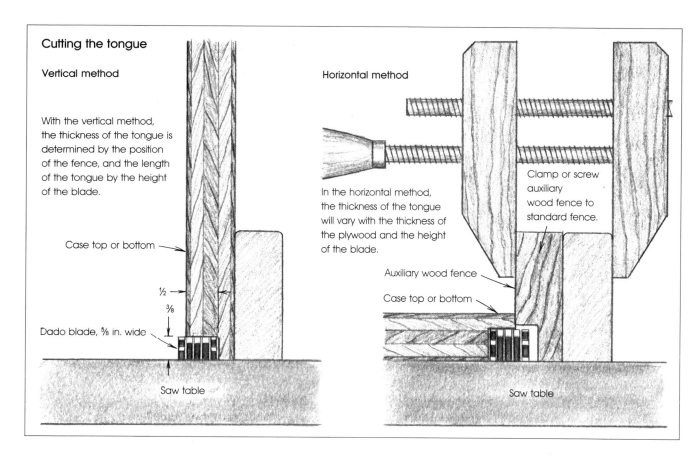

Cutting the tongue

Vertical method

With the vertical method, the thickness of the tongue is determined by the position of the fence, and the length of the tongue by the height of the blade.

Case top or bottom

½

⅜

Dado blade, ⅝ in. wide

Saw table

Horizontal method

In the horizontal method, the thickness of the tongue will vary with the thickness of the plywood and the height of the blade.

Clamp or screw auxiliary wood fence to standard fence.

Auxiliary wood fence

Case top or bottom

Saw table

created here can easily be accommodated by the spacers you'll use to install the cabinets.)

Next, move the fence into position. Using the scrap plywood as shown in the drawing at right on the facing page, make sure the plywood is flush with the outside of the blade, or the blade is a bit proud. It's much easier to sand a ¹⁄₁₆-in. excess off the ends of the case sides than it is to sand down the entire surface of the case top or bottom. (If you laminate the bottoms of your cases, as I do, make sure to use a laminated scrap to set the fence for these grooves.) As a safety precaution, always pull the power cord for the saw when performing this operation. When the fence is adjusted, reconnect the power and check the placement of the groove by making a test cut in another scrap of plywood, as shown in the drawing. With the fence set, cut the top and bottom grooves in all the case sides.

A sharp dado blade will make a smooth cut if the plywood is fed slowly. If the work is fed too quickly or if the blade is dirty or dull, the face veneer will chip, leaving a ragged edge that will have to be filled later. If you don't have a dado blade, you can make the grooves with several passes over a standard crosscut or plywood blade. I sometimes use this method if I'm making only one or two grooves. The bottom of the groove won't be as clean as one produced by a sharp dado blade, but this won't interfere with the joint. Certainly, if you're making a whole kitchen, it will pay to buy a good dado blade.

Cutting the other half of this joint—the tongue—is equally straightforward, but you have two options, as shown in the drawing above. You can either stand the plywood on edge or pass it flat over the dado blade. In the first (vertical) method, the thickness of the tongue will be determined by the distance between the blade and the fence. This is a machine setting and will produce a

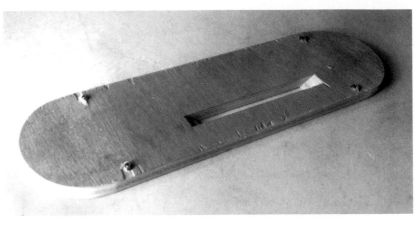

This throat plate (shown in place above left and upside-down above right) was custom-made to fit a dado blade. The four screws are used to adjust its height level with the saw table.

tongue of uniform thickness, regardless of any irregularities in the thickness of the plywood. In the second (horizontal) method, the thickness of the tongue is determined by the height of the blade and will vary with the thickness of the plywood sheet.

For the sake of accuracy, I prefer to use the vertical method whenever possible—especially on fir-core plywood, which is much more irregular than lauan or poplar-core material. But it can be difficult to control a large sheet of plywood passed vertically over the saw, so you should use the second method if you feel at all uncomfortable with the vertical cut. Using the horizontal method probably won't affect the quality of the joints cut in lauan or poplar-core plywood, but most fir-core plywood is so irregular that you'll have to adjust the height of the blade for every tongue. (If you have a shaper, you can obtain a consistent tongue dimension by feeding the stock flat.)

In any case, the tongue is cut with a ⅝-in. wide dado blade, so you'll need a new throat plate to fit the wider blade (photo, above). Remove the original throat plate and use it as a pattern. Transfer its shape to a piece of plywood, and cut it out with a jigsaw or bandsaw. Lower the dado blade and install the new throat plate. Start the saw and slowly raise the blade through the plate.

Now you are ready to make your trial vertical cuts. Cut them out of scrap plywood and try them in the finished grooves cut in the case sides. First, adjust the distance between the fence and the blade until you can cut a tongue that will slip into the groove with friction, but by hand force alone. Then adjust the height of the blade to determine the length of the tongue. Start with the blade a bit low and gradually raise it until the tongue is about ⅟32 in. shy of the depth of the groove. If the blade is too high, the tongue will bottom out in the groove, which will prevent a good joint. If the tongue length is the exact depth of the groove (⅜ in.), you will run into a problem if the grooves are not perfectly consistent from piece to piece. The ⅟32-in. space allows for slight variations in the depth of the grooves, and it provides a place for excess glue to run out. Without this space you may encounter hydraulic problems when it comes time to assemble the case.

For the horizontal method, the length of the tongue will be determined by the position of the fence, its thickness by the height of the blade. (Since the length of the tongue is less than the width of the ⅝-in. dado blade, you'll need to bury the exposed portion of the blade in an auxiliary wood fence, as shown in the drawing on p. 89.) Adjust these settings and make a trial cut. Lower the blade to make a thicker tongue, raise it to make a thinner tongue. If the tongue is too short, move the fence away from the blade. If it's too long, move the fence to cover more of the dado blade. (Of course, you'll have to do this with the saw running to enlarge the groove in the auxiliary fence.) Using this method, the thickness of the tongues will vary slightly if the plywood is not of consistent thickness, so it's wise to check every other piece as you cut. Remember, if you're using laminated stock for the case bottoms, you'll have to set up two different cuts—one for the laminated stock and another for all the rest. Only one setup is required with the vertical method.

Backs   The last operation before assembling the cases is to cut the ¼-in. thick plywood backs. They must be perfectly square because they will be used to square the cases. I also make them ¹⁄₁₆ in. smaller than the outside dimensions of the cases to avoid having to trim off any excess. (Remember to cut the backs so that the grain is oriented vertically inside the cases.)

When all the joints and the backs have been cut and before the cases are assembled, all interior case surfaces must be sanded smooth. It's a lot easier to sand flat sheets than to sand the inside of a plywood box. It could be argued that sanding is best done before any joints are cut to avoid changing the thickness of the tongues, but the plywood requires only a light touch-up to remove the scuff marks. Use 150-grit paper in an orbital sander. This is the last sanding the cases will require. Once assembled, their insides will be relatively safe from further scuffing.

Special cases   Most kitchen cases have another case on either side and a countertop above, so their outside surfaces needn't be finished. But if one or both ends of a case will be exposed, as in a peninsula or island cabinet, special care must be taken in constructing it. Once again, there are two options. You can increase the width of the exposed plywood sides by ¼ in. to cover the edges of the back, or you can cover the edges by applying a finished piece of plywood to the entire case side, as shown in the drawing on p. 30. In the first method, you'll have to cut a ¼-in. by ¼-in. rabbet at the rear edge of the side to conceal the back. This works well, but I prefer to use the second method because it allows me to standardize my components and operations. The time I save in construction (not to mention mistakes) more than makes up for the extra materials. The exposed plywood face should be sanded after the cabinet has been assembled.

If the case side will be veneered or laminated with plastic, I take a different approach. In this situation, I find it's quicker to make the back a trifle oversize, and simply run it past the sides of the cases. The protruding edges of the back are easily trimmed flush with the case side using a trimmer bit and router. The side is then ready for veneer or plastic laminate.

Assembling the cases

After all the inside case surfaces have been sanded, blow the dust out of the joints. Then run a bead of yellow, white or hide glue in the grooves and spread it with a brush. Assemble the four sides of the case as shown on pp. 92-93. Place the top and bottom in one side, making sure the edges are flush. Then install the second side. Use pipe or bar clamps, if necessary, to hold them lightly together and relatively square, as shown in the photo on p. 82. I use clamps only if the joints are too tight to go together without a little persuasion. You can hold the case pieces together (and roughly square) without clamps by simply tacking a piece of scrap diagonally across the back edges of the case, as shown in the bottom photo on p. 93.

Next, fasten the case together so that you can remove the clamps and go on to assemble the next one. There are many effective ways to fasten a case—from hand-driven screws to air-driven staples. They all get the job done, although some methods are much quicker than others. If you drive the screws by hand, I recommend using 1¼-in. No. 6 drywall screws—they are hardened and

Start assembling the case by running a bead of glue in the groove and inserting the tongue, making sure that the edges of the sides, bottom and top are flush.

much stronger than ordinary wood screws. Bore the holes first using a counter-sink bit, and drive the screws with a drywall gun or clutch drill, if you have one. To speed things up, you can use hi-lo drywall screws, which cut their own holes without preboring. But beware—the drywall gun or clutch drill can shoot these screws right through the material if you're not careful.

These days, I fasten the cases with air-driven, 1³⁄₁₆-in. narrow-crown staples (an electric stapler won't do the job) instead of using nails or drywall screws. The pneumatic stapler is incredibly fast—no clamping or preboring is neces-sary—and the staples won't wander the way a screw or nail might. I can assem-ble the cases for an average kitchen in less than an hour with the pneumatic stapler, compared to about three hours using nails or screws.

If one side of the case will be exposed and will not receive a finished face, you won't want to use any fasteners in the exposed joints. Instead, clamp the case overnight. Stand the case upright with two ¹⁄₂-in. strips of wood on top to hold the clamps off the surface, or place it on its side on the bench, as shown in the photo on p. 82. Then clamp the top joint, using ³⁄₄-in. sq. clamping blocks on both sides. The clamping blocks will restrict clamping pressure to the joints. (Any pressure applied below the joints will cause the case sides to bow.) When the top of the case is clamped, turn it over and do the bottom. You can remove the clamps and hold the case square with diagonal braces, as shown in the bottom photo on the facing page.

Finally, install the backs and square the cases. (Use strips of carpet remnants or two long scraps of wood to protect the front edges of the case when you lay it face down to attach the back.) Run a scant glue bead around the back edge

Place the top and bottom of the case in the grooves cut in one side, and then install the second side.

Tack a diagonal brace between the back edges of the case side and the top or bottom to hold it square.

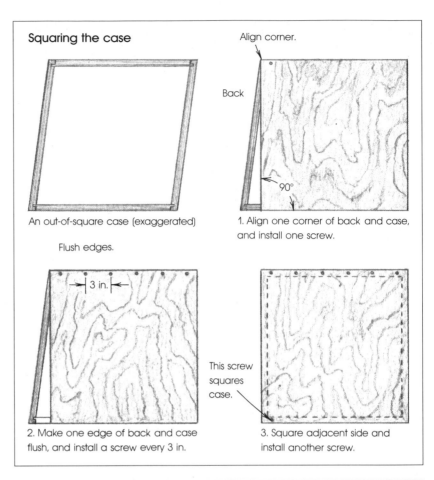

Squaring the case

An out-of-square case (exaggerated)

Align corner.

Back

90°

1. Align one corner of back and case, and install one screw.

Flush edges.

3 in.

2. Make one edge of back and case flush, and install a screw every 3 in.

This screw squares case.

3. Square adjacent side and install another screw.

Install the back to square the case. You can use nails or screws, but a pneumatic stapler will do the job quickly, and it's easy to hold the case in position while you shoot the staples.

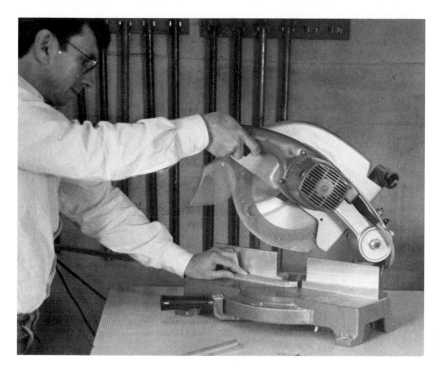

Make the edging strips slightly oversize and trim the miters to fit on the chopsaw.

of the case. Align one corner of the back with a corner of the case and drop the rest of the back into place. Then fasten it with one 1-in. No. 6 drywall screw or a ¾-in. narrow-crown staple, as shown in the drawing and photo on the facing page.

With only one fastener in place, the back can still swivel. Move it so that one of the edges of the back adjacent to the fastener is flush with the side of the case along its entire length. Then install a fastener every 3 in. If the case isn't already square, pull it into position by aligning the other edge of the back from the same corner and install another screw or staple at the far end of this edge. If the plywood back is square, the entire case will be made square by this action. Finish securing the back with fasteners on all edges. Let the glue set for about 20 minutes before proceeding with the edging. While the glue dries, you can assemble another case.

Edging I complete the front edges of my plywood cases with hardwood trim, which covers and protects them. The wood should be ¼ in. thick and wide enough to cover the edge. I make most of my edging ¹³/₁₆ wide, or slightly wider than the ¾-in. thickness of the plywood I use, so that I can trim it to the exact thickness with a router and a trimmer bit after it is installed. This way the trim is perfectly sized to the thickness of the plywood. Because I usually laminate the bottoms (and shelves) of my kitchen cases, the bottom trim must be about ⅞ in. wide to accommodate the extra thickness of the laminate.

Just about any hardwood will do, but I like to use maple or oak because of their color and grain. Also, I like to match the edging used on the drawer faces, doors and countertop. The edging should be mitered at the corners. This can be tricky to fit, but the work can be done neatly and quickly using a power miter box, or chopsaw, fitted with a 10-in. carbide cutoff blade (photo, above). I used to use a Lion miter trimmer, which slices the wood cleanly with its sharp, guillotine-like blade, but it just isn't as fast as the chopsaw. Make the pieces a bit long and pare them down to size in small increments until you get a tight miter.

I cannot overemphasize the importance of using straight-grained stock for the edging. Select your material carefully or you'll regret it when you trim the

Trimming edges with a router

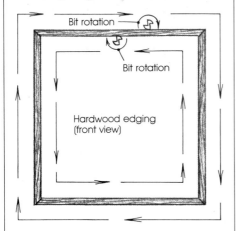

Bit rotation

Bit rotation

Hardwood edging
(front view)

Run the router clockwise around the outside
of the case, and counterclockwise within.

edging and the wild grain tears out. Later on, when you're trimming the faces of the cabinets, it's even more critical to work with straight-grained stock, so you may as well start with good material now.

To attach the edging, turn the cases on their backs and spread a light coat of yellow glue on the plywood edge. Attach the strips with 1-in. brads driven either by hand or with a pneumatic gun (photo, below). If you nail the brads by hand, remember to predrill the holes to avoid splitting the wood. The nail gun drives the heads of the brads slightly below the surface of the wood, but they should be countersunk a little more with a nail set. In either case, the holes must be filled with wood putty and later sanded. You could also skip fasteners altogether and just clamp the edging until the glue dries.

After the glue has dried, usually overnight, I use a 1-in. trimmer bit and a router to trim the edging flush with the sides of the case. I like to set the cabinets on a low table, with the edges facing up, and then run my router over the edges (top photo, facing page). On the first pass the router should be run around the outside of the case in a clockwise direction, and around the inside in a counterclockwise direction, as shown in the drawing at left. You will have to grip the router firmly on the inside pass because the action of the cutter will be to push the work away. This sequence will prevent tearout.

Once I've made an initial cut over all the edges, I usually make another complete pass, reversing the router's direction of travel. This ensures that all the excess wood has been removed. The router will leave rounded inside corners on the cabinet. These don't look bad, but they may interfere with the marking guides used to locate hinges and slides, so I square them up with a sharp chisel.

When all the edging has been trimmed, fill the brad holes with wood putty and sand them smooth. ZAR wood putty works well for this, but I often make my own by mixing sanding dust with lacquer to the consistency of putty. To ensure that the sanding dust won't be contaminated with dust from another wood, I vacuum out the sanding bag of the belt sander before starting the project. (Excess dust is stored in a jar for another job.) This gives me a good color match and a quick-drying binder that bonds well with the lacquer finish.

If you're skilled with a belt sander, you can use a 100-grit belt to make quick work of the edging (bottom photo, facing page). But a belt sander can destroy your work just as quickly, so use an orbital sander if you're not sure you can control the belt sander. The orbital sander takes longer, but it does a good job.

Glue and nail the edging strips in place. If you nail the brads by hand, make sure to predrill the holes, and fill them with putty before finishing.

Use a laminate-trimming bit to make the edging flush with the plywood (above). After all the nail holes have been puttied, sand the edging lightly with a belt or orbital sander (left).

Shelf supports After the edges are complete, I bore the holes for the shelf supports. If you drill them before assembling the cases, make sure the holes are oriented properly. If you wait until the cases are assembled, there's little doubt about where the holes should go. (If you plan to use the mortised pilaster strips shown on p. 45, you'll have to dado or rout the grooves before assembling the cases.) A No. 8 drill bit works fine for the 5mm European supports I like to use (shown in the photo on p. 46). I space the holes 1½ in. apart to provide for versatile shelf placement, without making the cases look like they've been machine-gunned. Since people rarely store anything that's less than 4 in. tall, I start the lines of holes 4 in. from the bottom of the case.

For speed and accuracy, you can use a boring template made from a scrap of ¾-in. plywood. My template is about 5 in. wide and ¼ in. shorter than the

A boring template ensures that shelf-clip holes will line up in the finished case. Align the bottom and one edge of the template with the bottom and the edge of the case and clamp or wedge it in place while you drill.

inside of whatever case I'm making. Mark the lengthwise centerline on the plywood template and drill ¼-in. dia. holes every 1½ in. along it as shown in the photo above. Place the bottom hole about 4 in. to 6 in. from the bottom of the template and leave about 10 in. between the top hole and the top of the case (allowing 5 in. for a drawer). Make sure you clearly mark the bottom and the top on both sides of the template—it's very distressing to find that you have used the wrong end.

To use the template, lay the case on its side and clamp the template tightly against the bottom of the case, with one edge aligned with either the front or back edge of the case. The holes will not line up and your shelves will tip if the template is not placed properly. (A wedge can be used instead of clamps to hold the template in position. I have a set of wedges for this purpose—each one is about 8 in. long and cut from ¾-in. sq. stock.) Use a stop on your bit to keep from drilling right through the side of the case. You can purchase drill-bit stops in different sizes, but I make my own from ¾-in. square stock. Bore a hole in the end grain of the stock and cut the wood to whatever length is needed. Then slip the block over the end of the drill bit, leaving about 1¼ in. of bit exposed to bore the holes (¾ in. for the template and ½ in. for the hole depth).

To cut clean holes, the drill bit must be sharp, and it must be fed into the work at a moderate speed. If you have a dull bit or if you ram the drill in, the surface of the plywood will tear and chip. In any case, take a quick pass over the holes with a sheet of fine sandpaper to smooth any rough edges that might have been raised by the boring.

Moving cases Building a kitchen in a small workshop can be a juggling act fit for a circus. The cases are continually shifted to make room for subsequent operations. Do your back a favor and get a partner to help out. Or, if you have to work alone, as I do, consider the lifting technique I've devised. Simply grab the top edge of the case and pull the cabinet against your thighs. Then bend your legs slightly to lift the case (photo, below). This avoids risking a heavy lift with your back, and the cases can be maneuvered effectively around the shop.

Even with this technique, you're bound to slide the cases around on the floor every now and then. This will nick their edges and scrape their sides, and any contact with a concrete floor is likely to transmit moisture. To avoid these problems, I attach skids to the tops of my cases and place them upside-down. Even if water happens to leak into the shop, the skids usually keep the cases dry.

My skids are made of scrap plywood, particleboard or pine, about 1½ in. wide by ¾ in. thick, and 1 in. longer than the case is deep. The skids protrude on opposite sides to keep the case from hitting a wall. I fasten two skids to the bottom of each case with air-driven staples, but you could tack them with 1¼-in. nails. Knock the skids off with a hammer when you're ready to install the cases.

Do your back a favor and use your leg muscles for lifting and moving cases.

rawers are the most difficult part of cabinet work. With four sides and a bottom, each one is a bit like a small, shallow case. But cases are immobilized between the countertop, base and adjacent cases, while drawers move freely, only loosely tied to the case by two slides. Drawers are also subjected to constant stress—not only from the loads they carry, but also from frequent opening and closing. Drawer joints must be well made to withstand these stresses, or eventually they will fail.

Either finger joints or dovetails will make a strong and attractive drawer corner, and a glued-in plywood bottom will help to stiffen the whole assembly. Although both types of corner joint can be cut by hand, they also lend themselves to step-by-step machine procedures that can be mastered with minimal practice. Since I prefer machined finger joints, I'll describe how to make them later in this chapter. If you prefer dovetails, however, or would like to explore some other drawer joints, see the sidebar on pp. 104-105.

Dimensioning drawers A mistake made while making drawers can have nasty consequences. An incorrect dimension or an improperly cut joint can mean remaking a whole drawer, or worse yet, lots of drawers. Before you can begin making the drawer, you must determine the type of corner joint and the slide you intend to use, as well as the interior case width and the height of the drawer, as shown in the drawing on p. 102.

All slides are slightly different. The side-mounting Accuride slides I use require ½-in. clearance per slide, plus an extra ¹⁄₁₆ in. per pair, to provide some leeway in drawer construction and installation. As I mentioned in Chapter 2, it's a good idea to wait until the cases are built before making your final drawer drawings. Plans change, and cases may wind up bigger or smaller than you anticipated; also, the plywood thickness may vary enough to affect the size of the drawers.

When the case is built, simply measure its inside width to arrive at the outside width of your drawers. The inside dimension of a 24-in. wide case (built of ¾-in. plywood) should be 22½ in. Allowing 1¹⁄₁₆ in. for the two Accuride slides, the drawer should be 21⁷⁄₁₆ in. wide. Plan to take the full 1¹⁄₁₆-in. clearance—it's much easier to shim the slides out than it is to shave fractions of an inch of stock from the sides of a finished drawer.

I usually place one drawer at the top of each base case, and I typically make it 20 in. long and 3½ in. high. The length is 2¾ in. shorter than the full inside depth of the case (including the ¼-in. hardwood edging on the front of the finished case). I leave this extra space to accommodate unanticipated plumbing and hardware connections. The front of the drawer will be covered with a nomi-

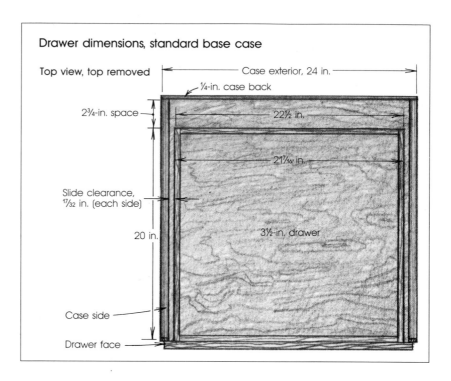

Drawer dimensions, standard base case

Top view, top removed

Case exterior, 24 in.

¼-in. case back

2¾-in. space

22½ in.

21⁷⁄₁₆ in.

Slide clearance,
¹⁷⁄₃₂ in. (each side)

20 in.

3½-in. drawer

Case side

Drawer face

nally 5-in. wide face (as explained on p. 30), which allows ¾ in. for the thickness of the top of the case, and ½-in. clearance above the drawer sides and ¼-in. clearance below, as shown in the drawing at the top of the facing page.

So, based on these dimensions, the finished drawer is 20 in. long by 21⁷⁄₁₆ in. wide by 3½ in. high. I add another ¹⁄₁₆ in. for the finger joints (or ⅛ in. to each drawer side) to arrive at the working length of the drawer stock. I use ½-in. thick stock for small to medium-sized drawers (up to 28 in. wide) and ⅝-in. stock for larger drawers (up to 36 in. wide). This makes the drawers a little more delicate than the case material, but plenty strong. Load and hardware are two other factors that should be considered when planning drawers—heavy loads and/or cheap slides call for heavier stock.

Ordering stock The use of hardwood for drawer stock is almost unheard of in manufactured cabinets. You'll more often see pine, vinyl-covered particleboard or sometimes even molded plastic. Woods such as poplar and pine are certainly easier to work and are much less expensive than oak, and they will make an acceptable drawer. But, for the sake of consistency, I prefer to make my drawers from the same wood that I use to trim the faces—usually oak, birch or maple. In combination with tight-fitting finger joints and full-extension slides, hardwood drawer construction will place your work in a class of its own.

If your drawer stock warps, it will be difficult to cut and assemble the joints. So whatever wood you choose, select clear, dry, straight-grained stock. If you have access to a jointer and thickness planer, I strongly recommend jointing and planing your own stock, rather than purchasing pre-planed boards. Rough stock is less expensive, and by planing the stock yourself, you can be assured of flat, straight drawer sides. To minimize warping, I try to plane my stock, cut the joints and glue the drawers before the wood has a chance to warp. Once the drawer is assembled, the wood is unlikely to move much.

I have found that it is usually a good idea to order as much as 25% more wood than your drawings call for. The extra stock will come in handy if you make mistakes, which you will surely do in the beginning. And as you prepare

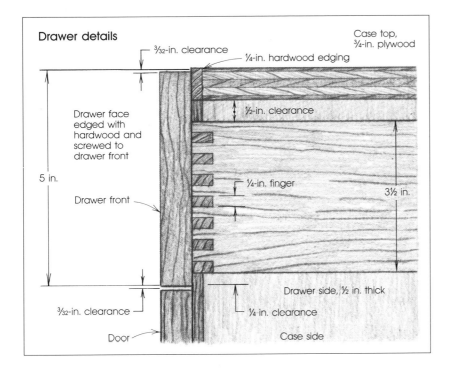

Drawer details

Case top, ¾-in. plywood

³⁄₃₂-in. clearance

¼-in. hardwood edging

½-in. clearance

Drawer face edged with hardwood and screwed to drawer front

5 in.

¼-in. finger

3½ in.

Drawer front

³⁄₃₂-in. clearance

¼-in. clearance

Drawer side, ½ in. thick

Door

Case side

the drawer sides, you'll probably discover knots or checks that weren't evident before. If you bought enough material at the start, you'll be able to select the best stock without having to shop for more, and you can plane and saw it all at the same tool settings. And you can always use a few extra pieces to set up the finger-jointing jig.

To minimize waste, look for rough stock that's slightly larger than the final width of the drawer sides (or an even multiple of it). Stock 4 in. or 8 in. wide is ideal. Boards 12 in. wide could be ripped into three drawer sides, but such wide material is hard to find and priced at a premium. Use 4/4 (1-in.) rough stock to get ½-in. to ¾-in. thick finished sides. The 20-in. by 21⁷⁄₁₆-in. drawer described above can be cut from a rough board 8 in. wide by 43 in. long. Of course, rough stock that's half as wide will have to be twice as long.

Preparing stock Begin making drawers by cutting the boards to rough length. Then joint one face and one edge, rip it to width and plane it. Care must be taken in machine-planing to remove an even amount of material from both faces, or the board may warp. I generally plane my stock in ¹⁄₁₆-in. increments, turning the board over with each pass through the planer. Cut the planed stock to length, making sure to allow an extra ⅛ in. on each side for trimming the joint later on.

After the stock is cut, check the boards for blemishes and orient them so that the nicest surfaces are showing. Then mark the corners lightly with a pencil. Once you begin cutting the joint, these marks will help you keep all the parts in order. With everything well marked, you can concentrate on *how*, rather than *what*, you're cutting. Any identification system that works for you is fine. I arrange the four drawer sides "out" side down. Then I mark each one with an X on the inside face where the slot for the drawer bottom will go, and a "Left A," "Right A," "Front A" or "Back A" on the bottom edge. All the parts for one drawer are identified with the same letter. I prefer to cut the corner joints before cutting the slot for the bottom so that I can make sure the slot will not show in the finished drawer.

Cutting a finger joint   I used to marvel at perfectly fitted finger joints. I avoided them for years because I was sure they were time-consuming to cut and fussy to fit. I elected instead to make router-cut dovetails. When I finally tried finger joints, I found them much easier to make, although they are exacting in their setup. And because the cuts are made on the table saw rather than with a router, they are less tiring and much faster to make than machine-cut dovetails. This is how I make finger joints.

Setting up the table saw is the first step. Install a ¼-in. dado blade on the saw and make sure that it is square to the table, and that the miter gauge is square to the blade. (Don't use a wobbler washer instead of a standard dado blade because it will make an arc-shaped cut that will be visible in the final joint.) If the stock is an integral multiple of the finger width, which looks best, your drawer parts will start on one edge with a pin and end on the other edge with a slot. The ¼-in. dado blade cuts seven slots and seven fingers in the 3½-in. wide door stock. Then screw or bolt an auxiliary wooden fence to the miter gauge to

Dovetails and other drawer joints

As I noted in this chapter, the finger joint is exceptionally strong, and I use it often. A well-made dovetail is just as strong, however, and many people prefer the look of a dovetailed drawer. You also may want to consider the much simpler tongue-and-groove joint, or even the modular European design, in which the slide hardware is an integral part of the drawer sides.

The machine-cut half-blind dovetail makes a handsome drawer joint, and the groove for the drawer bottom is entirely hidden by the drawer front at left.

Machine-cut dovetails   I first made machined dovetails in order to avoid the fussy precision that's required to make finger joints. Because machine dovetailing relies on a router and template, I thought all I had to do was set up the guides and switch on my router. I soon found, however, that such work could be very fussy indeed. My dovetailing jig needed to be kept clear of sawdust, so it had to be blown out with compressed air before inserting each piece of stock. I also had to make sure that each piece was precisely positioned and held tightly in place. Even with all that care, my dovetails still came out wrong now and then. But machine-cut dovetails are certainly attractive (photo, left), and with practice, they're not that difficult to set up. I usually make half-blind dovetails. One advantage is that the groove for the drawer bottom won't show if you cut it through a tail in the drawer side.

There are all kinds of commercial dovetailing jigs (a few of which are listed in the Resource Guide), and they range in cost from about $100 to $200. Be sure to consult the instructions that come with your unit, as dovetailing jigs vary greatly among manufacturers. In any case, you'll need at least a 1-hp router, and a carbide-tipped dovetail bit that fits the jig and template, as shown in the photo on the facing page. My Porter-Cable dovetailing jig requires a ½-in. dovetail bit. Carbide bits lasts longer than steel, and will hold a keener edge.

The drawer stock should be the same thickness as for finger joints (½ in. to ⅝ in.

thick). With half-blind dovetails, the drawer sides can be about ½ in. shorter. (The drawer front and back are the same length as the finger-jointed versions, because the tails should overhang the sides by ¹⁄₁₆ in. on both ends.)

When you insert the dovetail bit in the router, take care that the bit does not bottom out in the collet. Routers vibrate considerably, and if the bit is fully seated, it may work itself out of position, which will affect your cut. To install the router bit properly, slip it fully into the collet, then pull it out slightly before tightening the collet nut.

Setting the router's depth of cut is fussy work, but stick with it until you get it exactly where you want it. When the jig is set up, make a test cut. If the joint is too loose, lower the cutter a hair and try it again. Raise the cutter if the fit is too tight. (You'll be glad you made plenty of extra drawer stock.)

The pieces should fit together snugly, with no more than a light tapping with a mallet. Make sure no dust or debris prevents good contact between the drawer stock and the jig—if you have compressed air in the shop, and a little patience, you'll get nice joints. It's a good idea to check the fit of your joint after every fourth cut, or once for each drawer you make.

With all this fiddling around, you may be wondering about the relative merits of cutting dovetails by machine. You can cut a neat dovetail joint by hand, of course, but that requires a fair amount of patience and practice, and a whole

help support the drawer sides as they are being cut. The auxiliary fence is essential for two reasons. First, it provides a way to clamp the work. Even more important, the auxiliary fence holds the guide pin that indexes the cut, ensuring accurate fingers.

Next, set the height of the blade to $1/16$ in. more than the thickness of the stock. If the stock is $1/2$ in. thick, for example, set the blade to a height of $9/16$ in. When the side and front of the drawer go together, the pins on the front will overhang the drawer sides by $1/16$ in., and the excess wood will be trimmed off with a sharp hand plane or a belt sander. This allowance ensures that the pins won't be too short. If that occurs, you'll have to plane down the sides to salvage the drawer, which is a lot of extra trouble and may even require that you shim out the slides.

After the height of the blade has been adjusted, run the auxiliary fence across the $1/4$-in. wide dado blade. Then remove the fence from the miter gauge and make a mark one slot-width away from either edge of the first cut, as shown in

other set of skills. (See the Resource Guide for the titles of some books and videos that show you how to make hand-cut dovetails.)

Other joints   A much simpler drawer joint than the half-blind dovetail is the tongue and groove. It's the same joint that I use for cases, except that here you'll be using solid stock instead of plywood. Although I prefer the finger joint or the machine-cut dovetail, it should also be possible to get good results with the tongue and groove. You can even use it to make plywood drawers if the exposed plywood edges don't bother you. The tongues should be cut

with a dado blade, and the $1/8$-in. wide grooves can be cut with a standard carbide rip blade. With the tongue-and-groove joint, it is essential to glue the plywood drawer bottom in its groove for added strength.

There are lots of other drawer-joint possibilities, including all of the miters shown in the drawing on p. 87. Which one you choose depends mainly on your tools and skills, and personal preference.

Before leaving the discussion of alternative drawer joints, it's worth considering the latest Grass slides, which are actually built into the sides of the drawer. These are made of epoxy-coated metal (like the other Grass slides)

and attach to the drawer front and back with screws or 10mm ribbed dowels. Typically, the drawer front, bottom and back are cut from plywood or medium-density overlay. The stock is drilled to accept the dowels, and the drawer is assembled in a special clamp. The result is a neat, practical drawer, though it can be made only with three-quarter extension slides. You may find it tempting to use this system to cut both the cost and the time needed to make drawers, but to my eye, this modular approach will never equal the beauty of a dovetailed or finger-jointed hardwood drawer, equipped with high-quality full-extension slides.

This Porter-Cable router jig produces a clean, tight-fitting dovetail joint, although it takes some practice and attention to get it right.

Cutting finger joints. After marking and cutting a ¼-in. wide slot in the wood fence, make a second slot ¼ in. away from the first (above left and center). Then fit and glue a hardwood pin in the first slot (above right). Hold the top edge of a scrap of stock against the pin to cut the first slot (below left). Slip each slot over the pin to cut the next one (below right).

the photo, above left. Place the fence and miter gauge back on the table, and align the mark so that the next cut will make another slot, leaving a ¼-in. wide pin between the two slots (photo, above center). Clamp the fence to the miter gauge in this position, and screw it in place. Make a ¼-in. thick by 2-in. long hardwood guide pin, fit it snugly and glue it into the original slot, as shown in the photo, above right.

Now use a piece of scrap drawer stock to test the jig and fine-tune it. Standing the scrap on end, as you would a drawer side, butt it against the guide pin and saw a slot (photo, below left). Place this slot over the guide pin and make another cut. Use the second cut to index the third, and so on, until the entire

width of the stock has been milled (photo, facing page, bottom right). Turn the stock end for end and repeat the process. Then cut the scrap in half and fit the two ends together. The ideal fit should be hand tight (photo, bottom left). If the joint is too tight, loosen the screws that attach the auxiliary fence to the miter gauge and tap the fence to move the guide pin closer to the blade. If the fit is too loose, move the guide pin in the opposite direction. Tighten the screws, and try it again. If the tapping does not bring the jig into proper alignment, you will have to move the auxiliary fence and start over again.

If you are having trouble maintaining a consistent fit, something is loose. Save yourself a lot of grief later and spend whatever time is required to fine-tune the setup in the beginning to get a good fit. Try to wiggle the jig from side to side. If the jig moves and the miter gauge doesn't, tighten the screws, or try a fresh setup. If the miter gauge is loose in the saw-table slot, peen along the top edges of the miter-gauge bar with a hammer. If you overdo it, sand or file the tight spots.

When you're satisfied with the fit of the joint, proceed to cut the rest of the drawer stock. I start by holding the top edge of each 3½-in. wide drawer side against the guide pin, which will result in a pin at the top and a slot at the bottom. When you've finished the slots at one end, turn the board end for end but keep the same edge facing the hardwood guide pin. If you turn the board over, one end will receive a pin at the top while the other will have a slot, and the drawer won't go together.

After you've cut the slots on all the drawer sides, you can turn to the drawer fronts and backs. This time, the cut must begin with a slot. To set up for this, take the scrap stock that was correctly joined and place it over the guide pin, so that the first pin in the scrap covers the space between the slot in the jig and the guide pin. With the scrap held firmly in this position, butt the drawer fronts and backs against it and cut the top slot, as shown in the photo at right. After this first slot has been cut on both ends of all the remaining front and back pieces, remove the scrap and place this slot over the guide pin to cut the sub-

When the joint has been cut at both ends of the test piece, cut the board in half and check its fit (below left). The matching drawer front and back begin with a slot to match the pins on the sides. Holding a piece of scrap over the guide pin in the fence (below right), push the drawer front or back against the scrap and cut the first slot.

sequent slots as you did before, stopping to check the fit every so often to make sure that the jig hasn't slipped.

Good organization is the key to successful drawer joinery. Imagine the confusion that can result from a disheveled stack of parts for two dozen drawers of five different sizes. Label all your parts clearly and keep all your drawer sides together, separated from the backs and fronts. Also make sure that the top edges all face the same direction. You'll save yourself a lot of trouble and wasted drawer parts.

Fitting the bottom   After all the finger joints have been cut, you are ready to cut the drawer bottoms and the grooves they fit in. For the bottoms, I use ¼-in. hardwood plywood, cut from the same material used for the case backs. I prefer birch or oak plywood with one flat-cut A face, which matches the rest of the case material. You can use solid wood instead of plywood, of course, but remember that solid stock will expand and contract across the grain as it absorbs and gives off moisture. If you use solid wood, you'll have to allow some extra room in the groove to accommodate this movement, and you must not glue it into the groove.

The grain in the bottom traditionally runs across the drawer, or parallel to the front. That's because solid-wood bottoms are usually nailed to the back of the drawer and allowed to expand and contract in an enlarged groove in the drawer front. Of course, if you're using plywood you can run the grain from front to back and even bookmatch a veneer if you really want to get fancy. You might not want to bother with bookmatched veneer for kitchen cabinets, but remember that this style of cabinetry is equally suited to the office or living room, where specially veneered drawer bottoms can be highly desirable. In any case, obtain the plywood for your drawer bottoms before you start making the joints so that you can check its fit in the grooves. And with the plywood on hand, you'll be able to glue the drawers up right away, before the sides have had a chance to warp.

First cut the drawer bottom to size. I fit mine in a ¼-in. deep groove cut in the drawer front and back and both sides, allowing about ¹⁄₃₂-in. clearance in the bottom of the groove for excess glue. Simply add ⁷⁄₁₆ in. to the inside dimension of the drawer to arrive at the overall width and length of the bottom. Dry-fit the finger joints before you cut the bottom to check your inside dimensions and to determine the location of the bottom.

If you position the groove to coincide with the bottom slot on the drawer front and a pin on the side, as shown in the drawing below, the only place you'll

The drawer-bottom groove exits through a slot in the front and back. In the front, this will be covered by the finished drawer face.

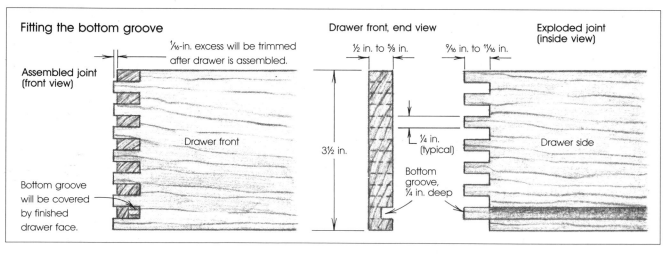

Fitting the bottom groove

Assembled joint (front view)

¹⁄₁₆-in. excess will be trimmed after drawer is assembled.

Drawer front

Bottom groove will be covered by finished drawer face.

Drawer front, end view

½ in. to ⅝ in.   ⁹⁄₁₆ in. to ¹¹⁄₁₆ in.

3½ in.

¼ in. (typical)

Bottom groove, ¼ in. deep

Exploded joint (inside view)

Drawer side

be able to see the groove is at the back of the drawer. As shown in the photo on the facing page, the groove that exits at the front of the drawer will be covered by the finished face. With ¼-in. finger joints, this means that the bottom of the ¼-in. groove will be ¼ in. from the bottom of the drawer.

If the plywood you're using is exactly ¼ in. thick, you can use a ¼-in. dado blade to cut the groove. Run a test groove on a piece of scrap and check the fit of the plywood—it should be an easy fit, but not sloppy. Then set the rip fence of the saw ¼ in. away from the blade and begin cutting the grooves. Make sure to place the inside face of your drawer sides face down on the saw, with the bottom edge against the fence. This may sound elementary, but it's amazingly easy to ruin a lot of good stock if you're not paying attention.

If the plywood is slightly less than ¼ in. thick—and most standard and metric plywood usually is—you'll have to make two cuts with a standard carbide blade. (Most ¼-in. dado blades cannot be adjusted to make a smaller cut.) This will take a little more time than with the dado blade, but the whole process goes rather quickly nonetheless. Set the fence so that the first cut defines one side of the groove, and run all the stock through (including one of the original finger-jointed test pieces). Then adjust the fence to cut the other side of the groove and make a trial cut on the test piece to see if the plywood fits. If the groove is too narrow or too wide, adjust the position of the fence until you've got it right. Then cut the rest of the stock.

If it is objectionable to run the groove through a slot on the drawer front, which it would be if the front were to be left unfaced, you'll have to make a stopped groove with a router and a straight-shank carbide bit. The same situation I described above regarding the ¼-in. dado blade holds true for the router. Unless the plywood drawer bottom is exactly ¼ in. thick, you'll have to make two passes with a ³⁄₁₆-in. router bit to get a good fit. If it's close, make a straight cut in a piece of scrap with your ¼-in. bit and test-fit the plywood. There are other bits that might be closer to the true dimension of your plywood, like ⁷⁄₃₂ in., but they are not always readily available, and unless they fit the plywood exactly, you'll have to make two passes anyway. A router table with a fence is most useful for this operation.

Alternatively, you could use ⅜-in. thick plywood for the drawer bottom and cut a ¼-in. tongue at the top that would fit exactly in a ¼-in. groove. The ⅜-in. material makes a sturdier bottom, but because I don't use it anywhere else in the kitchen, I use it only occasionally for drawer bottoms. For the best fit, use the vertical method for cutting the tongue, described on pp. 89-90.

When all the joints have been cut in the drawer sides and the bottoms have been trimmed to size, finish-sand the inside faces of the drawer and the top side of the drawer bottom using an orbital sander and 100-grit paper. These areas will be difficult to get at after assembly. The outsides and the edges of the drawer sides will be sanded later.

Assembling the drawer

If your work thus far has been accurate, assembling the drawers will be easy. Even so, take a few minutes to dry-fit at least one drawer before you glue. Select your worst pieces for the dry run—if they go together, you are ready to glue. Run a small bead of yellow glue in the bottom of the grooves and brush additional glue inside all the finger-joint slots. Then fit the parts together. Assemble the two sides and the front first, then slip the plywood bottom in the groove and cover it with the back. Pull the joints together with a clamp if you have to, as shown in the photo at right, using 3½-in. long clamping blocks inside the joints at each end.

Check that the drawer is square by measuring diagonally between opposite corners or using a small square placed on an inside corner. You may have to

Clamp the finger joints together, using a small clamping block placed just inside the joint. Note that the fingers are about ¹⁄₁₆ in. too long—this excess will be trimmed off after the glue has dried.

Clamp diagonally across the drawer to square it. Remove the clamp after the drawer is square.

rack the drawer a bit to get it square. If pushing on the corners won't do the job, try tightening a clamp diagonally across the corners, as shown in the photo above. Release the clamps and check the drawer again—it may spring back a bit. When the drawer is square, remove the clamps and place it on a flat surface to dry. When the glue has skimmed over but before it hardens completely, use a sharp chisel to trim the excess from inside the drawer. I usually let my drawers dry for one full day before trimming the joints flush.

You can use a low-angle block plane or a belt sander to remove the 1/16-in. long tails on the finger joints, but the sander is much quicker. If your drawers will receive a covering face (and all of mine do), you can round over the top and bottom edges of the drawer with a router. This is a nice visual detail that also makes the drawer more inviting to the touch. Use a round-over bit half the thickness of the stock (i.e., use a 1/4-in. bit for 1/2-in. stock). Secure the drawer, top side up, on your workbench and run the bit all around the inside, and then around the outside on both sides and the back. On the bottom of the drawer, run the bit only on the outside of the sides and back. Leave the front edges square—they will look cleaner where they meet the face.

Finally, sand the outside of the drawer to the same finish as the inside. This should remove any nicks or rough spots that may have resulted from assembling the drawer or from trimming the finger joints.

After sanding, all the drawers should be finished. They get hard use and need a tough finish, so I use water-white lacquer. (Finishing is described in Chapter 9.) Make sure to finish the entire drawer—if you leave the bottom or back unfinished, the drawer may warp. After finishing, you're ready to install the drawer slides and hang the drawers in their cases.

Installing drawers

It's best to hang the drawers while the cases are still in the shop. If you wait until they're installed at the site, you'll wind up on your knees, trying to squeeze inside them to work. In the shop, tools can be conveniently arranged and the cases can be placed on their sides at a comfortable working height. This will permit you to position and install the slides with a minimum of juggling. Believe me, this simple trick makes life a lot easier when you have a kitchen full of drawers to hang, and I wish I'd discovered it long ago.

The following description applies to the Accuride #C3037 20-in. slides that I use. It is generally applicable to other side-mounted, full-extension slides, but you may have to modify the process or change the measurements for a different brand or style of hardware.

As described in Chapter 3, there are two parts to the Accuride full-extension slide: the mounting rail, which is attached to the drawer, and the sliding mechanism, which screws to the inside of the case. Once the hardware is installed and the sliding mechanism is fully extended from the case, the mounting rails engage a hook on the back of the slide and drop over a plastic clip on the front of the slide. On Accuride slides, the mounting rail is reversible and may be attached to either side of the drawer, while the sliding mechanism is designed to be mounted on one side of the case or the other.

Mounting the rails is easy, and, as usual, I avoid marking and measuring whenever possible. Instead, I use the hardware itself as a boring template. To do this, assemble the two parts of the slide and place them against the side of the drawer and aligned with the bottom. (This is easily done by placing both the drawer and the slide on a flat work surface.) Then, move the slide forward so that the front end of the mounting rail is flush with the front of the drawer, as shown in the photo below.

Using a ⅛-in. drill bit for hardwoods like oak, bore pilot holes for two of the three or four screws that will attach the mounting rail to the side of the drawer. These holes should be ⁷⁄₁₆ in. deep for a ½-in. thick drawer side. (Use a depth gauge or homemade stop block, as described on p. 98, to keep from boring through the drawer side.)

After the first two pilot holes have been bored in the drawer side, install two screws to keep the mounting rail from moving and remove the sliding mechanism. Then prebore and install the remaining screws in the rail. Assemble the

With the drawer and slide placed flat on the bench, align the front of the slide with the front of the drawer.

other rail and slide and mark the holes on the other side of the drawer. Then bore and mount the second rail.

With the rails installed, the sliding mechanism can be mounted to the inside of the case. If you are installing slides for the first time, it's a good idea to mount your first pair to the case using only two screws. That way, you can try the slides out before fastening them permanently, and you will be able to correct their placement with the remaining screws. Once you are satisfied with the way the slides work, you can mount the other slides the same way.

To position the sliding mechanism in a standard base case, measure down 5 in. from the top of the case (4¼ in. from the inside of the top, if you've used ¾-in. plywood). This is where the bottom of the drawer face will rest. As I explained on p. 30, my 5-in. high drawer faces actually measure 4²⁹⁄₃₂ in., allowing ³⁄₃₂-in. clearance between the top of the drawer face and the underside of the counter.

If the mounting rail has been attached to the drawers as described above, the centerline of the screw holes on the sliding mechanism should fall exactly

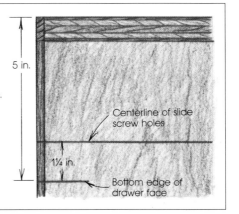

Installing slides

1. Mark the bottom edge of the drawer face.

2. Mark the centerline of the slide screw holes along front edge of case.

3. Extend center line across inside of case.

These measurements are designed for the Accuride full-extension slide (#C3037). Modify them for the slide you use.

5 in.

Centerline of slide screw holes

1¼ in.

Bottom edge of drawer face

Align the slide with the front edge of the case and center it over the pencil line to install the front screw, as shown at right. A fitting block can be used to locate the position of the rest of the slides for standard installations.

1 in. above the bottom of the drawer. (This distance is for the Accuride slides I use, but it will vary with different hardware. Make sure to check your slides before installing them.) Mark the centerline along the front edge of the case, 1¼ in. above the bottom of the drawer face, as shown in the drawing on the facing page. The extra ¼ in. accounts for the clearance between the bottom of the drawer and the bottom of the face. This mark should be 3 in. from the inside of the top of the case. Use a square or a straightedge and a pencil to extend the centerline along the inside of the case.

Now cover the centerline with the sliding mechanism so that the pencil mark is visible in the center of all the screw holes and the slide is flush with the front of the case (photo, facing page). Then bore a pilot hole at the front end of the slide and install one screw. As shown in the photo below, extend the slide out of

Extend the slide and center it over the line that's marked on the case side to install the rear screw.

Test-fit the drawer before permanently attaching the sliding mechanism to the inside of the case.

the case to gain access to the rear screw holes, and install a second screw near the back. Flip the case over and repeat the process on the other side. Your pilot holes need only mark the center of the screw—it is easy to drive the fasteners into plywood. If the side of the case will not be exposed, you won't need a depth gauge for your drill bit.

Now stand the case up and test-fit the drawer, as shown in the photo above. If everything goes well and the drawer hangs straight and slides easily without binding, remove the drawer and install the remaining screws that attach the sliding mechanism to the inside of the case. If there is too much side-to-side movement, loosen the screws that attach the slide to the case and slip a piece of veneer beneath it. Retighten the screws, and try the drawer again. If the drawer is too tight, you will have to remove the hanging rail and plane one or both drawer sides until the drawer fits the case properly. If even this doesn't work, you will have to make a new drawer.

When you have the slide positioned properly, you can make a fitting block to help you align the slides in the other cases. This block is simply cut to fit between the top of the slide and the top of the case.

If you've got a lot of drawers to hang at once and you are using the same slide for all of them, you can save even more time by transferring the screw-hole pattern for the slide to a template. It takes me about as long to make the template as it does to mount two drawers without one. But I can mount drawers about four times faster when I have a template, so it usually pays to make one, even when I only have three pairs of slides to install.

You can use just about any material for the template—¼-in. Masonite or plywood will do fine—but I use acrylic because I have lots of plastic scraps left over from various workshop projects. I also find that it's easier to position the template if I can see through it. My template is essentially a T-square with a long plastic blade, 2 in. wide by 22 in. long. The top of the T is made of wood, about 2½ in. wide by 7 in. long. The blade is centered on the top of the T, and a series of ⅛-in. guide holes is bored down the center of the blade. Use a spring clamp to hold the template in place while you bore the holes in the side of the case.

For cases with more than one drawer or with drawers of different sizes, the installation process is the same, and I always use the bottom edge of the drawer face as a reference point. Install the mounting rail to the drawer sides first. Then mark the location of the bottom of the drawer face on the case and measure up the appropriate distance for your hardware to establish the centerline of the sliding mechanism.

If you want to make use of the speedy dowel mounts of the 32mm system but have not prebored the grid of holes on the inside of the case, you'll have to bore 10mm-dia. holes to install the slide dowel mounts. A light-duty slide may require only two dowels to support a small drawer and its contents, but a larger drawer will require a third or fourth dowel. There are manufactured jigs available for limited-production 32mm installations, and a few suppliers are listed in the Resource Guide on p. 184.

hen you walk into a European-style kitchen, the first thing you see is a roomful of faces. It's not that the kitchen is crowded with people, though. The faces that you see form the fronts of the cabinets, and the kitchen's visual impact is conveyed entirely by the size, shape, color and design of the faces the maker has installed. In this sense, the faces and the casework are really two independent parts of the cabinetwork.

Simply defined, a face is a panel of plywood that has been covered on both sides with plastic laminate or veneer, although in certain instances, faces (especially for drawers) can also be of solid wood. Drawer faces are screwed directly to the drawer fronts; a door face is really the door itself and is mounted to the case with concealed cup hinges.

Since the edges of plywood and particleboard aren't particularly attractive, cabinet faces are always edged with plastic laminate, solid wood or veneer. Which one you choose depends on the look you want your kitchen to have. Laminate edges work well with laminate-covered faces, although they give the cabinets an austere, almost clinical look. Solid-wood edging, on the other hand, adds a touch of warmth that I find quite appealing, and it's more resistant to dings and dents than laminate. If you've decided to use hardwood plywood for the faces, it can be edged with veneer, but again, veneer isn't as durable or attractive as solid-wood edging.

I occasionally use solid wood for drawer faces and, of course, these don't need to be edged. Because of the risk of warping and swelling of large panels, however, solid wood doesn't work well for doors. If you want a solid-wood door, I suggest using a frame-and-panel design with stiles wide enough to accommodate European cup hinges (usually about 2½ in.).

Building faces

As you've discovered in previous chapters, building the casework is not complicated. The faces, however, take more effort because although they're quite straightforward in design and construction, their simplicity puts an extra burden on the cabinetmaker to do careful work. The faces of European-style cabinets form a nearly unbroken plane across the fronts of the cases so it's important to align every element with its neighbor. Like the grout lines that accentuate any misplacement of ceramic tiles, the slim clearance gaps between cabinet faces will highlight the effects of sloppy fitting.

I usually allow ³⁄₃₂ in. between adjoining faces in a run. This means that the width of each door and drawer face will be ³⁄₃₂ in. less than the width of the

Doors and drawer faces in a variety of colors and materials give the European-style kitchen its characteristic sleek look.

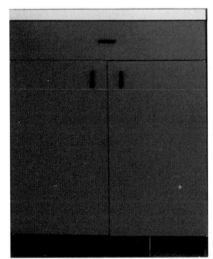

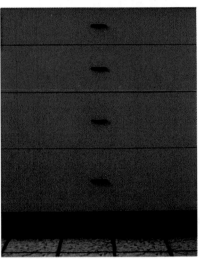

cabinet, as discussed on pp. 26-31 and shown in the drawing at right. There's nothing absolute about this $\frac{3}{32}$-in. clearance, and you could make it slightly more or less. But over the years I've found that this allowance has proven visually and functionally acceptable. It allows enough space to adjust the swing of the door, but it's not so wide as to be visually disturbing.

When determining the size of a face, remember that you're calculating overall size, so include the edging. To determine face sizes, carefully measure the overall sizes of the cabinet, then subtract for the clearance gap. A cabinet with a drawer above a door should have a $\frac{3}{32}$-in. space between the two faces as well as between the countertop and the top of the drawer face, as shown in the drawing at right. Similarly, the faces in a bank of drawers should also be spaced $\frac{3}{32}$ in. apart, so you have to reduce their heights accordingly. No allowance need be made at the bottom of the door (or a bank of drawers) because it doesn't butt up to anything.

Preparing faces for edging As I said in Chapter 4, $\frac{3}{4}$-in. birch or lauan plywood makes an excellent substrate for plastic-laminated cabinet faces. Using the no-fault method of laminating (described in Chapter 5), I glue the laminate to oversize pieces of substrate, and then cut the faces to their final size. (The conventional method is to size the core and then trim the plastic later with a laminate-trimming bit. If you prefer to laminate the plastic after the plywood has been cut to final size, you will have to make sure that the edges of the substrate are square and smooth; otherwise, the trimmer bit won't leave a crisp surface for the edging.)

Also, some laminate-trimming bits leave the plastic slightly proud of the plywood edge, and this will keep the edging from seating properly. You can feel this protruding lip with your finger or see it by eyeballing along a straightedge placed across the edge. If you fail to trim the laminate flush, most of the clamping pressure will be exerted on the plastic rather than on the plywood when the edging is glued on. This may cause the plastic to buckle and delaminate from the plywood, particularly in the area immediately around the edge of the panel, as shown in the drawing below. Viewed at a shallow angle, the delamination will look like a bubble along the edging. It's best to avoid the problem but if it does occur, it can sometimes be remedied by placing a cloth over the bubble and heating the area with an iron set at the temperature specified for polyester fab-

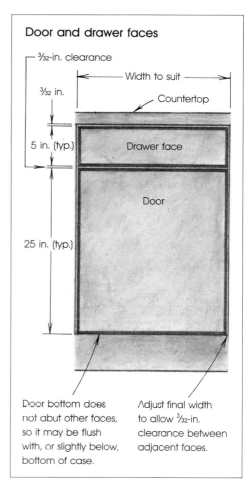

Door and drawer faces

$\frac{3}{32}$-in. clearance

Width to suit

$\frac{3}{32}$ in.

Countertop

5 in. (typ.)

Drawer face

25 in. (typ.)

Door

Door bottom does not abut other faces, so it may be flush with, or slightly below, bottom of case.

Adjust final width to allow $\frac{3}{32}$-in. clearance between adjacent faces.

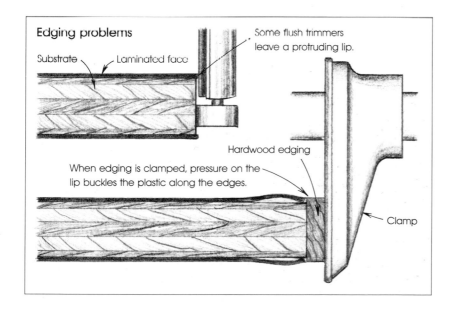

Edging problems

Substrate

Laminated face

Some flush trimmers leave a protruding lip.

Hardwood edging

When edging is clamped, pressure on the lip buckles the plastic along the edges.

Clamp

ric. Apply the heat for about 20 seconds, then clamp the bubble, using a block of wood beneath the clamp to distribute the pressure. If this technique doesn't work, the edging will have to be cut off on the table saw, which will square the edge of the panel and flush the laminate at the same time. Then lift the bubble a bit, apply fresh contact cement and clamp.

Edging the faces Once the cores for the faces have been cut to final size, the edging can be made and glued on. I use solid-hardwood strips almost exclusively for edging. Besides being more durable than either plastic laminate or veneer, solid wood is nicer looking, and it's easy to add attractive design details by subtle shaping.

I like to make my edging about ¼ in. thick, a dimension that's both visually pleasing and thick enough to clamp easily. This thickness is appropriate for faces that are covered with either plastic laminate or hardwood veneer. Make the edging ¹⁄₁₆ in. or more wider than the face's thickness to allow for flush trimming after it has been applied. So in your calculations allow for the thickness of the core, plus the ¹⁄₁₆-in. thick plastic on both sides, plus a little extra for trimming. If you're using ¾-in. plywood as a substrate, for example, the edging should be ¹⁵⁄₁₆ in. wide. I start with 5/4 boards (about 1¼ in. thick), which I first thickness-plane to ¹⁵⁄₁₆ in. before ripping them into ¼-in. strips. To provide one clean edge for gluing, joint the board between rips.

Make all your edging at one time to ensure consistent dimensions throughout. If some of the strips emerge wavy or crooked, start afresh with another board with straighter grain. Wavy stock is difficult to glue up, and later, when it's time to flush up the edging with a hand plane, wavy grain will be more likely to tear out.

There are two ways to join edging at the corners: a miter or a butt joint. I think a well-done mitered corner looks better, though it is more difficult to

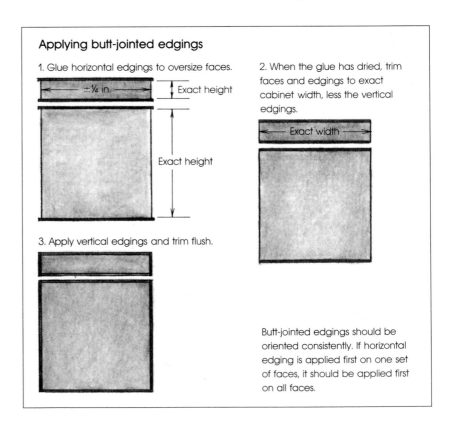

Applying butt-jointed edgings

1. Glue horizontal edgings to oversize faces.

± ¼ in.   Exact height

Exact height

2. When the glue has dried, trim faces and edgings to exact cabinet width, less the vertical edgings.

Exact width

3. Apply vertical edgings and trim flush.

Butt-jointed edgings should be oriented consistently. If horizontal edging is applied first on one set of faces, it should be applied first on all faces.

achieve. But a neat butt joint is better than a sloppy miter, so you'll have to assess your own skills.

I've developed one trick to make butt-jointed edging easy to apply. To start with, the faces should be ripped to their exact height but left about ¼ in. wider than the finished size. Then cut the horizontal edging longer than the width of the face and glue it to the top and bottom edges, as shown in the drawing on the facing page. Spread yellow glue and then seat the edging, sliding it back and forth a bit to make the glue tacky. This will help hold the wood in place during clamping. You can also use masking tape to hold the wood in place. Scrap stock as long as the edging makes a good clamping pad that will help to distribute pressure evenly along the joint.

If you use pipe clamps, ½-in. wooden shims placed beneath the pipes will hold them away from the surface of the face. This will keep clamping pressure parallel to the edging and will also prevent the iron pipes from staining the wood if they come in contact with the glue. There should be some squeeze-out all along the edge between the hardwood edging and the plywood; scrape off the excess or remove it with a damp rag to save cleanup time later. The strength of glue increases as the glue cures. It will reach full strength in a day or two. The clamps can be removed in as little as 30 minutes, but I leave them on at least two hours because I can always do other work while the glue cures.

Next, with a trimmer bit in the router, trim the edging flush with the front and back surfaces of the face. Then cut the panels to their exact final width, less the thickness of the vertical edging (step 2 in the drawing on the facing page). This way you'll be cutting the horizontal edging flush with the edge of the panel in the same operation, which saves a lot of fussy fitting and ensures a perfect butt joint.

When all the vertical edges have been trimmed, glue the remaining edging to the faces. After the glue has set, trim the excess edging on the table saw (photo, below), using a block of plywood to provide a reference edge against

After the butt-jointed hardwood edging is applied, trim off the excess on the table saw. Use a block of plywood to register the edged panel against the fence.

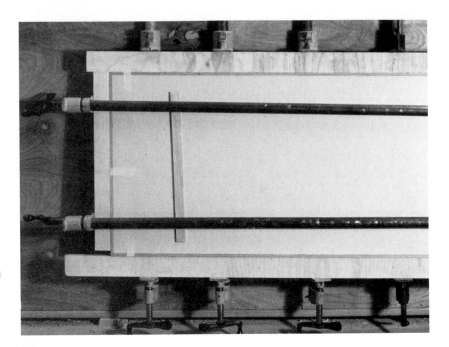

To achieve a tight fit at the corners of mitered edging, all four pieces must be clamped at the same time. Tape the edges to hold them in place while you're setting up the clamps. Wood shims beneath the pipes will protect the oak edging from staining.

the fence. Be consistent in the way you orient the butt joints. If you apply the horizontal edging first on one face, do the same for all the other faces.

If you wish to miter the corners of the edging, you'll have to trim all the plywood panels to their final size before applying the edging. Measure the two long sides, mark the edging and cut a miter on both ends, using a chopsaw with a 60-tooth carbide-tipped crosscut blade. A Lion miter trimmer (often used by picture framers) also will cut a good miter. Either way, the pieces must be cut perfectly. If they're too long or too short or if the angle is inaccurate, the miter won't close. I like to cut the edging slightly long first, and then trim a hair off, testing the fit between cuts. If I cut too much off—nobody's perfect—I just use the piece on a shorter side. That's why I cut the longer edging strips first.

As each face is fitted for edging, I glue and clamp opposing sides. Then I flip the face over and clamp the ends, as shown in the photo above. Again, taping the edges will help hold the edging in place. Fitting mitered edging is much fussier work than fitting butt-jointed edging, particularly because all four edges have to be clamped at once. But I think it's worth the extra effort.

Flush-trimming mitered edging Once the glue has cured, the edging must be trimmed flush with the surface of the face. I do this in two steps. With a 1-in. long trimmer bit in my router, I remove most of the excess. As shown in the photo at left on the facing page, the bearing runs against the face, leaving the edging slightly proud of the panel surface. To avoid tearout, run the router from right to left, then make a final cleanup pass in the opposite direction.

Next, trim the slight lip that remains with a hand plane set to take a fine shaving (photo at right, facing page). This may take some getting used to, but with practice—and as long as you keep the tool level—you can get a sharp plane iron to ride across the surface of the plastic without scratching it. The important things to remember are to plane with the grain and to keep the plane sole flat on the surface of the laminate. If the idea makes you nervous, just try to cut into a piece of scrap laminate with a plane. You'd have to angle the plane to get it to dig into the plastic and even then, I don't think you'd do any damage.

If you do accidentally nick the laminate while hand-planing, you may be able to hide the blemish by using the damaged side as the backside of a drawer

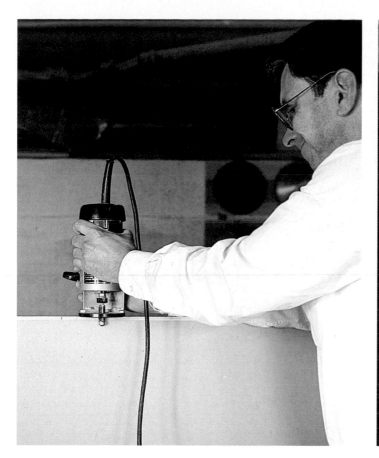

Once the glue has dried, the edging is trimmed flush with the panel's face. Use a laminate-trimming router fitted with a trimmer bit to remove most of the excess stock (above left). Then finish the job with a hand plane.

face or a door. Small nicks can be filled with Kampel SeamFil (see the Resource Guide on p. 185), a putty-like filler for plastic laminate. SeamFil can be bought or mixed to match the colors of most contemporary laminates. To keep the plane from tearing out the edging at the corners, plane toward the center of the edging from each corner.

How do you know when to stop planing? One indication is when the plane no longer cuts. Another is when the slight build-up of glue squeeze-out disappears, exposing a clean, crisp joint.

After trimming the edging flush, chamfer or round it over with a sharp chamfer or quarter-round router bit equipped with a ball-bearing pilot. Feed the bit into the work slowly, and you will be rewarded with a surface that requires no sanding. The back corner of the edging, which faces the inside of the cabinet, should be eased with 100-grit sandpaper.

One final note about the advantages of hardwood edging. Many plywoods and fiberboards have very thin veneer. As a result, it can be difficult to plane the edging flush with the face of the panel without damaging the face veneer. Relatively thick veneers (1/28 in. or more) can be sanded to repair a nick if the damage isn't too deep. As an alternative to planing, careful sanding with 100-grit paper on a belt sander will get the edges flush. It's very easy, however, to sand through the face of a veneered panel. I've done it many times, and I've seen the best craftsmen do it, too. A belt sander cuts aggressively, so you must be very careful. Once the edge is flush, sand the entire panel with an orbital sander, starting with 100-grit paper and progressing through 120, 180 and then 220-grit paper. This advice also applies to the edging that is applied to the front edges of all interior shelves.

Making and installing pulls

While the cabinet faces establish a kitchen's feel, it's the thoughtful little details that add visual texture to what might otherwise be a featureless expanse of plastic laminate. One such detail is drawer and door pulls. Pulls are a personal item, like an earring or a tie tack.

There are basically three ways to add a pull to a door or drawer face. The quickest way is simply to buy or make a pull (it doesn't necessarily have to be wood) and screw it right to the surface of the face. A stile glued to the edge of a plywood face provides plenty of raw material from which to shape a pull, while you can rout or carve a pull right into a solid-wood face. (Because of its tendency to expand and contract, solid wood is generally used only for drawer faces.)

Factory-made pulls   In recent years, European hardware manufacturers, particularly in Germany and Italy, have exported to this country a rich variety of well-designed pulls and knobs made of wood, metal and plastic, a few of which are shown in the photos below. These pulls are well suited to European-style cabinets, and many are available by mail order (see the Resource Guide on p. 185). Commercial models come in three basic styles—surface mounted, edge mounted and inset. I won't go into great detail about factory-made pulls, but I can give some general advice.

First of all, buy the pulls before you begin work on the cabinets. Commercial surface pulls, for example, come in all shapes and sizes, with endless combinations of mounting-screw locations. It's better to know ahead of time what you're dealing with than to have to remake drawer and door faces to accommodate some particular feature you thought your store-bought pulls would have. If you

Plastic pulls (right) are available in a wide varieties of shapes and colors. The wooden pulls (below) may be installed in a routed recess or screwed directly to the drawer face. (Plastic pulls are courtesy of Hewi, Inc., of Allendale, N. J.)

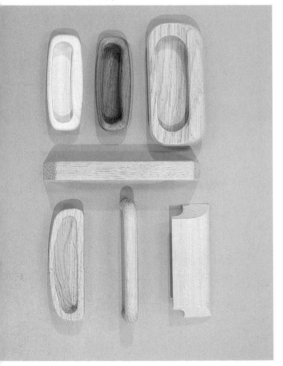

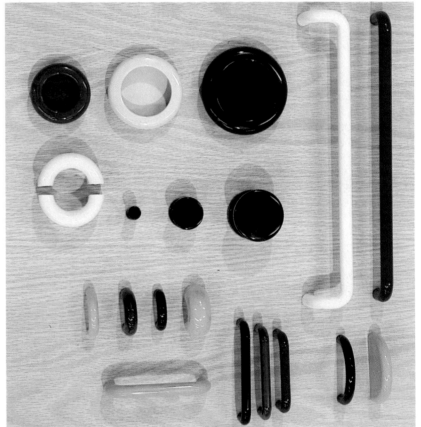

think that the pull might be discontinued, buy extras. It's not uncommon to have to replace a broken or worn pull.

Mounting screws are generally sold along with the pulls, and there's often a choice of lengths. Most mounting screws are 1 in. to 1¼ in. long and are intended for standard ¾-in. thick faces. That length is fine for doors. But in my system, the combined thickness of the drawer front and face is about 1¼ in., so I try to get 1⅝-in. long (or longer) screws. It's a good idea to purchase these from your pull supplier, since much of this hardware is imported and will have metric threads.

Pulls can be attached to the faces before or after the faces are mounted to the drawer fronts. If you attach them first, you won't need extra-long screws, and the screw heads will be concealed once the face is mounted, making a cleaner-looking job. On the other hand, the screws will be inaccessible should you want to tighten the pulls or exchange them for a different design in the future. You could bore access holes in the drawer front to get at the mounting screws, but it's a lot easier just to use the longer mounting screws and be done with it.

The placement of the pulls is as variable as the pulls themselves. Personal taste will determine where on the door or drawer they ought to go. As a general rule, however, surface-mounted pulls look best centered on a drawer face, while door pulls should be mounted near the top edge of a base-cabinet door and the bottom edge of an upper-cabinet door. The best way to proceed is to place the pull where you think it should be and judge for yourself.

Surface-mounted pulls   If you're bored by the thought of store-bought pulls or just want something different, you can make your own. Making pulls involves a lot of extra work and certainly isn't for everyone, but I've seen many a prospective client run an appreciative hand over my custom-made pulls. It sells casework every time.

The simplest pull, and one that I've used successfully, is the cylindrical wooden pull shown in the photo at right. These can be turned on a lathe, but I find it easier to cut them on the drill press, using a plug cutter. Plug cutters are available in diameters up to 1½ in. and up to 3 in. long. I make my pulls 1 in. in diameter and about ⅞ in. long. I use the same type of wood for the pulls as for the edging and begin with stock a little thicker than the pulls will be long. With the board clamped to the drill press, I run off an entire job's worth of pulls at once, making a few extras in case of mistakes or poor grain or color. For reasons you'll understand in a moment, I stop the plug boring just shy of the full thickness of the board, so the plugs remain temporarily captive in the holes.

Cylindrical wooden pulls are fastened to the cabinets with machine screws passed through holes in the door or drawer face and into brass or steel threaded inserts let into the back of each pull. Threaded inserts come in various sizes and shapes, and the size hole required for an insert will depend on several factors. Inserts that are meant to be hand-threaded into the hole will require a slightly larger-diameter pilot hole than those that are meant to be power-driven. For example, brass inserts require a larger hole than steel ones of the same size because brass is softer. Also, in the very hardest woods, like ebony, the hole should be just a hair smaller than the diameter of the external threads. If the hole is too small, either the insert won't go in or it will split the pull. I bore the holes for the inserts while the pulls are still attached to the board, so I won't have to clamp them individually to the drill press.

I don't generally use brass inserts because they're too soft, particularly in hardwoods, where the extra toughness of steel inserts makes them easier to drive. True, steel may react chemically with oak, but the insert is concealed by the pull, so any staining won't be visible. Even steel inserts can be difficult to drive in straight, though. I've found a neat trick for accomplishing this, which

You can add a personal touch to your work with these simple wooden cylindrical pulls.

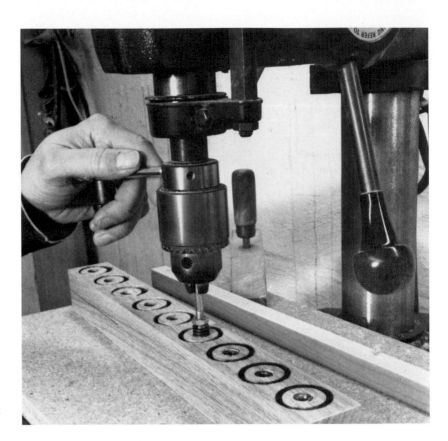

Mount a cut-off bolt in the drill press and turn the drill chuck by hand to install the inserts. Then bandsaw the pulls free of the plug stock and sand them smooth.

saves me lots of effort, especially if I have dozens of pulls to make. I cut off the head of a hex-head machine bolt sized to fit the insert's inside threads (usually ¼-in. diameter) and chuck it in the drill press with the bolt threads on the bottom. I thread an insert onto the bolt and turn the chuck by hand as I lower the insert into its hole, as shown in the photo above. When all the inserts have been screwed in, I resaw the board on the bandsaw to cut the pulls free. This operation is quite safe, as long as you keep your cut well away from the inserts. If you should accidentally saw into the inserts, though, you will ruin the blade and the pulls.

These round pulls look good on just about any cabinet design, but they're not always appropriate. Some people find their smooth sides hard to grasp, and they are especially difficult on heavy drawers or doors. You wouldn't want them on a file drawer, for example. You can improve the grip on this pull by cutting a notch into one or both sides of the cylinder. I do this by boring a hole across the pull while it's still attached to the board or by sanding a notch into the pull after it's cut free.

Yet another simple pull can be made by using the plug cutter to cut half-wafers in stock about ⅜ in. thick. Clamp two pieces of stock together at their edges, center the plug cutter on the seam, and bore away. The resulting half-wafers can be attached with glue and drywall screws driven from the inside of the door or drawer. Wafer pulls are suitable only for delicate applications, not for large or heavy drawers.

Stile pulls   Of all the various pulls I make, I like glued-on stile pulls best. One chief advantage is that they require no pattern at all. Over the years, I've experimented with various stile widths, finally settling on 2 in. as the best choice (photos, facing page). The stile can be glued to a vertical or a horizontal edge,

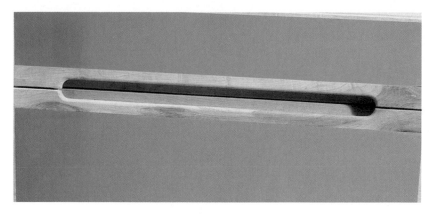

Solid-wood stiles glued to the drawer face in place of edging provide plenty of material for routing pulls. In this cabinet, routed maple stiles have been glued to the top of the door and the bottom of the drawer face to form matching pulls.

depending on whether the pull will be for a door or a drawer. In either case, the size of the plywood panel will have to be adjusted to allow for the stile's width.

The stile can be added to an already edged face, or it can be glued on in place of one of the ¼-in. edging strips. The method you choose depends on the look you want. If the stile is glued to edging that has been chamfered or rounded, a shadow line results, highlighting the stile. A stile installed in lieu of edging will appear cleaner and will form a more integrated part of the door or drawer face. Obviously, if you want wooden stile pulls, you'll have to make and install them as you're edging the faces. If you've chosen commercial pulls, you can go ahead and install the faces when the edging is complete and add the pulls later.

The simplest stile pull is the round pull shown in the photo below. The cut-out is simply a hole, 1⅛ in. in diameter or larger, bored on the drill press using a Forstner bit. Once you've decided on the location of the pull, simply bore the hole and then shape the edges of the hole to provide a comfortable and secure finger-hold.

After the hole has been bored, clamp the workpiece in a vise so that the front of the stile faces up. Then round the edge using a ¼ in. bearing guided round-

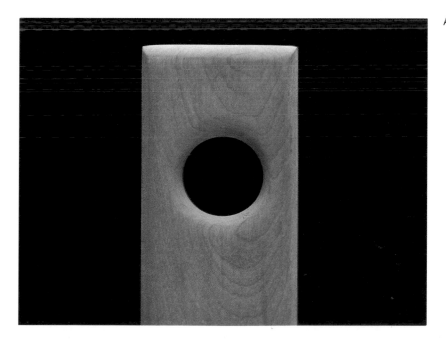

A round pull routed into a 2-in. wide stile.

Once its overall shape has been cut out, the pull's front edge is rounded over (above left) with a router. Then the back is shaped with a cove bit guided by a pilot bearing (above right). The finished pull is shown at right.

over bit, as shown in the photo at top left. Then flip the piece over and use a ⅜-in. bearing-guided cove bit to hollow out the back of the pull for the finger-hold (top right photo). Although I used to be rather precise about the exact depth of this cut, I don't bother to measure it anymore. Instead, I start by making a small cut, then drop the bit a little on each successive pass. After three or four passes with the cove bit, the pull is done, except for sanding.

The pull is the first place that you touch a cabinet, and it must be silky and inviting. Don't spare the labor here because you'll regret it every time you open a drawer. I find that the best approach to sanding pulls is to use a combination of hand and machine sanding. I start with an orbital sander, then sand by hand. I begin with 100 grit, then go to 120, 180, and finally to 220 grit. Sand all the parts evenly and be sure to get the finger-hold as smooth as possible.

You can vary the design further by making a split-round pull, which I often use on adjacent door stiles (bottom photo, facing page). To make one, rip a

A backup plate, a thin piece of wood glued to the back of the stile, closes off the back of the split-round pull.

board into two 2-in. wide stiles, then clamp them together and bore the hole. This method preserves the grain of the wood and the circular shape of the cutout. Now round over the front edge of the hole and cove the back, as for the round stile pull. A split-round stile pull needs a backup plate (photo, above left) to close off the opening, so the pull won't look like a bottomless dark hole in the front of the cabinet.

Yet another variation of the basic round pull is the elongated version shown at right in the photo below. To make one, bore two holes to form the ends of the cutout pull and remove the waste between them with a jigsaw. To get the waste cut perfectly straight, I follow with a router and trimmer bit, guided by a straight piece of plywood clamped to the back of the stock along the outside edges of the holes.

Elegant wooden stile pulls can be made using only a drill press and a router. The elongated pull (below right) was made by connecting holes bored in two boards temporarily clamped together.

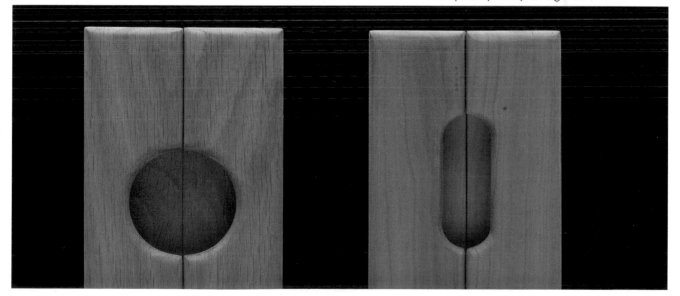

Inset pulls An inset pull is a shaped hole or slot cut through the door or drawer face. To provide a finger-hold, a cove is routed into the backside of the opening, as described for the stile pulls. Generally, I would only make an inset pull in solid wood because through-routed slots in plywood aren't very attractive. However, it is also possible to cut the pull in a piece of hardwood let into a plywood drawer face or door.

The inset pull shown in the photo below is one of my favorite inset designs. It was inspired by furniture I once saw in a book about Charles and Henry Greene, two turn-of-the-century architects best known for their skillful blending of Arts and Crafts with Japanese motifs. I wanted to incorporate the Greene brothers' sense of rich, individual character in my own cabinets. This pull can be routed directly into a solid-wood drawer front or into a stile, which is then glued to a door or drawer face. If you choose the stile approach, the pull's shape can be routed into a pair of stiles that have been temporarily clamped together. When they are separated and glued to faces, the stiles will form pulls in adjacent doors or drawers.

The process for making inset pulls is called pattern routing, and it ensures consistent results because the same pattern is used to guide the router for each pull. Making an accurate pattern is really the only tricky part of making the pull; using the pattern as a guide makes the machining go pretty quickly. To begin, I draw a full-size outline of the cutout portion of the pull on a piece of ¾-in. plywood. As the drawing on the facing page shows, the pull's shape is defined by a series of ¼-in. radius circles joined by straight lines. When laying it out, though, I don't bother drawing in the radii. Instead, I simply mark the centers of the eight circles and bore them out with a ½-in. dia. Forstner bit. This method produces a cleaner, smoother curve than I could ever achieve by hand.

When the holes have been bored, I jigsaw the lines that connect their outside edges. With a mill file and 80-grit sandpaper, I shape the outside radii and smooth the pattern so the pilot bearing on the router bit will have an even surface to run against.

Once the pattern is completed, I make a test pull on a piece of scrap. Using the pattern as a guide, I bore the holes at each outside corner first. Then I jigsaw almost up to the edge of the pattern. Then I turn the pattern over and use a 1-in. long bearing-guided trimmer bit to shape the cutout to the pattern. Finally, I

The inset pulls in these solid wood drawer faces were cut with a router, following a plywood pattern. This design also can be routed into a stile, which is then ripped in half and mounted on adjacent door or drawer fronts.

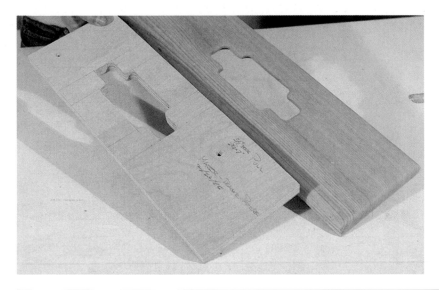

The decorative pull in the solid-oak drawer face, at right, is easily made by following the plywood router pattern, at left.

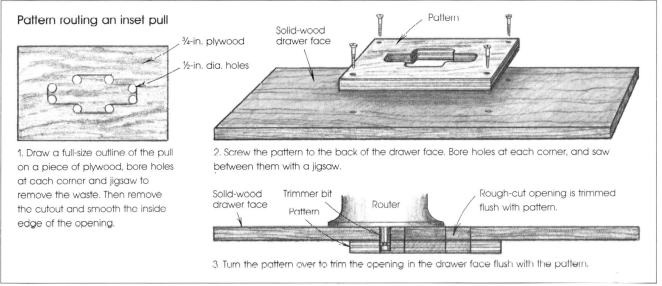

Pattern routing an inset pull

¾-in. plywood

½-in. dia. holes

Solid-wood drawer face

Pattern

1. Draw a full-size outline of the pull on a piece of plywood, bore holes at each corner and jigsaw to remove the waste. Then remove the cutout and smooth the inside edge of the opening.

2. Screw the pattern to the back of the drawer face. Bore holes at each corner, and saw between them with a jigsaw.

Solid-wood drawer face

Trimmer bit

Pattern

Router

Rough-cut opening is trimmed flush with pattern.

3. Turn the pattern over to trim the opening in the drawer face flush with the pattern.

round the inside edges of the pull, cut the cove on the backside and sand the pull smooth, as described for the stile pulls on p. 128.

When I'm satisfied that the shape is exactly right, I perform each machining operation on all the pulls I want to make. Working this way ensures that all the pulls will be identical and saves endless resetting of the router's cutting depth. Also, if you are working on a stile, it makes sense to shape the pull before the stile is glued to the drawer or door face. That way, if you make a mistake cutting it, you haven't ruined the whole face. If you are shaping a drawer pull, the pattern can be screwed to the back of the face, since the screw holes will be hidden when the face is mounted.

Once the pull is cut into a drawer face, the face can be screwed directly to the front of a drawer, provided that the front is made of the same material as the face. If it isn't, the contrasting wood will show through the cutout. To remedy this, you can let into the drawer front a piece of wood of the same species used for the face, or glue on a ³⁄₁₆-in. thick hardwood plate to the back of the cavity, as described on p. 129.

Mounting drawer faces

When the edging around all the drawer faces is complete and any inset or edge-mounted pulls have been installed, the drawer faces can be attached to the drawers. Before installing them, however, it's a good idea to finish the edging, as described in Chapter 9. Alternatively, you could install the faces (and doors), check all the fits and then remove them for final finishing, but this method is much more involved.

Mounting the drawer faces is straightforward, but requires careful work since the $\frac{3}{32}$-in. clearance gaps between faces must be accurately maintained. To begin, bore and countersink the inside of each drawer front for four 1-in. long drywall screws. An unusually large drawer, say 30 in. wide, should get six screws. I use only drywall screws unless they're not available in the particular size I need. Self-starting "hi-lo" drywall screws do not require pilot holes, and they are hardened so their heads won't get chewed up, even when they are power driven.

On a case with lots of drawers, it's best to fit the top drawer first, then work down, using $\frac{3}{32}$-in. shims to keep the spacing even between drawers. There's good reason for working in this order. If you start at the bottom and make a mistake, you won't have much room to maneuver against the countertop at the top. Working from the top down is less of a problem because the bottom drawer face doesn't butt up against anything. If your measurements are off a little, you'll have plenty of room to make adjustments.

Start by centering the top drawer face on the width of the case. Next, butt the drawer face tightly to the underside of the countertop (or to a scrap piece of plywood that serves as the countertop) and mark where the bottom edge of the face hits the case. To allow for the clearance between the top of the face and the counter, I make a second mark $\frac{3}{32}$ in. below this and use it to align the face for attachment. You can also place a $\frac{3}{32}$-in. shim between the counter and the top of the drawer face. Then attach a couple of short lengths of double-faced tape to the drawer front, align the face with the pencil marks on the case, and press it firmly against the tape to hold it in position. You can also use quick-setting hot glue in place of the tape, but if the glue is too viscous, it will prevent the surfaces from fully seating.

With the tape holding the face in place, pull the drawer out of the case and clamp it temporarily with a pair of handscrews (photo, facing page). Drill a

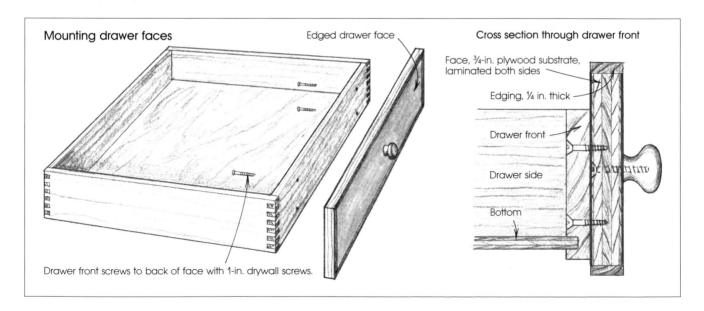

Mounting drawer faces

Edged drawer face

Cross section through drawer front

Face, ¾-in. plywood substrate, laminated both sides

Edging, ¼ in. thick

Drawer front

Drawer side

Bottom

Drawer front screws to back of face with 1-in. drywall screws.

With the drawer face taped and clamped to the drawer front, screw holes can be prebored and screws driven to fasten the two together. Make any adjustments before sinking all the screws.

shallow hole in the plastic laminate through the holes you that bored in the drawer front and drive the fastening screws. If you sink only one or two screws in each face at first, you'll be able to install all of the drawer faces and make minor adjustments before driving the rest of the screws. With the top drawer in place, follow the same procedure to mount the remaining drawer faces. As you work, check frequently to see that your drawer faces will align with those on adjacent cases.

Mounting cup hinges and hanging doors

After the drawer faces have been installed, the doors can be hinged and mounted. You could start with the doors, of course, but if the drawers are done first, you can remove them from the cases and give yourself a little more working room to mount and adjust the hinges. As I mentioned in Chapter 3, concealed cup hinges make hanging a door a snap compared to the process needed for standard leaf hinges.

All cup hinges mount in a similar fashion. The cup fits in a 35mm-dia. mortise bored in the back of the door, and its pivoting arm attaches to a base plate, which is screwed to the inside wall of the case. Adjustment screws on the arm (and sometimes the base plate) allow the door to be moved in three planes, for

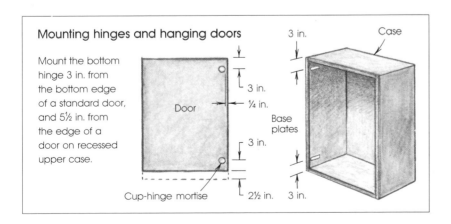

Mounting hinges and hanging doors

Mount the bottom hinge 3 in. from the bottom edge of a standard door, and 5½ in. from the edge of a door on recessed upper case.

Door

3 in.

3 in.

¼ in.

3 in.

Cup-hinge mortise

2½ in.

Case

3 in.

3 in.

Base plates

3 in.

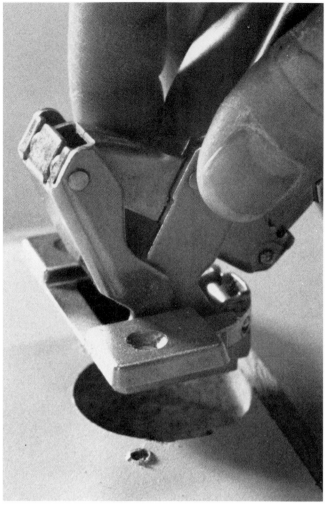

Concealed cup hinges are installed in 35mm-dia. mortises bored on the inside face of each door. Although it's expensive, a carbide bit (above left) bores an accurate mortise quickly. Two screws secure the hinge cup in the mortise (above right).

leveling and for adjusting the clearance gap between adjacent doors and/or drawer faces.

On both base and upper cabinets, I lay the case on its side on the bench to install the cup hinges. This allows me to position the door as it will be when it's finally hung, and it simplifies aligning the hinges and the base plates. I begin hanging the door by boring mortises for the hinges.

Using a 35mm-dia. mortising bit like the one shown in the photo above left, bore shallow cup mortises in the door. This specialized bit, available through most hinge suppliers, is worth its cost, since the hinge's strength relies on a tight-fitting mortise. In a pinch, however, a 1$\frac{3}{8}$-in. Forstner bit will also work. Set the drill-press depth stop at $\frac{9}{16}$ in., which allows plenty of room for the cup but won't risk punching through the door face. Set up a fence on the drill press so that the edge of the mortise is about $\frac{1}{4}$ in. from the edge of door. Once the mortises are bored, press the cup in place and fasten it with the two small screws provided (photo, above right).

I bore the hinge mortises 3 in. on center from the top and bottom of the doors to allow plenty of clearance for the bottom and top of the case. The bottom hinge on upper-cabinet doors is mounted 5½ in. from the bottom to allow for the 2½-in. light-fixture recess that I usually build into the cases. If you wish, you could mount the top hinge 5½ in. from the top edge of the door, too. This would make it possible to mount the door on either the right or left side of the cabinet, since the hinge mounts are equally spaced.

To hang the door, fasten the matching base plate to the inside of the case wall, aligned with the centerline of the hinge cup. Each manufacturer's hinge plates are different. The adjustable Grass base plates I often use are mounted $^{15}/_{16}$ in. from the front edge of the case, while the non-adjustable Grass base plates mount $^{9}/_{16}$ in. from the edge. Normally, the hinges will be shipped from the factory with an information sheet (and sometimes a paper template) detailing their mounting instructions. Also, most of the European hinge manufacturers sell an adjustable plastic or metal jig that locates both the hinge cup mortise and the base plate (see the Resource Guide on p. 184). Some of these jigs will even locate the base plates and drawer slides on the case side before the case is assembled. You can also make your own base-plate mounting jig, as I have. I use my jig, shown in the photo below, to prebore the screw holes for the

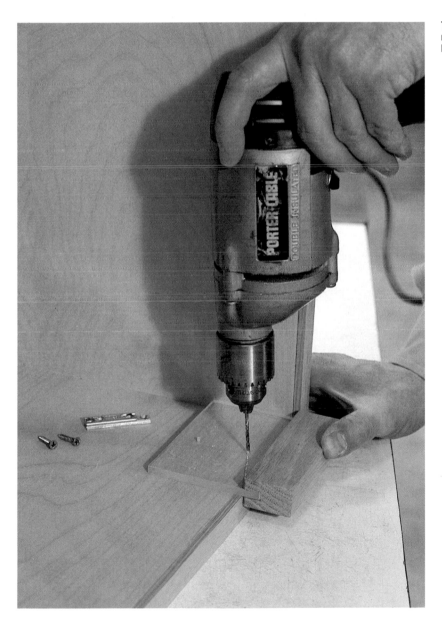

This simple Plexiglas jig locates the base-plate mounting holes the right distance from the top, bottom and front edge of the case.

These two doors are vertically misaligned. Adjusting the hinge-arm screws, as described on the facing page, will realign them.

Horizontal adjustment
Locking screw
Vertical adjustment
Base plate

All the adjustments to this Grass #1203 cup hinge are made on the hinge arm, which slides on the base plate. Position the arm on the base plate so that the door is the right distance from the front of the case, then lock it in place with the center screw. Adjust the door's height by turning the screw on the right (in the elongated slot), and its lateral position by turning the screw on the left.

base plates. The jig, which can be easily made from a small piece of Plexiglas and a scrap of wood, ensures uniformly accurate screw holes from case to case, and speeds the work considerably.

Once the plates are installed, I set the case upright and slide the hinge arms onto the base plate. All the adjustments to the Grass #1203 cup hinge in the photo above and to hinges like it are made on the hinge arm. The center locking screw in the arm is snugged down to lock everything in place.

Adjusting the hinge is as easy as installing it. When the door is in place and the locking screw is tight, close the door and examine it. If it stands too far from the front edges of the cabinet, loosen the locking screw and push the door in a little, and then retighten. If the door binds, loosen the locking screw and pull the door away from the cabinet a bit, then retighten. Next, check to see that the door is perfectly level by sighting along the bottom of the countertop or, if possible, along a neighboring door or drawer face. Correct any misalignments by adjusting the appropriate screw on the hinge arm, following the instructions that come with the hinge.

On the Grass #1203, the screw on the right (in the elongated slot) adjusts the door's height. (Depending on the brand of hinge, this screw may be located on the hinge arm or on the base plate.) Adjust the door's lateral position by turning the screw on the left. Of all the hinge brands I've tried, I like Grass hinges best because all of these adjustments are made directly. With some of the other hinges, you must first loosen another setscrew before you can make your corrections.

Doors can be hung on the cases in the shop, but once the cabinets are installed in the kitchen, you will probably have to adjust them again to account for any racking that has been caused by out-of-plumb or twisted walls. Also, as the doors are opened and closed, the hinges tend to loosen up over time and will require occasional readjustment.

pplying a durable, attractive finish to kitchen cabinets is a crucial part of making them. Even an ordinary wooden object like a cutting board or a spoon can be made beautiful by careful finishing, and even the most precise cabinet work will look sloppy without the right finish. As with other furniture in the home, the finish protects the cabinet from dirt and moisture and provides some resistance to the dings and dents of everyday use. There are literally hundreds of ways to finish wood, but if you don't have a finishing routine of your own, you might want to adopt my system. This chapter describes the finishes I use. For specific product information and manufacturers' addresses, see the Resource Guide on p. 184.

How you've designed and built your cabinets will have a lot to do with the finish that goes on them. If your cabinets are laminated inside and out with no wood edging, there will be no finish to apply. You'll need only to clean the laminate thoroughly to remove all traces of dirt and contact cement. A mildly abrasive cleaning powder (not Comet or Ajax) or a soft cloth dampened with lacquer thinner will remove stubborn spots of contact cement. When the laminate surfaces are thoroughly clean, buffing with a commercial furniture polish like Jubilee or Pledge will add a nice luster.

If you've used wood pulls and edging on the cabinets and countertops, they will need a finish, as will all the wooden parts of the drawers. I've boiled my finishing procedures down to three choices: penetrating oil, lacquer and varnish, each of which has its advantages and disadvantages.

Penetrating oils, such at Watco Danish Oil Finish, give good results with few headaches. Bought by the gallon, they are relatively cheap, and aside from brushes and rags, they require no special equipment to apply. One of the beauties of an oil finish is that it's very thin and doesn't form a film, so it allows the wood's figure to show through in a way that lacquer or varnish can't quite match. Oil finishes are easy to repair, too. A damaged or stained area can be sanded down and then re-oiled without much ado. The repair will look lighter at first than the surrounding finish, but will eventually darken to blend in with the original surface.

On the negative side, oils aren't very resistant to water and dirt, and will stain when subjected to the frequent soaking that some kitchen surfaces receive. In that sense, penetrating oil is a high-maintenance finish that requires renewal every few years, or more often if exposed to heavy use. If ease of application and a rich, clear surface appeal to you, oil is the thing. If you want to finish and be done with it, oil is a poor choice.

My favorite finish is nitrocellulose lacquer. It's more involved to apply than oil, but lacquer has some real advantages over oil. Chief among them is that it's lightning-fast—you can begin finishing in the morning and install the cabinets in the afternoon. Lacquer is definitely the best choice for wooden drawers. It protects them from dirt and is more water resistant than oil. Lacquer is a solvent-release finish, which is to say that it consists of a low percentage of solids dissolved in volatile solvents. When the material is sprayed or brushed on, the solvents evaporate, leaving behind a thin, semi-permeable film. Lacquer is very versatile, too, and is available in many gloss ranges and even in different colors. It is moderately resistant to abrasion, but when aged will sometimes chip or peel. A damaged lacquer film is usually easy to repair with spot sanding, spraying or brushing. If you ever get tired of it, a lacquer finish is easy to strip with lacquer thinner.

If sprayed, lacquers require extensive equipment, including a compressor (or low-pressure spray unit), a spray gun, an air hose and an explosion-proof spray room or booth. This last item is essential—lacquers are extremely flammable and deadly if mishandled, so I do most of my spraying outside. Make sure you've taken all the safety precautions before spraying. Brushing lacquers, which are widely available in local paint stores, are a good alternative to spraying. Although slower to apply, they require less cleanup and give good results without need for a spray booth or without moving outside. Even when brushing lacquer, though, be sure to wear an organic-solvent respirator so you won't be overcome by the fumes.

Varnishes, both polyurethane and alkyd-resin types, are the most durable finishes for kitchen cabinets, at least for small-shop application. They form a tough, thick film that's highly resistant to moisture and dirt. In addition, varnishes stand up well to alcohol, something that can't be said of lacquers and oils. Available in several gloss ranges, alkyd resins and polyurethanes have improved greatly since their early days, when they buried the wood beneath an unappealing heavy layer of gloss. Although they're extremely durable, varnishes do yellow with age and will sometimes chip. This damage is hard to repair because a fresh coat of varnish, particularly polyurethane, won't always adhere well to a

Machine-sand all the wood surfaces with successively finer abrasives, starting with 100 grit and finishing with 220.

cured coat, so your fix might create a bigger mess than you started out with. I use varnish only when exceptional wear resistance is needed.

Once you've decided on a finish, you must prepare the wood to receive it. The steps I'll describe here apply generally to all three finishes, and I'll explain where additional steps are required for each. Before going into the details, I should note that I prefer to complete the finish—sanding, spraying, buffing and waxing—before the hardware is installed. This keeps drawer slides, pulls and other attachments from getting gummed up with finish.

The quality of a finish depends a lot on the smoothness of the wood surface beneath it, so sanding is a fundamental part of finishing. I begin by sanding all of the wood surfaces with 100-grit paper, followed by 150 grit and 220 grit. It's tempting to shortcut this progression through finer grits, but if you do so, you risk leaving deep scratches and swirls that will show up in the finished work. I use a cloth-backed resin-coated paper made by United Abrasives. This paper has a silicon-carbide abrasive that holds up extremely well.

Wherever possible, I use an orbital finishing sander, like the one shown on the facing page. (Mine is made by Porter-Cable.) Where wood edging abuts plastic-laminated panels, however, you risk marring the plastic with an electric sander, so protect it by holding a piece of wood over the adjacent plastic, and sand the edge by hand, as shown at right. I use scraps of sandpaper left over from the orbital sander to reach into corners where the sander won't go. When I've sanded the wood to 220 grit, I blow off the dust with compressed air and wipe the surfaces with a tack rag before applying finish.

If I'm spraying the edging with lacquer or varnish, I mask off the plastic with tape and paper to protect it from overspray (photo, below). I use the same method auto-body shops employ, which is to apply one layer of tape to the plastic, right next to the wood edging. Next, I place sheets of newspaper over the broad areas of plastic and secure the paper to the tape with a second layer of tape. I don't mask if I'm oiling or brushing on a finish. If you work carefully, the occasional wayward drop of finish can be easily wiped off with a rag.

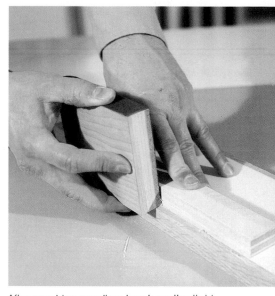

After machine-sanding, touch up the tight spots by hand using a cork-faced sanding block, and protect any adjacent plastic laminate with a piece of wood.

Mask off the plastic laminate with newspaper and tape before spraying a finish.

Oils

I use Watco oil most of the time because it delivers reliable results and is available locally. Other brands of oil include Behlen's Danish Oil (made by Mohawk Finishing Products) and Penofin Natural (made by Performance Coatings, Inc.). These oils vary in chemical composition but generally consist of natural oils like linseed or tung with additives that improve hardness and speed drying. Although I haven't tried them all, their product-information sheets suggest that they have similar characteristics.

To apply an oil finish, you'll need plenty of lint-free rags (try cotton waste, often available from auto-supply stores) and drop cloths if you're working on site. Although oils aren't generally toxic, you may wish to wear rubber gloves and an apron, plus an organic-solvent respirator. As they cure, oils oxidize, producing heat that might result in spontaneous combustion. Oily rags should be soaked in water and hung outside or kept in fireproof metal containers.

Unlike lacquer, oils isn't environmentally temperamental and can be applied on site or in the shop with little worry about adverse temperature or humidity. Of the three finishes mentioned here, oil is the least sensitive to dust, but I still try to work in a room that's as free of dust as I can make it.

Oil can be brushed, wiped or sprayed on, but in any case, the excess should be wiped away after it has had a few minutes to penetrate. The surfaces should

Finish-sand the oiled woodwork with 220-grit wet/dry paper. The slurry of sanded particles will help to fill the grain of the wood and will harden when the oil polymerizes.

still be glossy after this first coat, and if you note some dull spots apply more oil to them. It's hard to make a really bad mistake with an oil finish. You can apply too much and wait too long to wipe it off or apply too little and wipe it off too soon. In either case, the results will still be acceptable. Some oils, if left standing on a wood surface too long, will get gummy and difficult to remove. Usually a fresh coat of oil will dissolve the residue.

You can apply any number of coats of oil, but I find that two or three coats are adequate. One trick that produces a smooth finish is to hand-sand with 220-grit wet/dry paper while the first coat is still wet (photo, facing page). The sanding dust will be trapped by the oil, and the resulting thin slurry will be worked into the pores of the wood as the excess oil is rubbed off, acting as a filler. Sanding an oiled surface is sloppy work so find a place that can withstand the drips and runs, either in your shop or on floors protected with drop cloths.

I usually leave the oil to dry overnight. You can't do anything else in the shop once the oil is applied and still wet. If you leave finishing until the end of the day, the shop will be usable the following morning. When the last coat of oil is thoroughly dry, which usually takes three or four days, I apply a coat of Butcher's wax or Watco Liquid Satin Wax, which improves water resistance and keeps the finish from looking dried out.

Lacquer

Sprayable woodworking lacquer is not as readily available as most other finishes, so you may have to order it from your local supplier. I prefer the nitrocellulose lacquers meant for wood to the acrylic lacquers often sold as automobile finishes. Wood lacquers are cheaper than auto lacquers, and their working properties are more suited to small-shop application. In general, they spray more easily, adhere better and dry more quickly.

There is a vast selection of nitrocellulose lacquers, ranging from clear to opaque and bold, solid colors. Many so-called clear lacquers have a yellow or orange appearance in the can, and this can impart an undesirable tone to the wood. I try to use water-white lacquers, which, as their name suggests, are clear and without color. Although there are certainly differences among brands, the most important thing to consider about a lacquer is its gloss. Lacquers are sold in a range of glosses, from dead flat to high gloss. When you order lacquer, specify the gloss you want or buy a high-gloss lacquer and adjust the gloss yourself by adding a flatting agent, available from the same company that makes the lacquer. Keep in mind, though, that the slightly cloudy film produced by the flatting agent will be more susceptible to scratching than a full-gloss film.

One major problem with lacquer is that it's intolerant of temperature and humidity fluctuations. If you're finishing in hot, humid weather, say 80°F or 90°F with humidity to match, you can expect to encounter blushing, the appearance of a milky white film caused by moisture trapped in the lacquer. Adding a retarder (also available from the lacquer supplier) will cause the lacquer to dry more slowly, allowing the moisture to escape. Another common problem, orange peel, occurs when the lacquer develops a bumpy surface because it dries too quickly in hot weather, before it's had a chance to flow out properly. Thinning the lacquer, adding retarder or spraying at a lower pressure will help.

You can minimize lacquer problems by spraying in a spray booth or spray room with good ventilation and at a temperature recommended by the lacquer manufacturer. It's imperative that lights, fans and fixtures be explosion-proof and that a fire extinguisher be kept nearby. In addition to the fire hazard, there's the mess of overspray, so no matter how careful you are, it's never a good idea to spray cabinets on site. If you live in a mild climate, you can spray outside on calm days when the humidity isn't too high, and I do it whenever I can. One nice thing about lacquer is that it "flashes," or dries to the touch fairly quickly, so it doesn't attract dust for more than about five minutes after it's sprayed. Even if you are outside or in a well-ventilated booth, however, you'll still need to protect your lungs with an organic-solvent respirator.

For spray finishing, I have a Sears gun that I usually operate at about 30 psi. If you don't have an air compressor and don't want to buy one, you might consider purchasing one of the low-pressure spray systems recently introduced to the market. These have a self-contained, turbine-type compressor and a bleeder-style spray gun that supposedly produces less overspray and waste than conventional high-pressure guns.

Once the wood has been sanded to 220 grit and dusted clean with a tack rag, I spray one coat of a lacquer-based sanding sealer. The sealer provides a good base for subsequent lacquer coats and it contains zinc stearate, which powders up when sanded, lubricating the paper and leaving a smooth surface. For best results, sand the sealer coat with 220-grit open-coat paper or with paper that also contains zinc stearate. When the sealer is perfectly smooth, dust the surface again with a tack rag and apply the first of three lacquer top coats.

I use a gloss lacquer for the first coat, even if I want to end up with a satin finish. Since it contains no flatting agents, a gloss lacquer is clearer and defects show up better, so they can be fixed before subsequent coats are applied. Before spraying, make sure the lacquer is thinned correctly. The most precise way to do this is to time how long it takes a thinned sample of lacquer to pass through a viscosity cup, a small funnel with a calibrated opening. I've found it more practical simply to thin the lacquer one-to-one with a thinner supplied by the same manufacturer. Using the right lacquer thinner is important because they're not all the same. Some thinners are "leaner" than others, with a greater percentage of volatile solvents that might make the finish dry too rapidly. Ask your supplier to recommend a thinner for whatever lacquer you're using.

Once the first coat is dry, finishing will go quickly because you don't have to sand between coats and can usually recoat within an hour or so. The top, or final, coat should be rubbed down with 0000 steel wool after the lacquer is thoroughly dry and hard, which usually takes one to four hours, depending on the temperature and humidity. This rubout will dull the finish to a low gloss. Polish it with a clean cotton rag if you want a sheen. If you want a higher gloss, polish the surface with automobile rubbing compound and an electric buffer fitted with a lamb's-wool bonnet.

Lacquers can be brushed, but don't expect good results by brushing a spraying lacquer. Brushing lacquers have fewer volatile solvents so they dry more slowly, allowing them to flow out and blend in the brush marks. One of the most popular brushing lacquers is Deft Clear Wood Finish. Deft is a nitrocellulose lacquer to which alkyd-type resins have been added to improve flexibility and toughness. It is available in gloss and in semi-gloss, which has stearates added to make it easier to sand.

Preparation for brushing lacquers is the same as for spraying lacquers but you don't need to use a sealer—the first coat of a brushing lacquer serves as its own sealer. Two or three coats of brushing lacquer should be sufficient and because there's no worry of overspray, you can apply it on site. Be sure, however, to have plenty of ventilation and use an organic-solvent respirator. Rub out brushed lacquer as you would sprayed lacquer.

Varnishes

Every paint store sells dozens of brands of varnishes, and I'm sure many of them are excellent. Basically, there are three kinds of varnishes: the old standby oleo-resinous type made from natural oils, often tung oil; alkyd-resin types, in which natural oils, commonly linseed or soya, have been chemically altered to improve application and durability; and polyurethanes, which consist of oils treated with di-isocyanate, a material that improves hardness. Polyurethanes are chemically related to plastics and are therefore among the toughest of finishes.

I haven't tried every varnish on the market so I can tell you only what works for me. I've had the best luck with McCloskey Heirloom Finish in semi-gloss. This product is an alkyd-resin varnish available in three gloss ranges. Three coats of the semi-gloss produce a lovely finish that's very hard but not too shiny. Again, the look is different from that of oil or lacquer so I use McCloskey only when the extra protection is needed.

Varnish can be applied with a brush or sprayer. In either case, it takes much longer to dry to a hard surface than does oil or lacquer—as long as a few days to a week. Varnish manufacturers sometimes recommend starting with a thinned coat that acts as a sealer; McCloskey sells a product called Tungseal Clear Penetrating Finish that's recommended as a sealer. Frankly, I get good results by applying the first coat straight out of the can, unthinned. Once dry, the first coat should be sanded smooth with stearated 220-grit paper, after which the second coat is applied. Allow sufficient drying time for the first coat. If the film is not hard, it will quickly gum up the sandpaper and you'll know you've jumped the gun. Two coats of varnish (plus the sealer) are usually enough to protect the wood. If you want extra protection, apply a third coat, after sanding, of course. The last coat should be rubbed with 0000 steel wool, and then burnished with a clean cotton cloth to make the finish feel smooth and silky.

Whether you're using tried-and-true lacquer or experimenting with some exotic finish, it's a good idea to make your own test pieces. Take a few scraps of wood of the same variety you intend to use for your kitchen trim and sand them, just as you would a finished cabinet. Then finish each piece, and mark on the back which finish is being used. These small samples are easy to make, and you'll get an idea of how much work it takes to produce the finish. Even better, though, you'll be able to compare the finishes with relatively little effort. Don't forget to compare your samples under various conditions, because what looks great in the daylight isn't always inviting under fluorescent.

You can brush on lacquer or varnish for a nice finish. Sand between coats with 220-grit paper, then finish with steel wool and buff with a cotton cloth.

COUNTERTOPS & BACKSPLASHES

Chapter 10

After the cases are built and finished and the hardware and faces are attached, you are ready to tackle the countertop (and backsplash). Many of the procedures involved in making countertops are variations of techniques you have long since mastered in building the rest of your cabinets. Specifically, plastic lamination and wood or plastic edging are the two primary ingredients in most countertops, and their application varies mainly in scale from the procedures you employed earlier to make doors and drawer faces.

I have saved this discussion of countertops until now, not only because it is the very last step (before installation) in the sequence of building a kitchen. The countertop is also the one item in a kitchen that does not allow for mistakes. As a work surface, it is used (and often abused) constantly, so it must be flat, rigid, well finished and resistant to moisture. And it is the largest, single visual element in the kitchen. It is what ties the cabinets together, and if it doesn't do this job well, it detracts from all the work that preceded it.

As a rule, countertops tend to be very big and fragile—until they are attached to the cases. They involve large sheets of material, which are expensive and unwieldy to store and to prepare. Once the counter is finished, it usually takes two people to carry it—and there is always the risk of a cracked lamination or a dinged edging. For all these reasons, it's not unusual to farm out the construction of the countertop and backsplash to a company that specializes in this type of work. As I mentioned earlier in the book, there's nothing dishonorable in doing so. In fact, I've found that such manufacturers are usually able to sell me a completed countertop according to my own specifications for not much more than I would pay for the materials alone.

Still, there are good reasons to build your own countertop. It's probably the last chance you'll get to incorporate any unusual design features or materials you've been considering. And the more elaborate the countertop design, the more money you'll save by making it yourself. This chapter begins with the basics of countertop construction, followed by a discussion of some interesting countertop options and instructions for making the backsplash.

Countertop construction

I make my countertops 25¾ in. wide (including the edging) and 1½ in. thick, built from two layers of ¾-in. plywood, particleboard or medium-density fiberboard. Of all the countertop materials I've used, I prefer ¾-in. marine-grade lauan plywood—it is very stable and more resistant to moisture than either particleboard or MDF. I find the 1½-in. thick stock to be just right—visually and

On the underside of this countertop, plywood strips have been glued and stapled to reinforce the top.

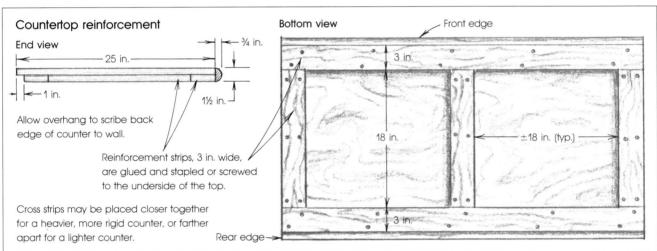

Countertop reinforcement

End view

25 in.

¾ in.

1 in.

1½ in.

Allow overhang to scribe back edge of counter to wall.

Reinforcement strips, 3 in. wide, are glued and stapled or screwed to the underside of the top.

Cross strips may be placed closer together for a heavier, more rigid counter, or farther apart for a lighter counter.

Bottom view

Front edge

3 in.

18 in.

±18 in. (typ.)

3 in.

Rear edge

practically. A thinner counter looks fragile, while a thicker one may dwarf the cases it sits upon. What's more, the two ¾-in. layers of plywood or particleboard are easy to work with, and they provide ample support for a large counter.

The counter needn't be two solid sheets of ¾-in. laminated material. To lighten the weight and save material, I usually employ 3-in. wide reinforcement strips for the bottom layer, spaced strategically as shown in the photo and drawing above. One strip is glued and stapled or screwed along the front edge, and another is attached 1 in. inside the back edge. (If there will be no backsplash, the back edge of the counter must be scribed to fit the wall. This is more easily done to a single layer of material, and the process is described in Chapter 11.) These strips are then connected by a series of 18-in. long cross strips, spaced approximately 18 in. apart.

For the top layer, I begin with a 25½-in. wide sheet. After the reinforcement strips have been attached to its underside, I rip the counter on the table saw to get a smooth front edge for whatever edging I plan to apply. (Run the back edge of the countertop along the saw fence, and remove only what's necessary to even up the front.) With about ¼ in. sliced off in this step, the countertop is still 1¼ in. wider than the depth of my standard base cases (24 in., including the doors and drawer faces). Part of this may be used up in scribing the back edge of the counter to the wall, and whatever is left over—perhaps an inch—will simply leave me with a small space behind the cabinets. My countertops typically overhang the doors and drawer faces by ¾ in., or the thickness of the wood edging that I usually apply, which seems to look just right. If you will be using plastic edging and you want to maintain the same overhang, simply add the ¾-in. width of the wood edging to the width of your countertop material.

If the counter is long, or shaped in an L or a T or anything other than a straight run, you'll have to build it up from two or more pieces. (Since ¾-in. plywood and particleboard are available in 16-ft. sheets, if you can handle the material in your shop you can go well beyond a standard 8-ft. long counter before you'll have to add extra pieces.) Draw a plan of the counter from dimensions taken on site. If you can wait until your cases are installed, it will be easier to determine the actual layout.

Rip the top sheet(s) of your counter substrate to width and length and attach all the 3-in. wide strips (except for the ones that span the seam at the front and the back) to the top pieces. I use yellow glue and pneumatic staples or 1¼-in. long flat-head wood screws to hold the strips in place. Make sure to place your fasteners far enough away from the front and back edges of the counter that you won't run into metal when you trim the front edge or scribe the back.

If you need to join two countertop pieces, crosscut their mating ends to get a tight-fitting joint and reinforce it with a 24-in. wide plywood or particleboard plate. The plate should be centered over the seam and should fit tightly between the 3-in. wide reinforcement strips, as shown in the drawing below. Where the countertop must make a right-angle bend, apply the reinforcement strips and the seam plate in the pattern shown at right in the drawing. Wait until the glue is dry before moving the countertop. I like to do this job at the end of a day so it can cure overnight.

If the walls are very irregular or if the run of cabinets does not form a 90° angle, these factors will have to be taken into account when you build your countertop. You may have to make the counter wider, for example, to leave more room for scribing the back edge to an out-of-square corner. It is much

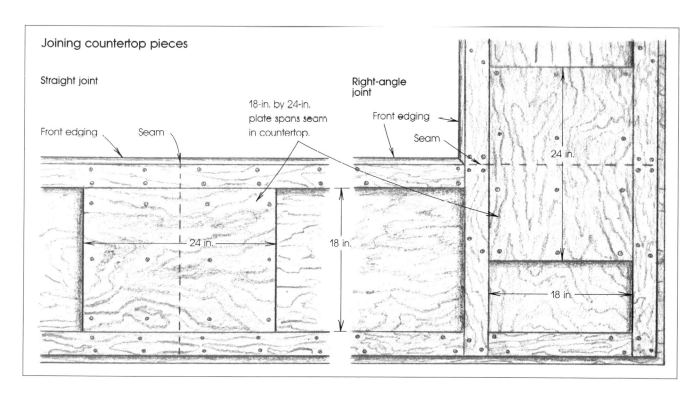

Joining countertop pieces

Straight joint

18-in. by 24-in. plate spans seam in countertop.

Front edging   Seam

Right-angle joint

Front edging

Seam

24 in.

24 in.

18 in.

18 in.

easier to join both the adjacent cabinet runs and the counter in an L-shaped kitchen if the angle between them is 90°, or close to it. If it is not, you'll have to allow for this discrepancy in the angles of your corner pieces.

Laminating the surface   If you prefer wood edging, as I do, the surface will have to be laminated before you apply the edging. I use only matte-finish, solid-color laminates for my countertops. Glossy and textured finishes may be visually striking, but you're looking for trouble if you use them on a hardworking surface like a kitchen counter.

Following the no-fault process described in Chapter 5, laminate the surface before you trim the countertop to its final width. Note, in particular, the seaming method described on pp. 80-81. A countertop installation should have as few seams as possible. Seams collect dirt and are likely inroads for moisture. You can avoid seams by using long sheet materials, or you can disguise them by inlaying a decorative hardwood strip, as shown in the photo on p. 81.

For an L-shaped corner, you can join two pieces of laminate in a right-angle or mitered seam. (If you make a right angle, be sure that the seam in the laminate is not directly above the joint in the substrate.) Or, if one leg of the L does not extend more than 60 in., you can buy 61-in. wide laminate and avoid a seam entirely. Obviously, you won't be able to employ no-fault lamination on an L-shaped (or curved) countertop. Instead, you'll have to follow the traditional method described in Chapter 5. Cut the substrate to its final dimensions and apply the overhanging laminate. Then trim the plastic using a router and a laminate-trimmer bit.

Remember that any countertop openings (for the sink, electrical outlets, etc.) can be cut either before or after the surface laminate is applied. As I mentioned in Chapter 5, you can reduce the risk of breaking a countertop with a large opening by leaving the cutout partially attached to the rest of the counter until it is installed. (If you cut the corners in the shop, it will be easy to connect them on site using a jigsaw.) Large openings may be reinforced along their edges with the same 3-in. wide strips that you've used to brace the underside of the counter. Pay particular attention to the placement of screws or staples in these strips, however, to avoid chewing up your sawblade.

Once the surface laminate has been installed, even up the front edge on the table saw, preferably fitted with a 72-tooth to 80-tooth, crosscut laminate-cutting blade. Check the cut of your blade before you slice into the countertop—you've invested too many expensive materials at this point to risk making a bad cut.

Wood edging   When the plastic is on and trimmed, the wood edging can be applied. If the countertop includes a corner, miter the adjacent pieces of edging before attaching them. If you glue the wood on first it will be much more difficult to fit a crisp miter, especially at an inside corner.

You can shape the edging in many different ways, but I like the ¾-in. wide bullnose, or half-round, profile, shown in the photo and top drawing on the facing page. It is about 1⅝ in. thick, or slightly thicker than the countertop, and is applied in the same manner as the edging on doors and drawer faces, discussed in Chapter 8. Quarter-round molding, rounded edging and chamfered edging are a few other attractive alternatives. All of them can be cut with the router, following the same two-step process I use for the bullnose.

First, glue and clamp the edging to the front edge of the countertop using yellow glue. When the glue has dried, use a 1-in. trimmer bit to remove most of the excess wood on both the top and the bottom of the counter, and plane the edging flush with a hand plane (photo, p. 152). Then form the bullnose, using a ¾-in. radius round-over bit in a router fitted with a ½-in. collet. This is a heavy cut, which I would not attempt with a ¼-in. shank bit. (If you don't have a router with a ½-in. collet, you can buy precut half-round molding, and very carefully

Hardwood edging protects the edge of the countertop and laminate and provides a warm accent to the broad expanse of plastic.

Making a bullnose edging

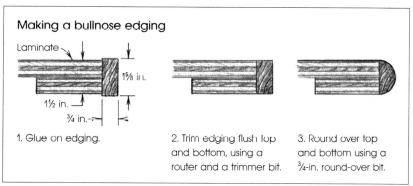

Laminate

1⅝ in.

1½ in.

¾ in.

1. Glue on edging.

2. Trim edging flush top and bottom, using a router and a trimmer bit.

3. Round over top and bottom using a ¾-in. round-over bit.

Hardwood edging profiles

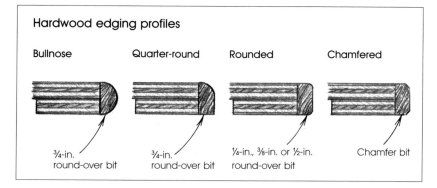

Bullnose

¾-in. round-over bit

Quarter-round

¾-in. round-over bit

Rounded

¼-in., ⅜-in. or ½-in. round-over bit

Chamfered

Chamfer bit

After the edging has been glued and trimmed to the countertop, use a hand plane to flush it with the laminate.

apply it to the edge.) This is too big a cut to make in one pass, so I make two passes on each edge. To minimize tearout, I run the router from right to left (against the rotation of the bit) for the first cut, then finish it off in the opposite direction. After routing, carefully sand the edge with an orbital sander, using 100-grit and then 150-grit paper.

Plastic edging If instead of a wood edging you decide to use plastic, you'll have to apply it to the edge before you cement the surface laminate (drawing, below). This will make the edge seam less visible in the finished countertop and much less susceptible to damage. The procedure is essentially the same for applying an edge laminate as for a surface laminate, but be sure to use plenty of contact cement. The substrate edges are very porous and will readily soak up a couple of coats of cement.

After the plastic edging is applied, it must be trimmed flush with the top surface of the counter. Use a router and bearing-guided laminate-trimming bit for this, and finish up by carefully filing any protruding laminate with a flat file. For the last few strokes, hold the file flat on the surface of the counter with one hand while you guide it at an angle with the other. You can use a belt sander instead of a file for this, but you must have perfect control. It's very easy to spoil the job by gouging the countertop with the fast cutting action of the belt.

Once the plastic edging is trimmed, apply the surface laminate. Then use a trimmer bit to make it flush with the plastic edging. Be sure that your bit cuts flush, or a little proud of the bearing surface, or you'll damage the edge laminate. If the bit cuts too close, you can attach a strip of tape to the edging and run the bearing along it. Finish the edge using a flat file or a sander.

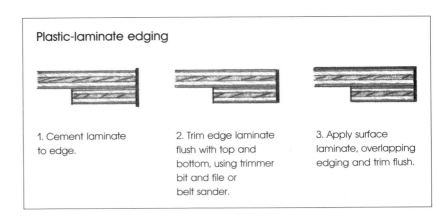

Plastic-laminate edging

1. Cement laminate to edge.

2. Trim edge laminate flush with top and bottom, using trimmer bit and file or belt sander.

3. Apply surface laminate, overlapping edging and trim flush.

A curved countertop offers some interesting design opportunities and can serve a practical function where an angular corner may be uninviting or dangerous.

Curved countertops

Most kitchens call for straight lengths of countertop, often running between two opposite walls. This design is an old standby, and it works well, but it isn't always exciting. Now and then a curved countertop seems the only solution to a difficult problem, or the only way to add spice to ordinary fare.

To make curved countertops, I use two different methods, depending upon whether the counter will be edged with wood or plastic. But in either case, I cut the curve in the substrate before applying the surface laminate. That way, if I blow the curve I'll be able to recut it without wasting a lot of expensive laminate.

Preparing for plastic edging The first method I'll describe is used when the countertop edge will be laminated with plastic. I begin by cutting a pattern for the curved portion of the countertop, using a 1 hp router and a trammel. The trammel is a straight rail of wood or metal with a pivot point on one end and an attachment for the router on the other, as shown in the photo below. The router is swung in an arc around the pivot point.

Some router manufacturers sell trammels that fit their routers, but you can make one easily enough. Begin with a piece of ¼-in. plywood about as wide as

A plywood trammel and a router can be used to make a pattern for a curved countertop. The router is screwed to one end of the plywood, and a nail through the other end provides a pivot point for the arc.

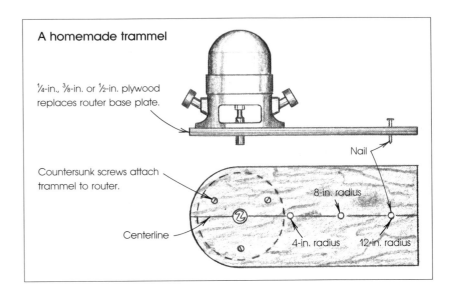

A homemade trammel

¼-in., ⅜-in. or ½-in. plywood
replaces router base plate.

Nail

Countersunk screws attach
trammel to router.

8-in. radius

Centerline

4-in. radius   12-in. radius

the router base plate, and about 6 in. longer than the radius of the arc you want to cut, as shown in the drawing above. Remove the router base plate and use it as a pattern to transfer the mounting holes and the opening for the bit onto one end of the plywood. (Draw a centerline along the length of the plywood, and center the base plate on it.) Then cut out the opening for the bit in the plywood using a jigsaw or hole saw, and drill and counterbore the holes for the mounting screws. Attach the router to the plywood, using the same mounting screws that held the original base plate.

Next, mount a ⅜-in. carbide straight bit in the router, and, with the tool unplugged, rotate the bit by hand so that the inside cutting edge is facing the pivot point. Measuring from this edge of the cutter, as shown in the photo below, mark the length of the radius along the axis line and drill a ¹⁄₁₆-in. dia. hole through the plywood at your mark. Now flip the router and trammel right side up and drive a No. 4 finishing nail or a No. 18 brad through the hole. The nail will be the center of the arc and the pivot point around which the router will

To cut a convex radius, rotate the bit so that its cutting edge faces the inside of the trammel. Then measure the radius from the inside edge of the bit along the centerline and drill a hole for the pivot point.

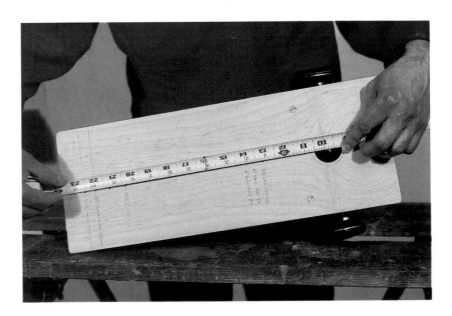

swing. If you do a lot of countertop work, keep the trammel after the job is done—it will come in handy again someday, I'm sure.

When the trammel is complete, it can be used to cut a neat pattern for the curved part of the countertop. The pattern can be cut from any sheet stock you have; I usually use ¾-in. particleboard. Arrange the trammel so that it will cut an arc of at least 90°. (The most you're likely to need is 180°, which will allow you to cut two curved corners on the end of a countertop.) Then drive the pivot nail firmly into the stock to fasten the trammel in place. Turn on the router, lower the bit about ³⁄₁₆ in. into the stock and move the router and trammel slowly about the pivot nail to cut the arc. Drop the bit another ³⁄₁₆ in. and make a second pass. Continue in this way until the stock is cut through, with a piece of scrap underneath your pattern so you won't cut into top of your workbench.

The router will probably leave stepped ridges in the edge of the countertop stock due to the multiple passes, so it has to be cleaned up. Even if the edge *looks* clean, I recommend a final cut. Pull the pivot nail and relocate it ¹⁄₁₆ in. closer to the cutter. (Move the nail to one side of the centerline to avoid breaking into the original hole.) This will tighten the radius of the arc by ¹⁄₁₆ in., which will be compensated for by the thickness of the edge laminate. (If you are edging a 180° arc with wood, you'll have to add ¹⁄₁₆ in. to the thickness of the edging.) If your arc is only 90°, however, the ¹⁄₁₆-in. discrepancy won't make a difference. You could achieve the same result by switching to a larger-diameter bit. With the router bit fully extended, make a final pass to leave a smooth vertical cut.

Take the pattern you've just made and trace its shape onto whatever material you intend to use for your countertop. Use a jigsaw to make a rough cut as close to the arc as you feel comfortable (⅛ in. is fine), as shown in the photo below. Remove the router from the trammel and replace its regular base plate. Then lightly nail the pattern to the underside of the countertop stock and use a 1-in. trimmer bit to cut the counter stock flush with the edge of the pattern, as shown in the photo and drawing on p. 156. (Make sure that the nails that attach the pattern won't interfere with the base plate of the router.)

As an alternative to using the trammel to make a pattern, you can always draw a freehand curve, cut it with a jigsaw and smooth it with a belt sander. Then use it

Trace the shape of the pattern onto the countertop and use a jigsaw to cut the plywood close to the line.

instead of the routed pattern, described above. You probably won't be able to produce as smooth a curve as you can get with a trammel, but this method is quicker and, for many applications, perfectly adequate. If an irregular flowing curve is what you're after, you'll have to cut it freehand anyway.

After the curve has been cut and smoothed in the top sheet of the counter stock, remove the pattern and apply a 4-in. wide reinforcement strip of ¾-in. plywood or particleboard to the edge of the counter, just as you would attach a 3-in. wide strip to a straight section. At the curve, you'll have to assemble a series of short strips to cover the edge, as shown in the drawing on the facing page. These should overhang the entire edge of the curve by at least ⅛ in. Use the jigsaw, as before, to cut the overhang back to within about ⅛ in. of the curve again, and use the router and trimmer bit to cut it flush with the edge of the top. (If your trimmer bit won't make a perfectly flush edge, use a belt sander to smooth it.)

If you have a shaper, the counter arc can be shaped in one pass, cutting through two ¾-in. thicknesses of stock. Use a straight cutter in the shaper with

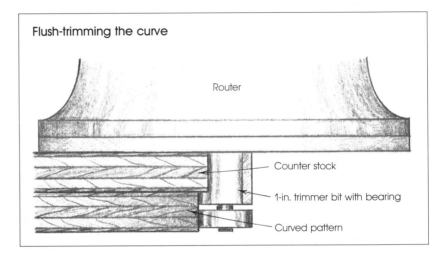

Flush-trimming the curve

Router

Counter stock

1-in. trimmer bit with bearing

Curved pattern

Nail the pattern to the counter and use a 1-in. straight trimming bit to trim the edge flush.

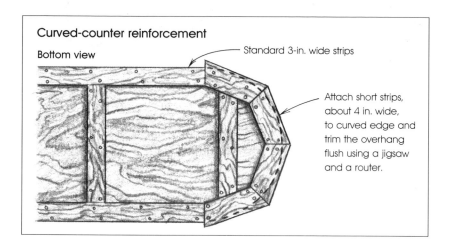

Curved-counter reinforcement

Bottom view

Standard 3-in. wide strips

Attach short strips, about 4 in. wide, to curved edge and trim the overhang flush using a jigsaw and a router.

a ball-bearing rub collar of the same diameter. Mount a pattern on the reinforced counter stock. Use a jigsaw, as described above, to trim the edge as close as you can safely get to the shape of the pattern. Then set the depth of the shaper cutter so that it will cut slightly more than the required thickness, or about $1\frac{9}{16}$ in. for two layers of $\frac{3}{4}$-in. plywood or particleboard. With the pattern rubbing against the collar, cut the arc. On a heavy countertop section, you'll need an extra pair of hands to make this cut.

Once the curve is finished, the counter will be ready for plastic edging. Most horizontal-grade laminates can be curved to take a 3-in. radius without heating. (Use a vertical-grade or postforming-grade laminate to bend a tighter arc—Wilsonart makes the most flexible laminate I know of.) The laminate is applied with contact cement in the usual fashion. Trim the edge with the trimmer bit, file or sand it flush, if necessary, and laminate the surface.

Preparing for wood edging   Making wood edging to fit a curved countertop can be tricky, especially compared to bending a strip of plastic laminate to do the same job. The safest way to do it is to work backwards—make the curved wood edging first, and then use it to mark the countertop for cutting.

There are various ways to make a curved wood edging. It can be cut from solid stock, steam-bent or laminated. Even when it's glued to the countertop, however, solid stock is weak because of the short grain that is exposed by the curve. Steam bent wood tends to spring back a bit toward its original shape—and not always evenly. I find that laminating offers the most reliable solution—the retention of the curved form is greatest.

I cold-mold $\frac{1}{8}$-in. to $\frac{1}{4}$-in. thick stock of the same species used for the rest of the straight edging and trim. The thin strips will take almost any bend I want without heat or steam. Six $\frac{1}{8}$-in. thick strips will form a $\frac{3}{4}$-in. wide laminated edging, which looks quite nice either chamfered or rounded with a $\frac{1}{4}$-in. radius. You can round or chamfer either edge, but again, I prefer the half-round bullnose shown on p. 151. It is even more pleasing in curved sections than in straight ones. Of course, whatever profile you've used on the straight sections of the counter should be duplicated on the curve.

For very tight radii (less than 2 in.), the edging can be bandsawn out of solid wood. I use this method only when lamination won't work. This will create a short-grain situation, which will invariably tear if the wood is machined. The material also will be quite fragile until it's applied and, even then, it could be easily cracked by a clamp during glue-up.

For a detailed description of how to laminate a curved edging, refer to pp. 158-159. When the edging is complete, cut the shape of the countertop to

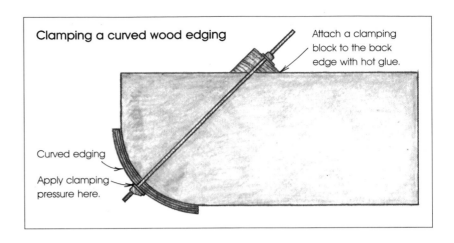

Clamping a curved wood edging

Attach a clamping block to the back edge with hot glue.

Curved edging

Apply clamping pressure here.

Laminating a curved edging

It takes longer to prepare to laminate a wood edging than it does to bend and glue it. First, you have to build a two-part mold for whatever radius you plan to shape (photo and drawing, below). You can use either plywood or particleboard, but plywood makes a stronger mold. The concave curve of the mold should have the same radius as the outside of the edging; the convex curve should have the same radius as the inside of the edging. A half-circle, or 180° arc, is the most you can incorporate in a two-part mold; larger arcs have to be built out of two or more smaller curves.

There are several things you can do that will make your mold more useful for future projects. You can make a half-circle mold, for example, even if you only need a quarter-circle right now. And you can stick to a common radius, such as

2 in., 3 in., 6 in. or 12 in. You also can design the mold to handle thicker stock, although you'll have to make up the difference between the thickness of your edging and the capacity of the mold by adding unglued plies during lamination. (These will drop off when the edging comes out of the mold.)

In any case, the mold must be at least as thick as the edging, or 1⅝ in. for my countertops. (I make my edging slightly thicker than the 1½-in. thick countertop, and trim off the excess after the edging is installed.) Again, if you build the mold out of three or four layers of ¾-in. material, you'll be able to use it to laminate wider stock. (You can always use the mold on narrower stock.)

Using a common center, draw the inside and outside radii directly on the mold stock. Make sure to add 2 in. of

straight run at both ends of the curve. This will give you material to join to the straight countertop edgings. Then cut the two mold sections on the bandsaw and sand the curves or use a router and trammel to smooth them.

When the mold is ready, cut the strips for laminating. Joint one edge of a 1⅝-in. thick board and use a bandsaw to rip the first laminate off the straight edge. (You can use a table saw, but its thicker blade removes a lot more material.) Make the strips slightly thicker than their final dimension. For most radii up to 12 in., I make ⅛-in. to 3/16-in. thick laminates; I use ¼-in. laminates to bend a larger radius. Stock 1/16 in. thick or even veneer may be required to bend a smaller radius. If you have trouble bending a particular piece of wood, try thinner stock. Always select straight-grained

You'll need a two-part mold to laminate a curved wood edging. This mold will handle up to a 180° bend—a larger curve will have to be pieced together. The mold shown in the drawing at right is designed to hold six ⅛-in. strips, and should be waxed before use.

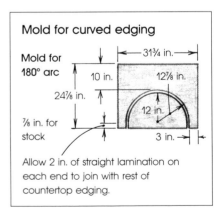

Mold for curved edging

Mold for 180° arc

31¾ in.

10 in.

12⅞ in.

24⅞ in.

12 in.

⅞ in. for stock

3 in.

Allow 2 in. of straight lamination on each end to join with rest of countertop edging.

match. Lay the laminated edging on the counter and trace the inside of the curve. Using a jigsaw, cut as close as you can to the waste side of the line and then carefully smooth the curve with a belt sander. If you overcut the line a bit, simply build the edge out with auto-body filler and file or sand it smooth.

You can cut the curve in the countertop before or after the reinforcing strips have been attached to its underside, but single-thickness material is easier to cut. Once you have the right curve in the top surface, it's easy to install the reinforcing strips and use the top as a pattern to cut them with a trimmer bit.

When the edge of the substrate has been prepared and is a perfect match for your wood edging, you can proceed exactly as you would for edging a straight section of countertop section. First apply plastic laminate to the surface, then trim the curved edge flush and attach the wood edging. To apply clamping pressure to the curved section of edging, I attach a small scrap block with hot glue to the back edge of the countertop, as shown in the top drawing on the facing page.

stock—a cross-grained strip may split before you get the mold closed, or it may split after the edging is released from the mold.

After each strip is cut, rejoint the ripped edge of the board and rip another, until all the strips have been cut. Then thickness-plane the strips to final dimension, using the jointed face on each strip as a reference surface. As you're ripping and planing the strips, take care to keep them in order so that the grain and color of the wood will be consistent when the edging is laminated.

The combined layers of stock should be exactly as thick as the intended thickness of your edging (and the space allowed for them in the mold). Then cut them to length, adding 2 in. at each end to join with the rest of the countertop edging. Use the following formula to calculate the length (L) of the strip:

$L = \pi r + 4$ in.

For a half-circle arc with a 12-in. inside radius (r), the calculation is:

$L = 3.14 \times 12$ in. $+ 4$ in., or 41.68 in.

Next, try the six ⅛-in. thick strips (if the mold is for ¾-in. material) in the mold. Lay the mold on a flat surface and stack the strips on edge between the two halves of the mold. Place one pipe clamp across the center of the mold and gradually tighten it. When the clamp has reached its full travel, place another clamp on either side, leaving enough room to turn the clamp handles. Then tighten the outside clamps until the first one is loose. Remove the center clamp and tighten the other two clamps completely. Unscrew the handle of the first clamp, replace it and apply pressure with it again. As the outside clamps loosen, unscrew their handles and replace them on the mold, as you did for the center clamp. Continue alternating pressure in this way until the mold is tight. If it starts to close unevenly, compensate by varying the pressure with the clamps.

When the mold is completely closed, make sure that all the strips are tight. If all looks well, undo the clamps in reverse order to take the mold apart. The strips

will have a lot of spring, so don't try to knock off the clamps.

Then wax the mold so that the glue won't stick and, using a 3-in. roller, apply yellow glue to one side of each strip (except for the last one in the lamination). Replace the strips in the mold, and tighten it as before. When the mold is fully closed, add another clamp or two across the open end to even up the pressure there (photo, facing page). Let this assembly dry overnight or even for a few days before opening the mold.

When the glue is dry, remove the edging from the mold and joint one edge; the plies sometimes slip during lamination and the edge may be uneven. I do this on the jointer to save time. When one side is flat, smooth the other side on the bandsaw or table saw and trim the ends with a handsaw, a chopsaw or a table saw (photo, below). Glue the curved section to the countertop first, then join the straight sections to it. I use a simple butt joint, but you can miter the joints if you like.

This table-saw jig holds the curved edging securely while its ends are trimmed square.

Granite (bottom) and marble are expensive, but they make elegant and practical kitchen countertops.

Natural countertops

I have a great fondness for natural materials. They are not only appealing to look at but are also often superior in use. One of the most beautiful natural countertop materials is polished granite. Check to see if your lottery number hit, though, before running down to the store. Granite runs about $50 per sq. ft., and can easily double the cost of an average kitchen. Most people who use it do so sparingly. But for a small counter, granite can provide a stunning accent.

Marble is softer than granite, but it can be found in a bewildering array of colors and patterns. It can even be bookmatched like wood. My local dealer has about 40 different samples, and they vary greatly in price. The radio-black marble I have used costs around $25 per sq. ft. Pure white marble can run as much as $70 per sq. ft.

Both marble and granite are available in thicknesses ranging from ⅜ in. to ⅞ in., and other dimensions can be cut on special order. Marble and granite are also available in tile form, and can be used in place of ceramics. Both materials can be cut and polished, and their edges can be rounded or chamfered, but these treatments require the use of special machinery, so you will have to order what you want.

Marble and granite are extremely heavy and will break if handled improperly, so sheets of these materials should be handled with care. Their great weight works to your advantage in the kitchen, though, as they needn't be secured to the cases. Just place the sheet of marble or granite in position on top of the cabinets. (A ¾-in. thick slab of marble or granite may require a bead of silicone to help keep it in place.)

Unfinished granite and marble will stain like wood, so they must be treated. Monument companies can polish either granite or marble, but be patient—they're accustomed to customers who can wait. You can treat the surface yourself by spreading a thin coat of cooking oil on it and then wiping it off. Marble polishes are available at most hardware stores.

Many people like to include a section of strip-laminated maple (or some other hardwood) in their kitchen countertop. Aside from its decorative quality, this so-called "butcher-block" counter makes an excellent surface for chopping, breadmaking or rolling pastry. (A traditional butcher block has an end-grain work surface and is generally quite thick.) You may purchase a pre-laminated hardwood countertop or laminate one yourself. If you buy the ready-made variety, all you will have to do is shape the edge, install it and perhaps finish it.

Avonite is one of several new synthetic countertop materials that look like granite and marble, but are much less expensive than the genuine article.

New materials   Until recently, there weren't many choices for kitchen countertop materials. You could have stone or wood, or perhaps stainless steel. Then came plastic laminate and its steadily increasing variety of patterns and colors. I still prefer conventional laminates, but in recent years, new synthetics have become available that mimic the oldest natural materials. Avonite and Corian are among these granite and marble look-alikes. Both are opaque, monolithic sheet materials with continuous color throughout. They are quite attractive and are available in sheets of various thicknesses.

Avonite (photo, above) and Corian are made of different materials, but are similar in application. Avonite is a polyester resin material, while Corian is an acrylic (see the Resource Guide on p. 184 for the manufacturers' addresses). They are available in a wide variety of solid colors and granite or marble patterns. Both can be machined with carbide tools and buffed to a high sheen, although they tend to scratch easily. (It's no suprise, however, that these materials are rough on cutting edges.) Perhaps their main advantage is that either material can be bonded to itself, using a special adhesive, to build up a thick edge. The adhesive fuses the layers together, making it difficult or impossible to see the seams. And the fused material can be sanded and polished to match the surface.

In general, plastics expand more than wood with changes in temperature, and less than wood with changes in moisture. This difference is especially problematic with Avonite and Corian. In an unheated cabin that is opened for a winter skiing weekend, the results can be disastrous. When the stove is lit to heat and dry out the room, the wood substrate will shrink and the plastic laminate will expand. Because Corian and Avonite are more susceptible to heat and moisture than standard plastic laminates, their manufacturers recommend using an elastomeric bonding agent like Silicone II to attach the laminate to the substrate. The flexible adhesive compensates for any movement.

Avonite and Corian are much more expensive than other plastic counter materials. At this writing, ¼-in. thick material costs around $10 per sq. ft., compared to about $4 per sq. ft. for Colorcore (described in Chapter 4) and $1 per sq. ft. for standard horizontal-grade plastic laminate. With a price ten times that of standard laminate, you wouldn't think these materials would be as popular as they are. But, next to marble and granite, they look almost cheap.

Given the extremely high cost of granite and marble, why not use a synthetic? For one simple reason—the natural materials have more visual depth. Only Nature's presses can create a high-density material of such exquisite beauty.

The backsplash

The backsplash, as its name suggests, provides a washable, protective surface at the back of the countertop. In form, style and material, the backsplash offers myriad possibilities, two of which are shown in the photo below and on p. 146. The backsplash can be a simple 4-in. to 6-in. high lip, molded into the counter surface, or a laminated panel that fills the space between the countertop and the upper cabinets, or even the ceiling. Materials range from ceramic tile and plastic laminate to marble, granite or varnished hardwoods.

While low backsplashes may be adequate in performing their protective task, they add nothing to the appearance of the cabinetwork. A full-height backsplash, on the other hand, can have a dramatic effect on the look of the cabinets. The upper cabinets no longer appear to hang awkwardly from the ceiling, but rather become part of an integral unit that flows smoothly from floor to ceiling. Full-height backsplashes, however, aren't usually favored by kitchen designers because it takes a careful mechanic to install them properly. Electrical outlets must be cut in precisely, and once a mistake is made an expensive laminated panel may be totally wasted. A full-height backsplash also adds to the cost of the kitchen, and this can be significant if it's made of granite, Corian or Avonite.

The joint between the backsplash and the countertop should be sealed with silicone caulk. This will prevent water from running under the backsplash and harming the wall surfaces behind. (You can use caulk or a decorative molding to conceal the seam between the top of a high backsplash and the bottom of the upper cabinets.) No matter how you apply it, the caulk will probably be visible, but you can make it less obtrusive. Look for a caulk that matches, or at least complements, the color of your laminate. (Kampel Enterprises, Inc., the makers of SeamFil plastic seam filler, also makes a caulk that is available in many colors to match a wide variety of laminates.) Plastic or aluminum moldings can be used where you can't match the color or material, but I don't use them. I think they're ugly, and they won't prevent moisture from seeping beneath the backsplash.

This full-height tile backsplash protects the wall behind the countertop and ties the upper and lower cases together visually.

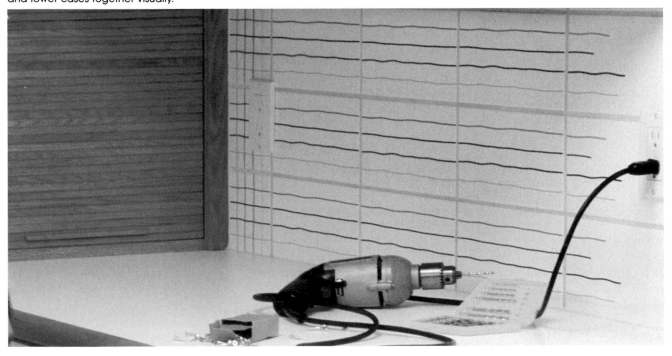

Low backsplashes A low backsplash—one that stops short of the electrical outlets—is a standard feature of kitchen designs because it's quick, easy and relatively inexpensive. One of the most common low backsplashes, shown in the drawing below, is actually an integral part of the postformed countertop. Postformed counters are manufactured with special equipment, and the prefabricated counters are distributed through retail lumberyards. They can be cut to length, in which case the exposed ends must be laminated to cover the particleboard substrate. A postformed counter is installed the same way as a custom-built countertop, by screwing up through the tops of the cases, as described on p. 179.

If you don't like the look of a postformed backsplash, there are other ways to provide inexpensive protection for the wall using plastic laminate. In some kitchens, the laminate is simply glued to the wall, using a metal trim piece to protect any exposed edges. This approach is quick and easy, though it looks shoddy if the wall itself is irregular. Another option is to laminate plastic to a plywood strip in the shop, then attach it to the countertop before the counter is installed. Of course, you can use materials other than plastic laminate to make a low backsplash. A single row of ceramic tiles can form a stunning accent, as can granite or marble. Tile should be applied to a plywood substrate, which is installed using one of the methods shown in the drawing on p. 165. Granite and marble are simply glued in place, without a plywood backing.

Full-height backsplashes If you need to cover a damaged wall or just want a dramatic effect, consider making a full-height backsplash. Any of the materials I've suggested for the countertop and the low backsplash can be used to make a full-height backsplash. But before you plunge ahead, assess your skills carefully. Cutting holes for electrical boxes in an expensive backsplash is nerve-wracking, and a small mistake will waste a lot of material. Remember also that, depending on the thickness of the backsplash material, the existing outlet boxes may have to be moved or extended to reach the new surfaces. Usually this can be done by screwing a box extender (available from an electrical supply store) to the existing boxes.

Installing a full-height backsplash takes some preparation. The best way to guarantee a first-rate job is to make a full pattern of the area to be covered. (Cardboard is adequate for this, though Masonite would be sturdier.) Start by making a quick sketch of the area to be covered, noting all dimensions and including the location of electrical outlets, switches, range hoods and the like. This needn't be a scale drawing, but to ensure accuracy all measurements

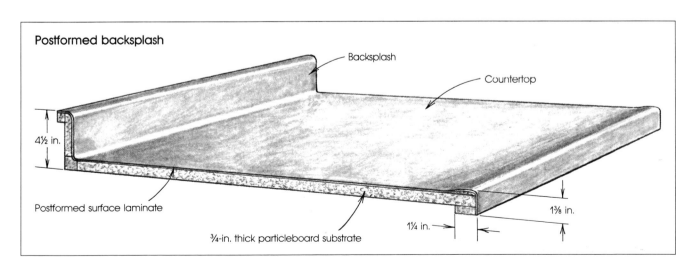

Postformed backsplash

Backsplash

Countertop

4½ in.

Postformed surface laminate

¾-in. thick particleboard substrate

1¼ in.

1⅜ in.

should be taken from the same reference point. Measure, say, from one wall or from a fixed point in the middle of the kitchen (the range, perhaps) and work out in both directions from there.

Now transfer all your measurements to the cardboard, taping sheets together as necessary (an appliance store is a good source of large sheets of cardboard). A carpenter's square will help you keep all the lines square to one another, though they may not be square on the wall. If you have a lot of electrical boxes to draw, buy a box and use it as a template for drawing the cutouts. When the pattern is complete, cut it out with a matte knife and check its fit above the counter, trimming it if necessary. If you accidentally cut away too much, add a cardboard patch (I stick them on with my trusty hot-glue gun) and trim it again.

Trace the pattern onto the plywood substrate and cut the plywood to size. Make sure to cut the bottom edge and the ends on the table saw, so you will have a straight, clean edge where the backsplash meets the countertop and at both ends. Use a jigsaw to cut along the top of the backsplash. This edge needn't be perfect because it will be covered with a finish molding. To make the cutouts for electrical boxes and other fixtures, bore a hole in the corners of each marked box. Then insert the jigsaw blade in one of these holes and cut out the box. Slip the plywood into position as you did the cardboard pattern, and check its fit. You can make the backsplash fit tightly to the underside of the upper cabinets, but it will be much easier to fit if you leave a small gap, which also will be covered by the molding.

Once you've cut the plywood (including any holes for electrical boxes) cut a piece of laminate slightly larger than the substrate. (Refer to p. 74 for some tips on how to align the laminate.) Then spread two coats of contact cement on both the laminate and the substrate and roll out the laminate as usual, covering the cutout holes in the plywood.

After laminating, use a bearing-guided trimmer bit to trim the excess laminate on all the outside edges of the backsplash. Then use a router equipped with a pilot bit to clean up the inside edges of the cutouts. The pilot bit, shown in the photo on p. 78, is guided by the straight section of the bit shank below the cutter and has a cutting point that can bore its own hole in laminate. It should not be used for regular trimming, however, or any place you can fit a bearing-guided bit, because the friction caused by the spinning steel will leave burn marks on the edge of the plywood and laminate. This isn't a problem in the backsplash cutout holes, because they'll be covered by caulk or hidden by switch plates.

Trimming holes in the backsplash is a breeze with a pilot bit—it's only finding the holes that's tricky. I turn the plywood over and bore one hole through from the back with the pilot bit, then finish the cut from the front. The bit will leave a slight curve at the corners of the cutouts, but this is a good thing—it prevents stress cracks.

If you plan to attach the laminate directly to the wall, map out the appropriate cuts by using the cardboard pattern as a guide, and cut the laminate to shape.

Fitting the backsplash A low or full-height laminated backsplash may be screwed to the back edge of the countertop from underneath, or fitted to the counter with a tongue-and-groove or dowel joint, as shown in the drawing below. Any of the above methods will make a good joint, but I prefer the tongue-and-groove joint—it's strong and easy to make, and it provides a continuous barrier to water. Saw or rout the ¼-in. wide by ⅜-in. deep groove in the back of the countertop before the countertop is installed. Then cut a matching tongue on the bottom of the backsplash. Make the tongue ⁵⁄₁₆ in. long to keep it from bottoming out in the groove. To play it safe, I'd still caulk the seam to prevent standing water from seeping under the backsplash.

If the countertop is too large or if you don't have the extra pairs of hands you'll need to manipulate it with the backsplash attached, you'll have to add it after the counter is in place. Countertop and backsplash installation is discussed on pp. 178-180.

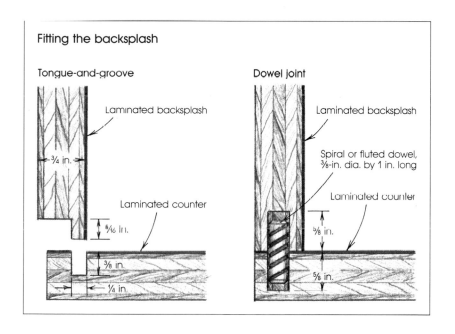

Fitting the backsplash

Tongue-and-groove

Laminated backsplash

¾ in.

Laminated counter

⁵⁄₁₆ in.

⅜ in.

¼ in.

Dowel joint

Laminated backsplash

Spiral or fluted dowel, ⅜-in. dia. by 1 in. long

Laminated counter

⅝ in.

⅝ in.

INSTALLING THE CABINETS
Chapter 11

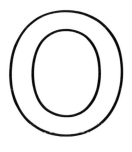nce the casework is complete and the doors, drawers and countertops are finished, installation isn't far behind. The upper cases must be mounted securely to the wall, and the base cases must be raised to provide a kick space at the floor and leveled so that the countertop will be at the correct working height. Without a level base, the lower cases would rack, and the doors would be almost impossible to mount. Most floors slope down, away from the wall, and the countertop will have the same pitch unless the case is leveled. A slight pitch is tempting to ignore, but when you put down the eggs for an omelet, you'll wish you had brought a bucket and a mop.

Before I describe how to install the cabinets you've worked so hard to build, I'd like to make one cautionary remark. As soon as the cases are done, but before all the drawers and doors are fitted, you may be in a hurry to install them. It's always gratifying to see the cases in place, and it's a relief to know that they're going to fit. Also, the tangible array of empty cases somehow justifies to your family or your client all those long hours of preparation. But whether you're building your own kitchen or someone else's, I urge you to wait. As soon as you install the cases, your spouse or client will pepper you with questions: "Are you going to put drawers here? Where will the shelves go? Will the counter be too high?" Such questions express a justifiable anxiety, but they'll slow down your work and make life miserable. If, on the other hand, you roll into the house and plunk the entire kitchen down in finished form, you'll look like a pro. Let me tell you a story to illustrate my point.

When I'm not busy making kitchen cabinets (or writing books about them), I make small decorative boxes, which I veneer with bookmatched burls. They're only a few inches square, but each box takes about 20 hours to complete. Several years ago I took a few of my finest examples to a highfalutin gallery on Madison Avenue in New York City. I removed them from a cardboard box, unwrapped the old towels that protected them and showed them to the owner. She admired them, but didn't take any to sell in the store. Not only was my pride wounded, but if this was my best work, I thought, how would I ever make it as a woodworker?

Pride heals, though, and six months later I decided to try again. This time I wrapped the same little boxes in fine tissue paper and placed them in a handsome wooden case, just big enough to hold them. I went back to the same gallery and showed them again to the same woman. This time she loved the boxes, and sold a bunch of them at fancy New York City prices. Though conditions at the gallery may have changed between my two visits, I suspect that the different result was due more to the change in my presentation. As I discovered with my boxes, appearances are indeed important—the proper presentation affects how well you do.

In the early chapters of this book, I outlined the major advantages of European-style cabinetry over traditional face-frame cabinetry—in the case construction, the hardware and in the design of doors and drawer faces. Another significant advantage of the cases I build over their traditional counterparts is in their method of installation.

The case sides of a traditional face-frame cabinet extend to the floor, where they are notched to create the kick space. The cabinet is leveled by trimming material from the bottom edge of each side to accommodate high spots in the floor, and for every adjustment the case must be turned over and a little more material sawn off. (The bottom of the case can also be shimmed, but if you have to shim very much you will wind up with an unsightly gap at the end of a run, which will have to be covered.) Once the cabinet is leveled, nails or screws are driven through the back of the case into the wall studs. The main problem with this system (besides its inefficiency) is that the walls in most homes are neither plumb nor straight. If the case is straight and level on the floor, there's a good chance it won't meet the wall. Shims must be used to fill any gaps between the wall and the case before nailing. Shimming might pull the cases out of square and will surely cause trouble if either the wall or floor settle.

European-style cabinets, on the other hand, are attached to the floor, not the walls, and they rest on an independent base system or a series of adjustable legs. It's true that floors are no more level than walls are plumb, but an independent base is easily adapted to irregular conditions. Like so many of the methods of construction I have outlined in this book—from cutting case joints to no-fault lamination and installing hardware—my approach to installation assumes the worst. With an independent base, the problems of sloping floors and out-of-square walls are anticipated and resolved with a minimum of fuss.

The base system

There are several types of independent base systems suitable for European-style cabinets, a few of which are shown in the drawing below. The one I most often use, shown at left in the drawing, employs two parallel plywood rails, ¾ in. thick by 4½ in. high, which run the length of the cabinets. I usually build the rails from scrap plywood left over from the case construction. If the run is greater than 8 ft. long or if I have only shorter pieces on hand, I butt another section of rail against the first and brace the joint with a 12-in. long plywood block, glued and screwed to the inside. Glued and stapled to the inside bottom edge of each rail is a ¾-in. sq. ledger strip of poplar, predrilled every 18 in. for No. 8 drywall

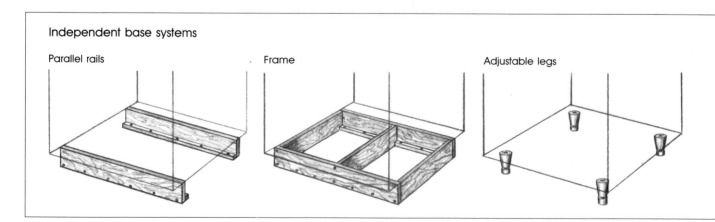

Independent base systems

Parallel rails   Frame   Adjustable legs

screws. (Any hardwood would do for the ledger strip, but poplar is cheap and easy to work.)

Although its position isn't crucial, I usually locate the front rail 2½ in. from the front of the door, and the back rail 2½ in. from the wall, as shown in the drawing below. The front recess creates a kick space for your toes when you stand at the counter. The 4½-in. height of the rails plus the 30-in. height of the cases and the 1½-in. thickness of the countertop brings the counter work surface to a total height of 36 in., which is standard in the industry. For a slightly lower or higher countertop, simply change the height of the rails. Be aware, however, that if you lower the overall height of the countertop too much, the range and dishwasher might not fit. And the farther you stray from the standard counter height, the more trouble you'll have when you try to sell the house.

Before you install the rails, get a copy of the floor plan, showing the cabinets (see the drawing on p. 7), and all elevation drawings (see p. 27), and refer to them throughout the installation process. Begin the layout by snapping a chalkline on the floor where the front of the cabinets will go. Next, snap a second line 2½ in. behind the first one to mark the position of the front rail. Then make a third line 2½ in. from the wall to mark the location of the back rail. It's more important that the back rail be parallel to the front rail than to the wall, so if there are any discrepancies make sure to maintain the parallel relationship of the rails.

To install the rails, place them along the chalklines, with the ledger strips on the inside. Screw through the ledger strips and into the floor with 2¼-in. long, No. 8 drywall screws, but don't tighten them all the way. If the floor is not level, the rails can be shimmed to level them along their length and with each other. Almost anything will work for shim stock—slim strips of hardwood, blocks of plywood, even cedar shingles and shakes. To maintain strong, continuous contact between the cabinets and the base, place these shims between the floor and the base, not between the base and the cabinet. Once the rails are shimmed level, drive the screws tightly into the floor. Where the run turns a corner, butt-join and screw the front rails together.

Another approach is to make an independent frame (shown at center in the drawing on the facing page). The frame resembles a ladder, with crosspieces between the front and back rails, and it provides an easily leveled foundation through which the bottom of the case is securely anchored to the floor. The independent frame provides much more rigid support than the twin rails, and I prefer it for peninsulas or islands, where the countertop is not supported by the wall. Also, you can build the entire base frame beforehand and install it at once instead of juggling separate pieces. Make the crosspieces from the same plywood stock and the same height as the front and back rails and screw directly

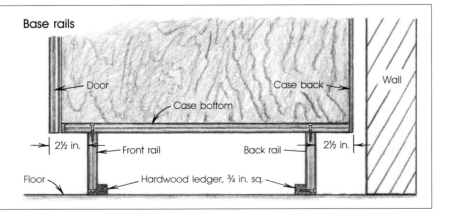

Base rails

Door — Case back — Wall
Case bottom
2½ in. — Front rail — Back rail — 2½ in.
Floor — Hardwood ledger, ¾ in. sq.

Corner frames

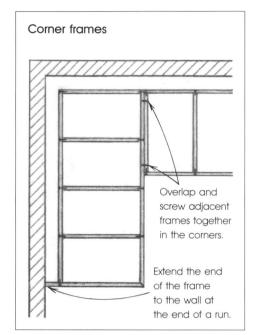

Overlap and screw adjacent frames together in the corners.

Extend the end of the frame to the wall at the end of a run.

through the rails to secure them. As before, attach the ledger strips to the inside bottom edge of the front and back rails. Extend the ends of the frame to the wall at the end of a run, and screw adjacent frames together where they meet in a corner, as shown in the drawing at left. This will make the understructure more rigid and much neater.

Adjustable legs   Instead of shimming the rails, you can use adjustable legs to level the cases. Several different types are made by various manufacturers, but they all work pretty much the same way. Four metal or plastic legs are screwed to the bottom of each case. The 4¼-in. high leg shown in the photo below may be extended by about 1 in. by turning the screw-adjusted foot at its base, making it possible to level the cabinets after they've been installed. Plywood shims can be added beneath the foot for even greater range of adjustment.

Once the cases are leveled, the legs are concealed behind an apron, or skirt, which may be made of hardwood or plywood covered with veneer or plastic laminate. The apron snaps onto the front legs with special clips that come with the legs. The clip shown in the photo snaps into a saw kerf cut on the inside of the apron. It can be moved sideways, which greatly simplifies installation. Some clips also lock in position with a setscrew.

When you decide where to locate the clips, snap them into the saw kerf and screw them to the back of the apron, if necessary. Then snap the apron onto the front legs. It's a slick system that allows the cabinets to be readjusted later, after the house has settled. It also makes the cabinets easy to move or to replace. (In Europe, cabinets are considered furniture, and people often bring their kitchen cabinets along when they move to a new house.) Also, the apron snaps off in an instant, whenever you need access to wires or pipes beneath the case.

For all their benefits, however, the leveling legs have one major disadvantage—they are not attached to the floor. You could screw through the backs of the cases into wall studs instead, but you'd have to beef up the case backs—a ¼-in. plywood back is not strong enough for this purpose. If the wall were out of plumb, which it usually is, you would also have to shim behind each screw to keep from racking the cases. After the screws are tight, check that the cases are level; then add more shims, if necessary, and readjust the height of the legs.

You can make your own adjustable legs with materials available in your local hardware store. As shown in the drawing below, simply screw threaded pipe

This 4¼-in.-high plastic leg offers quick installation and adjustment up to about 5¼ in. It bolts to the bottom of the case, and the foot unscrews to level the cabinet. The clip snaps into a saw kerf in the back of the apron.

Homemade adjustable legs

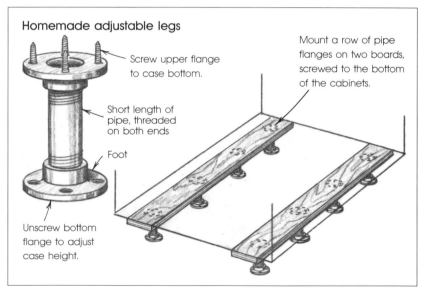

Screw upper flange to case bottom.

Short length of pipe, threaded on both ends

Foot

Unscrew bottom flange to adjust case height.

Mount a row of pipe flanges on two boards, screwed to the bottom of the cabinets.

flanges to the underside of the case and fit them with short lengths of pipe, threaded on both ends. A second flange threaded on the bottom of the pipe for a foot distributes the load. The height of the pipe leg is adjusted by turning the bottom flange.

Alternatively, you can attach a row of pipe flanges to two boards that are at least as wide as the diameter of the flanges and as long as the run of cases, as shown at right in the drawing at the bottom of the facing page. Place one board near the front of the cabinets and another near the back, as was described above for the rails. Then level the boards, place the cases on top and screw through the bottoms into the boards. (If you wish, you can screw the bottom pipe flanges into the floor before installing the cases.)

To fasten the apron to the pipes, I use wall-mounted tool holders, also readily available in most hardware stores. Screw them to the apron just like the commercial fittings described above, and then clip the apron onto the front pipe legs to enclose the space beneath the cabinets.

Installing base cases

The base cases should be planned, and if possible installed, around the appliances. If you have the appliances on hand, position them in the run before the cases are fastened in place, so that the cases can be situated around them with the appropriate clearances. Always read the installation instructions for the appliances before final installation. If the appliances have not arrived yet, you can get the installation instructions and recommended clearances through your dealer or from the manufacturer.

Be alert when the appliances are delivered—many dealers will switch appliances at the last minute if the ones you ordered aren't available. With dishwashers this shouldn't present a problem, but if the switch involves a refrigerator, it may. Refrigerators vary substantially in all dimensions—so much so that you may have to get another one or remake a case if you receive the wrong model. Also, you may find that the refrigerator door is hinged on the wrong side and will no longer fit your layout. (Refrigerator doors can sometimes be switched from one side to the other.) In any event, don't assume that whatever appliance is delivered will fit the space you've allotted. It isn't easy to move a heavy appliance through the house, and there's always a risk of damaging the woodwork

Install the appliances first, if possible, and fit the base cases around them. This freestanding range will interrupt the rails, which can either be cut out to make room or built around it.

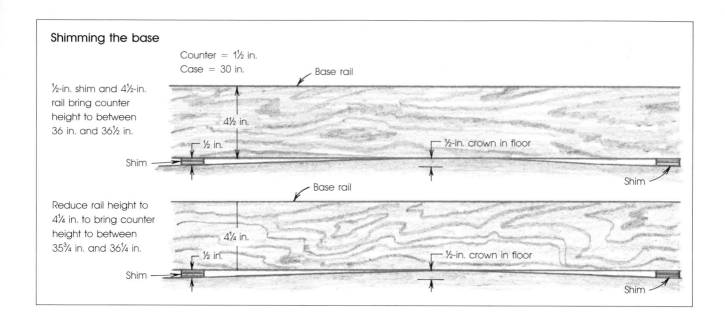

Shimming the base

Counter = 1½ in.
Case = 30 in.

Base rail

½-in. shim and 4½-in. rail bring counter height to between 36 in. and 36½ in.

4½ in.

½ in.

½-in. crown in floor

Shim

Shim

Base rail

Reduce rail height to 4¼ in. to bring counter height to between 35¾ in. and 36¼ in.

4¼ in.

½ in.

½-in. crown in floor

Shim

Shim

One kitchen—a case study

One bitter November day several years ago, I called on Malcolm and Suzi Moore at their new home in upstate New York. Standing around a kerosene heater in the cold and empty would-be kitchen, the Moores discussed their objectives. They had done their homework and had a good idea of what they wanted the space to contain. Malcolm had even drawn a floor plan, adapted from a kitchen they saw in a magazine. It didn't fit the rules, and I liked it right away.

The design they selected was a modified galley (drawing, facing page), open at one end but closed off by a large window at the other. The window would flood the kitchen with light, creating an open, airy feeling. On one side, the cabinets would be firmly anchored to a wall, and on the other side a double-wide peninsula of base cabinets would supply ample storage space and also separate the kitchen from the dining area. Although their design had only 8 lin. ft. of upper cabinets (2 ft. less than the minimum I normally recommend), it had an astonishing 18 lin. ft. of base cabinets.

After studying the floor plan, I measured the space for myself, even though Malcolm had already done so. Double-checking measurements is always a good idea, and in this kitchen, where one run of cabinets had to be tucked between two walls, accurate dimensions

were critical. As I looked around, I could see without measuring that one corner was seriously out of square. I also checked the ceiling height. People always say their ceiling is 8 ft. high, but it rarely is. The Moores' ceiling was 1½ in. low, and I decided to compensate for this by reducing the height of the molding above the upper cabinets.

After ironing out a few rough spots in the design, the Moores picked out a color for the plastic laminate, and we settled on a lightly stained oak trim to match. I made drawings of all the cases and ordered the materials and hardware. The plywood and oak were readily available, but the hardware would take a week to get and the plastic laminate could take up to three weeks. (You can wait as long as eight weeks for less popular colors or non-standard sizes.)

When the laminate arrived, I dropped most of it off with a firm that specializes in laminating countertops. (Despite the company's excellent reputation, the laminate on several doors bubbled after the heat and humidity of the first summer. Fortunately, I was able to heat the affected areas with an iron and clamped them to the substrate until the bond re-established itself.) While I waited for the laminated material to be delivered, I ripped up all the oak edging and made all the plywood base rails and the shelves. When the laminated panels

arrived, I cut them carefully to size and began building the cases.

The cases went together in a week, without fuss, and when spring finally arrived I was ready to install them. The long upper run had to fit between two walls so I left one end case unassembled. That way, I could install the rest of the run and make the end case slightly larger (by substituting a new top and bottom), if necessary, or cut it down to fit a tight space. Because of the out-of-square corner I'd spotted before and accumulated joint compound on the wall, I made the case about 1 in. narrower than the drawings called for. The gap created at the front of the case by the skewed wall would have to be filled with a spacer.

To support the base cabinets I used the parallel rail system instead of frames because the cases would be stabilized by the wall itself. Four parallel rails provided the foundation for the peninsula. A panel attached to the end of the peninsula would tie the exposed end together, and the wall to which the peninsula was anchored would hold the other end.

As the installation proceeded, a few typical glitches arose, and the system I developed over years of trials and innumerable errors came to the rescue. For example, the trim around the window kept the doors in the last cabinet

or the floors. So check the appliance as soon as it arrives. If it isn't what you ordered, send it right back.

Refrigerators and freestanding ranges interrupt the base system and divide the runs into separate sections. Each section must be made level with the surrounding sections. You can install long rails the full length of the run and cut out the sections where the appliances will go, or you can lay the rails in shorter sections that fit between the appliances. It's much easier to level one long rail than several short ones, but you'll have to make sure that the shims and fasteners aren't placed in the area that will be cut away when the appliance is installed. It's harder to level a rail installed in short sections, but once it's in you won't have to cut it out for the refrigerator or stove. I have used both methods and find them equally acceptable.

No matter what leveling method you use, try to maintain a counter height of 36 in. This isn't usually hard to do, but occasionally the floor will be significantly out of level, particularly in an older home. Where the floor rises and falls ½ in. or more over the run of the cabinets, simply shimming the rails, as shown in the drawing on the facing page, or adjusting the feet will raise the height of the countertop in places to 36½ in. In this situation, you can rip ¼ in. off the rails to keep the height of the countertop between 35¾ in. and 36¼ in. high. You can't shorten adjustable legs (unless you make your own), so if you plan to place

from opening all the way, which kept the slide-out trays from sliding out. But because I had allowed more clearance for the refrigerator than the manufacturer recommended, I had an extra inch to play with. I used it here, moving the cases 1 in. closer to the refrigerator, and installed a spacer at the wall.

Another problem occurred after the cases were installed, when the range that arrived turned out to be a drop-in unit instead of the freestanding stove that had been ordered. Luckily, I had not cut the countertop—I try not to do that until the appliances are sitting in the kitchen. The case to the right of the stove also had to be removed to install the vent. This was easily done by pulling the four screws that attached the bottom of the case to the base rails.

I installed tamboured cabinets on the wall over the peninsula, with electrical outlets in the back of the case for the small appliances that would be stored inside. But after carefully measuring for the outlet openings, I forgot to reverse the measurements when marking them on the backs of the cases. When I slipped the backs into place, the outlets were on one side and the openings were on the other. After correcting the cutouts, I fit a piece of ¼-in. plywood in the back of each case to cover my mistake. It was a little extra work, but my only loss was ¼ in. of depth inside the cases.

My next blunder was much more painful. Contrary to my usual practice, I had not yet made the drawers for one side of the peninsula. The faces were

made and the cases were installed with their doors. When I measured for the drawers I recorded the full case width instead of the net interior space. When I went to install the drawers, I realized at once that another weekend had evaporated. All four drawers had to be remade. Does anyone need four 22½-in. wide white oak drawers?

After that humbling experience, I began making shop drawings and cutting lists that include the full outside and inside width of the case, the space used by the drawer slides and the net width of the drawers. Combined with the standard case depth and drawer height, my new drawings give me all the dimensions I need. Now if I want to get

into trouble, I really have to go out of my way to do it.

The last major item was the peninsula countertop. It was a large and costly item, and after the outlet cutouts and the drawers, I was in no mood for a repeat. The peninsula required only the cutout for the sink, which mercifully dropped right into place. The balance of the installation came off without a hitch and, aside from the refrigerator, which had not yet arrived, the kitchen was in working order right on time.

The Moores' kitchen didn't go together quite as smoothly as I'd hoped—kitchens rarely do—but it wasn't too bad, and the results were worth the effort. You can just imagine what the tough ones are like.

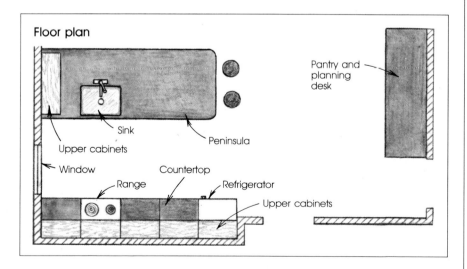

Floor plan

Pantry and planning desk

Sink

Peninsula

Upper cabinets

Window

Countertop

Range

Refrigerator

Upper cabinets

your cabinets on adjustable legs instead of rails or frames you may have to live with a slightly higher countertop. If the difference in the floor height is more than ¾ in. over the length of the run, it's best to level the floor before you are ready to install your cabinets.

Once all the rails or frames are fastened down, you may begin installing the base cabinets. In an L-shaped or U-shaped kitchen, start at a corner and work your way out. That way, if the run is a bit long or short, you won't have to fit the cases against a wall or another run of cases.

Installing the L-spacers   Before the cases can be secured to the base, you have to make and install the L-spacers that connect the end cases on adjacent runs. L-spacers are made just like doors and drawer faces. I use scrap pieces of ¾-in. plywood, faced with the same plastic laminate that was used in the rest of the kitchen and edged with the same ¼-in. thick hardwood, as shown in the drawing below.

To make an L-spacer, laminate and edge a panel about 5 in. wide and 30 in. long, to match the combined height of the doors and drawer faces in the adjacent cases. (As I discussed in Chapter 2, the combined height of a standard door and drawer face plus the space between them is actually $29\frac{29}{32}$ in.) Remember that the dimensions of the plywood must be ½ in. less than these overall measurements in order to allow room for the ¼-in. edging that will be added on all four sides.

When the panel is laminated and edged, rip it lengthwise into two pieces, 2 in. and 2¾ in. wide. Then form the L by screwing the pieces together along one edge, as shown in the drawing below, so that the exposed faces will reveal

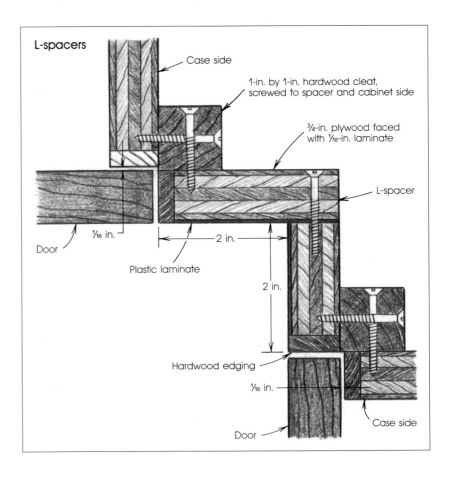

L-spacers

Case side

1-in. by 1-in. hardwood cleat, screwed to spacer and cabinet side

¾-in. plywood faced with ¹⁄₁₆-in. laminate

L-spacer

¹⁄₁₆ in.

Door

Plastic laminate

2 in.

2 in.

Hardwood edging

¹⁄₁₆ in.

Case side

Door

L-spacers made of ¾-in. plywood faced with plastic laminate connect the end cases on adjacent runs. They are installed before the cases are secured to the base.

2 in. on each side. Use 1⅝-in. long drywall screws, placed about 9 in. apart along the joint and 1 in. from both ends.

To mount the spacer to the cases, screw a 1-in. sq. hardwood cleat along each back edge. Then install the spacer by screwing through the cleats into the sides of the adjacent cases (or the front of a blind-corner case) with three evenly spaced, 1¼ in. drywall screws. In its final position, the spacer should protrude about ¹⁄₁₆ in. so that its front surfaces are flush with the faces in each run.)

Screw the spacer to the side of one case first, and then attach it to the adjacent case—from the outside, if possible, or from the inside of the case, if necessary. If all the screws are installed from the outside, you won't have any exposed screw heads inside the case, but the cases will be more difficult to remove later on, once the countertop is installed. If at least one of the cases is screwed from inside, you'll be able to remove the cases later without removing the countertop, but you'll have to put up with visible screw heads on the inside of the case.

When the two corner cases are in position and fastened together, begin attaching the remaining cases on both sides. You can use a handscrew clamp to hold the front edges of the cases together while their sides are counterbored and screwed together with 1¼-in. long drywall screws. Two screws front and back are sufficient, and the front ones may be hidden under the hinge base plates if you like. (You'll have to remove the base plates to do this.) I don't find it objectionable, however, to see neatly spaced fasteners inside a case. The screws will be less conspicuous if you line them up with the shelf-support holes.

Many cabinet manufacturers who use the 32mm system employ a special two-part, knock-down fastener to install cases. When both halves of the fasteners are tightened in the prebored sides of the adjacent cases, the cases will be perfectly aligned. If you haven't got the equipment to bore the precisely spaced grid of holes, you can still clamp the cases together and bore holes for these fasteners. Or you can use T-nuts (the kind with prongs that are hammered into the side of the case) and hex-head machine screws to get a very sturdy knock-down joint. Drywall screws are much faster, though, and perfectly satisfactory.

Attaching the cases to the base   After all the base cases have been fastened together, make sure they haven't shifted position and are still properly located between the walls, appliances and any other fixed obstacles. Then screw through the bottoms of the base cases and into the front and back rails of the base frame. I use four 1⅝-in. long drywall screws in the bottom of each case, countersunk and spaced 2 in. from both sides of the case. If you have been careful and consistent when you were locating your base rails, you should be able to hit the centers of the rails quite easily by measuring from the front of the case.

If the bottom and sides of the case are hardwood plywood, the countersunk screw heads can be concealed with a matching putty or even with wood plugs glued in place. (If you used softwood plywood, shame on you.) If the bottom is covered with plastic laminate, the screw heads can be puttied over with Kampel SeamFil. The putty can be scraped out if you ever need to pull the screws to remove the case.

A word of warning: Don't cover up these screws until the kitchen is complete. In spite of advance planning, I have yet to install a kitchen where there wasn't at least one base case that had to be moved for one reason or another. The plumber may need access to a pipe, or the ductwork for a heating vent may have to be moved away from the stove. With this case-and-base system, the screws holding any cabinet in place can be removed, and the cabinet can be pulled out and then replaced. In fact, I never conceal any of the screws that attach my cabinets to the base frame or to each other, because they are a functional part of the casework. Also, if the case has to be removed later—which happens more frequently than you can imagine—easy access to the screw heads will be greatly appreciated.

Trimming out the base As I mentioned earlier, the base can be made from scrap plywood left over from the cases. That's fine if the plywood veneer matches the hardwood edgings—if, for example, the rails are birch plywood and the doors and drawer faces have been trimmed with solid birch. But a birch rail won't look right if all the faces are trimmed with oak. If the base and the faces don't match, you'll need to cover the front base rail with trim. The trim will also conceal any shims that may have been used to level the cabinets, as well as the heads of the screws used to install the crosspieces in an independent base frame. As shown in the drawing below, you can hide the screws in a base frame without using trim, by screwing short hardwood blocks to the ends of the crosspieces. These vertical blocks, as well as the ledger strips that attach

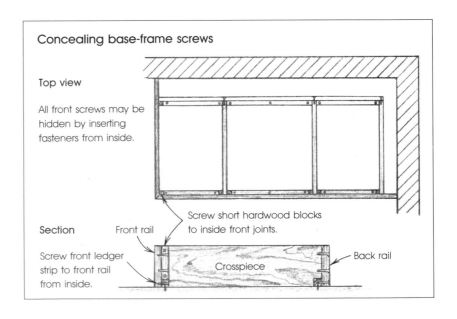

Concealing base-frame screws

Top view

All front screws may be hidden by inserting fasteners from inside.

Screw short hardwood blocks to inside front joints.

Section   Front rail

Screw front ledger strip to front rail from inside.

Crosspiece

Back rail

Base trim can be a subtle but attractive detail. There are several styles, including vinyl cove base (left), plywood (above) and hardwood trim (below). The finger-jointed sections highlight the cabinetwork.

the frame to the floor, may be screwed from inside the case, leaving no exposed screw heads.

Like the backsplash, this trim apron can be made out of a wide variety of materials to complement the cabinets and the rest of the kitchen. The black vinyl cove molding in the top left photo on p. 177 accents the bright red plastic laminate on the cases and ties the casework together, while the plywood base trim in the top right photo on p. 177 contrasts nicely with the black cabinets. If the kitchen floor will be tiled, you can also tile the front rail to form an attractive border around the base.

If you use hardwood trim, you can miter the ends of the trim sections wherever they meet in a corner or on a long run, or you can use the finger joint shown in the photo at the bottom of p. 177. The finger joint is attractive, easy to make and greatly simplifies fitting corners. All the joints are cut into equal fingers, the same length and width as the thickness of the trim material, usually ¾ in. Round over all edges with a ¼-in. quarter-round router bit and sand the joint and the rest of the trim thoroughly to a 100-grit finish before assembly. Because this joint is purely decorative, it needn't fit as snugly as the finger joints in the drawers. The real payoff comes when you put the pieces together. They will fit as nicely in a square or 45° corner as they will in a straight run. And you'll never notice if the trim is not perfectly aligned. Also, in front of the dishwasher or stove it will be easy to add a separate, removable piece of base trim, held in place by the finger joints alone. Prebore the hardwood trim and fasten it to the front base rail with finish nails, their heads set and filled with wood putty.

You could also use ¼-in. hardwood plywood left over from the drawer bottoms and case backs, as long as it matches the trim on the faces. (If you plan to use hardwood or tile, make sure to adjust the location of the front base rail to account for the extra thickness.) If you use plastic laminate or vinyl cove base, use a cove-base adhesive to apply it directly to the frame. Or you could apply the laminate to a separate strip of ¼-in. plywood, which in turn is glued to the front base rail with cove-base adhesive. Unlike contact cement, the cove-base adhesive will allow you to shift the plastic laminate (or the vinyl cove base) into position before securing it.

Installing the countertop and backsplash

After the base cases are secured to the frame, you're ready to install the countertop and backsplash. This is usually done before the upper cabinets are in place, because there's more room to maneuver. Also, if you plan to make a full-

Measure the front overhang of the countertop with its back edge pushed against the wall to determine its position before scribing.

Scribe the back edge of the counter by running a pencil along it, using a wood block as a guide against the wall.

height backsplash, the upper cabinets can rest on the backsplash itself. The countertop and the backsplash can be fastened together before they are installed, or the countertop may be installed first. If you install the counter first, make sure to cut any joints for the backsplash in the back edge of the counter or drill any screw holes beforehand (drawing, p. 165). If no backsplash is to be used, the counter's back edge must be scribed to get a tight seam at the wall.

Scribing the counter   Place the counter on top of the cabinets, and with its back edge pushed against the wall, measure the overhang at the front (photo, facing page). If the overhang is even along the length of the counter, it is properly positioned for scribing. If the overhang is uneven, shift the counter so that it overhangs the cases by the same amount all along the front.

My finished counters typically overhang the cabinets by ¾ in., which looks good with a ¾-in. wide bullnose edging. If you want the same overhang, subtract ¾ in. from the actual overhang and scribe the back edge of the counter at that distance from the wall. For example, if the existing overhang is 1¼ in. and you want a ¾-in. overhang, scribe the back edge of the counter ½ in. away from the wall. To do this, run your pencil the length of the countertop, using a ½-in. thick block of wood as a guide against the wall (photo, above).

Cut along this scribed line with a jigsaw and push the counter back into position. If it doesn't fit right, take it off and sand or file away any high spots. When the counter fits tightly against the wall and the overhang is a consistent ¾ in., the counter is ready to be installed. Run a heavy bead of caulk along the wall and press the back edge of the counter into it to keep water from running underneath. Then fasten the countertop in place by screwing up through the tops of the cabinets. I use four 1⅝-in. long drywall "grippit" screws in the top of each case. (Use six screws in cases over 30 in. wide.) These are screwed into the front and back reinforcement strips on the underside of the countertop.

If the countertop is marble or granite, you'll want to caulk rather than scribe it to the wall, and you won't have to screw it to the cabinets—its weight alone will hold it in place. To install a hardwood countertop, make sure to allow for some expansion and contraction across the width of the laminated top. This is easily accomplished by slotting the front screw holes in the tops of the cases.

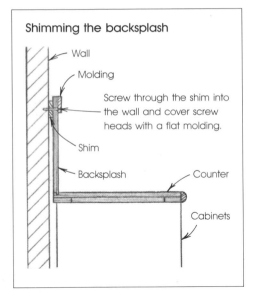

Shimming the backsplash

Wall

Molding

Screw through the shim into the wall and cover screw heads with a flat molding.

Shim

Backsplash

Counter

Cabinets

Installing the backsplash If you install a backsplash, there's no need to scribe the back of the counter to fit the wall—it won't be visible anyway. Most walls aren't flat, but a small bow won't be a serious obstacle to installing the backsplash. If the wall is not straight, simply cut a straight groove in the back edge of the counter (or prebore the dowel holes) so that the backsplash will clear the part of the wall that sticks out the most.

Attach the top of the backsplash to the wall with screws driven directly through the face of the backsplash into the wall studs. If the splash has been held away from the wall because of an irregular surface, you'll have to shim behind the top of the backsplash, as shown in the drawing at left, so that it will be plumb. Screw right through the shims along the top. Countersink the screw holes and cover them with putty or with a small, flat molding placed along the upper edge. Attach the molding with brads, set the heads and putty them. The exposed ends of the backsplash should be laminated.

If there are enough electrical outlet boxes near the bottom of the backsplash, say one every 36 in., simply drive a screw next to each outlet box directly through the face of the backsplash and into the wall stud to which the box is attached. Mark where the outlet cover plates will go and be sure to drive your screws so that they'll be hidden when the plates are installed. Secure the top of the backsplash as usual. After the top and bottom of the backsplash have been secured, caulk the bottom and any other joints with silicone.

Installing upper cases

Even though I like to make my cabinets as large as possible, I don't run my upper cases right to the ceiling because the ceiling, like the floor, is usually uneven—sometimes it's even worse than the floor. (The tops of the upper cases, by the way, should be solid plywood, not frames, since a frame would be visible from inside an upper case.) I leave a 3-in. space between the top of the upper cases and the ceiling, to match the kick space below the base cases.

I like to fasten straight runs of upper cases together before mounting them on the wall. A whole run of cases is heavy to lift, but it's so much easier to fasten them together on the floor that it's worth the effort. If the run is very long or if it turns a corner, break it up into two or more shorter runs.

As a rule, I prefer to install doors in the shop, where I can do the job quickly. It's also one less thing I have to do during installation. But I generally remove upper-case doors for installation. The upper cases are lighter and easier to handle without their doors and shelves. And the doors are easier to adjust than those in the base cases because they do not have to line up with a drawer or counter-top. If they are a trifle high or low it won't be noticed, as long as they're level.

Using handscrews, clamp the cases together so they are even along the top and flush along the front. Then screw the sides together as you did for the base cases.

With or without a backsplash The upper cases can be mounted directly on top of a full-height backsplash (top photo, facing page), or to a separate rail screwed to the wall above the backsplash (middle and bottom right photos, facing page). The rail will enable you to remove the counter and backsplash without touching the upper cabinets, and the counter usually needs replacement long before the cabinets. Make the rail about 1½ in. wide and ¹³⁄₁₆ in. thick so that it will be flush with the backsplash, which is usually ¾-in. plywood faced with ¹⁄₁₆-in. thick plastic laminate. If the undersides of the cases have been recessed for lighting, you'll have to notch the interior case sides over the backsplash or rail (drawing, facing page). Don't notch the exposed sides at the end of the run.

Next, prebore a 1-in. by ¾-in. strip of hardwood with ⁹⁄₃₂-in. dia. holes spaced on 16-in. centers to line up with the wall studs. These holes will receive the

Upper cases can be mounted directly on top of a full-height backsplash (photo at left) or on a separate hardwood mounting rail (photos, below). If you fit the rails between the cabinet sides, as shown in the bottom photo, you won't have to notch the sides of the cases around the rails.

Mounting upper cases

Lag screw, ¼ in. by 3 in., holds case to wall.

3 in.

Ceiling molding

¾ in.

1 in.

Hardwood mounting strip

Wall

Case top

Case back

Door

Case back

Case bottom

Recess for lighting

Case sides notched over backsplash and/or rail

Hardwood rail, 13/16 in. by 1½ in.

Backsplash

Molding, ½ in. by 2½ in., nailed to rail

Case side

¼-in. hex-head lag screws that attach the cases to the wall. Mount the strip to the top of the run of cases, as shown in the drawing, using two or three 1⅝-in. long drywall screws in the top of each case.

Raise the cases into position and rest them on the backsplash or rail. This will take all the weight, but you'll have to hold them against the wall to keep them from falling forward. Then insert a 3-in. lag screw with a washer into each of the holes you drilled in the top mounting strip and fasten the cases to the wall, with a lag screw in each stud. Once the first lag screw is in place the cases should not need any external support. Finally, secure the bottom of each case to the backsplash or wall rail with a single 1¼-in. screw and nail a molding under the cases to cover the mounting rail.

Never attach the upper cases to a ceiling soffit. Soffits are usually decorative and cannot be relied upon to support the weight of the cases.

If the upper wall is nearly plumb, no allowance need be made for straight runs of upper cases. If the wall is seriously out of plumb, however, shimming will be needed to correct it. Case runs that meet at a corner must be perfectly plumb, or nearly so, or the L-spacers won't mount and the doors on the corner cases will look askew and may even bump into the adjacent cases. Shim behind the upper mounting strip or the bottom of the cases, as necessary, and then tighten down the fasteners to secure the cases to the wall.

If you have to pull the bottoms of the cases away from the wall to get them plumb, make sure that you maintain a bearing surface of at least ⅜ in. on top of the backsplash or rail. Use a 1-in. thick mounting rail, if necessary, to get a beefier bearing surface. If this is still not sufficient, you'd better repair the wall before proceeding. (Your initial survey of the room should have revealed any discrepancies greater than ⅜ in. over the 39-in. rise of the upper cases.)

If you are not using a full-height backsplash, the hardwood mounting rail described above must be fastened to the wall to take its place. The mounting rail can be one long, continuous strip running beneath the entire run of upper cases, or you can fit a separate rail under each case. The latter method takes much more time to install, but you won't have to notch the case sides if the rail is not continuous. Either way, screw the mounting rail (or rails) into the studs with 2½-in. long No. 8 drywall screws. If the mounting rail is less than 2½ in. wide (the depth of the lighting recess), it will be visible only when the cabinet doors are open.

Corners between runs of upper cases are treated the same as they are on lower cases. Make and install L-spacers to cover the space between adjacent runs, and fit spacers wherever the end of the run meets a wall, as shown in the drawing on the facing page. If the case has been shimmed away from the wall, you'll have to conceal this gap wherever it is exposed at the end of the run with caulking or an applied molding.

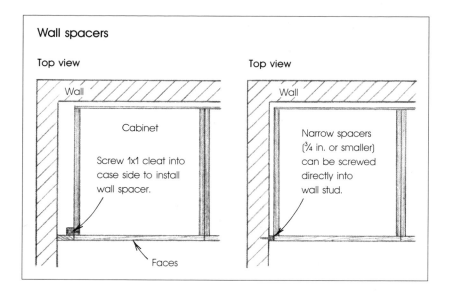

Wall spacers

Top view

Wall

Cabinet

Screw 1x1 cleat into case side to install wall spacer.

Faces

Top view

Wall

Narrow spacers (³⁄₄ in. or smaller) can be screwed directly into wall stud.

Trimming out the upper cases I usually install a ceiling molding above the upper cases of the same material and in the same style as the base molding installed in the kick space. I usually make the upper molding 2⅞ in. wide, or about ⅛ in. shy of the allotted space, and finish it before I install it. If the ceiling is uneven, you may have to scribe the molding to fit. Then screw through the tops of the cabinets from the inside to secure it. Align the face of the molding with the front edge of the case, without the door, so that there's no place for dirt to collect.

To install the ceiling moldings, prebore the tops of the upper cases with a ⅛-in. dia. hole and drive 1¼-in. No. 6 drywall screws into the molding. At first you will find that the screw will engage the case and push the molding away. When the molding is tight against the ceiling, the screw will start to penetrate the hardwood. Stop screwing as soon as the screw head is seated. Any further screwing will pull the molding down tight to the top of the case and expose a small gap at the ceiling. The small gap at the top of the case is not usually visible; it's the tight fit at the ceiling, which is visible, that you are trying to achieve.

Well-designed and neatly installed ceiling moldings add to the finished appearance of the case work. Many commercial kitchen manufacturers leave them out because it is difficult to fit them tightly to the ceiling. Promise you won't tell them my method.

Resource guide

Abrasives

United Abrasives, Inc.
P.O. Box 75
Willimantic, CT 06226
(203) 456-7131
Cloth-backed sheet abrasives that cost
more than paper, but last much longer.

Adhesives

Bostik Div. of Emhart
Boston St.
Middleton, MA 01949
(800) 343-8178
Their hot-glue gun is great for making a
quick fix or building a model.

Formica Corp.
155 Route 46 W.
CN 90
Wayne, NJ 07474
(800) 524-0159
(800) 624-1914 in New Jersey
Contact cement for applying
plastic laminate.

Franklin International
2020 Bruck St.
Columbus, OH 43207
(800) 826-2050
Good yellow glues for woodworking.

Ralph Wilson Plastics Company
600 General Bruce Drive
Temple, TX 76503
(800) 433-3222
(800) 792-6000 in Texas
Contact cement for applying
plastic laminate.

Countertop materials

Avonite, Inc.
12836 Arroyo St.
Sylmar, CA 91342
(800) 428-6648
Synthetics that look like marble
and granite.

Du Pont Co.
Corian Products
1007 Market St.
Wilmington, DE 19898
(800) 527-2601
Corian is a marble-like synthetic
sheet material.

Nevamar Corp.
8339 Telegraph Rd.
Odenton, MD 21113
(301) 569-5000
An impressive new abrasion-resistant
surface called ARP.

Fasteners

Duo-Fast Corp.
3702 River Rd.
Franklin Park, IL 60131-2176
(312) 678-0100
Pneumatic fasteners.

Equality Screw Co.
1850 John Towers Ave.
P.O. Box 1645
El Cajon, CA 92022
(800) 854-2886
Wide assortment of screws, including "hi-
lo" screws, "grippit" screws.

Paslode Corp.
Two Marriott Drive
Lincolnshire, IL 60015
(800) 852-5633 in Eastern states
(800) 323-1303 in Central states
(800) 852-8820 in Western states
Pneumatic fasteners.

Senco Products, Inc.
8485 Broadwell Rd.
Cincinnati, OH 45244
(800) 543-4596
Pneumatic fasteners.

Stanley-Bostitch
Route 2
East Greenwich, RI 02818
(800) 556-6696
These are the air fasteners I use.

Finishing supplies

Apollo Sprayers International, Inc.
11577 Slater Ave., Unit H
Fountain Valley, CA 92708
(714) 546-3100
Low-pressure spray equipment.

Binks Mfg. Co.
9201 W. Belmont Ave.
Franklin Park, IL 60131
(312) 671-3000
Compressors, spray guns.

Croix Air Products
520 Airport Road
Fleming Field
South St. Paul, MN 55075
(800) 328-4827
Low-pressure spray equipment.

Deft, Inc.
17451 Von Karman Ave.
Irvine, CA 92714
(800) 544-3338
Lacquer.

The DeVilbiss Co.
300 Phillips Ave.
Toledo, OH 43692
(800) 338-4448
Compressors, spray guns.

Garrett Wade Co.
161 Ave. of the Americas
New York, NY 10013
(800) 221-2942
Oils.

Graco, Inc.
P.O. Box 1441
Minneapolis, MN 55440
(612) 623-6000
Spray guns.

Grand Rapids Wood Finishing Co.
61 Grandville Ave. S. W.
Grand Rapids, MI 49503
(616) 459-4191
Lacquers, thinners, urethanes and stains.

Kampel Enterprises, Inc.
8930 Carlysle Rd.
Wellsville, PA 17365
(717) 432-9688
Kampel SeamFil for filling seams and repairing defects in plastic laminate.

The McCloskey Corp.
7600 State Road
Philadelphia, PA 19136
(800) 345-4530
Varnish.

Mohawk Finishing Products
Route 30 North
Amsterdam, NY 12010
(518) 843-1380
Lacquers and thinners, Behlen's Danish oil.

Performance Coatings, Inc.
360 Lake Mendocino Dr.
Ukiah, CA 95482
(800) 468-8820
(800) 468-8817 in California
Penofin Natural oil.

Randolph Products Co.
Park Place East
Carlstadt, NJ 07072
(201) 438-3700
Lacquers and thinners.

Seagrave Coatings Corporation
P.O. Box 187
Carlstadt, NJ 07072
(800) 426-0496
Water-white lacquer.

United Gilsonite Laboratories
1396 Jefferson St.
Scranton, PA 18501
(800) 845-5227
ZAR wood putty.

Watco-Dennis Corp.
19610 Rancho Way
Rancho Dominguez, CA 90220
(213) 635-2778
I use their natural Danish oil.

Wood Finishing Supply Co.
1267 Mary Drive
Macedon, NY 14502
(315) 986-4517
Oils.

Hardware

Accuride
12311 S. Shoemaker Ave.
Santa Fe Springs, CA 90670
(213) 944-0921
Superb, full-extension and ¾-extension slides. Slides for just about everything.

Amerock Corp.
4000 Auburn St.
Rockford, IL 61125
(815) 963-9631
Some useful interior cabinet hardware: lazy Susans and pull-out wire fixtures.

Julius Blum, Inc.
Highway 16-Lowesville
Stanley, NC 28164
(800) 222-7551 in North Carolina
(800) 438-6788 outside North Carolina
A full line of European hardware and machinery for the 32mm system: slides, hinges, shelf supports, installation jigs, adjustable legs, etc.

Fixture Hardware Mfg. Corp.
4116 First Ave.
Brooklyn, NY 11232
(718) 499-9422
Great heavy-duty shelf standards.

Grant Hardware Co.
High St.
West Nyack, NY 10994
(914) 358-4400
Some very good slides.

Grass America, Inc.
1202 Hwy. 66 S.
P.O. Box 1019
Kernersville, NC 27284
(919) 996-4041
The best of the European manufacturers. A full line of hardware and machinery for the 32mm system: installation jigs, slides, shelf supports, hinges, adjustable legs, etc.

Häfele America Co.
203 Feld Ave.
P.O. Box 1590
High Point, NC 27261
(800) 334-1873
A supermarket of hardware: slides, hinges, pulls, etc.

Hettich America Corp.
12428 Sam Neely Rd.
P.O. Box 7664
Charlotte, NC 28217
(800) 342-15322 in North Carolina
(800) 438-5939 outside North Carolina
A full line of European hardware and machinery for the 32mm system.

Hewi, Inc.
7 Pearl Court
Allendale, NJ 07401
(201) 327-7202
Door and drawer pulls.

Mepla, Inc.
909 W. Market Center Drive
High Point, NC 27261
(800) 334-1041
Another good source for European hardware and machinery for the 32mm system: slides, hinges, shelf supports, installation jigs, adjustable legs, etc.

Outwater Plastic Industries, Inc.
4 Passaic St.
Wood Ridge, NJ 07075
(800) 526-0462
Many lines of cabinet hardware: wire pull-outs, lazy Susans, etc.

Dave Sanders Co., Inc.
107-111 Bowery
New York, NY 10002
(212) 334-9898
Mail-order slides and hinges of major European manufacturers. A very complete selection. Also, "grippit" screws.

The Woodworkers Store
21801 Industrial Blvd.
Rogers, MN 55374
(612) 428-2199
Mail-order source of Accuride slides, pilasters, threaded inserts, pulls, etc.

Plastic laminates

Formica Corp.
155 Route 46
Wayne, NJ 07470
(800) 524-0159
(800) 624-1914 in New Jersey
A complete line of plastic laminates.

Ralph Wilson Plastics Company
Wilsonart
600 General Bruce Drive
Temple, TX 76503
(800) 433-3222
(800) 792-6000 in Texas
The best in plastic laminate. Wilsonart pays particular attention to your needs, especially the gripes.

Plywood and veneers

Maurice L. Condon Company, Inc.
250 Ferris Ave.
White Plains, NY 10603
(914) 946-4111

Connecticut Plywood
P.O. Box 10236
9 Andover Drive
West Hartford, CT 06110
(203) 560-0060

The Woodshed
1807 Elmwood Ave.
Buffalo, NY 14207
(716) 876-4719

Tools

AEG Power Tool Corp.
3 Shaw's Cove
New London, CT 06230
(800) 243-0870
Hand-held, portable power tools: drills,
screw guns, etc.

Delta International Machinery Corp.
246 Alpha Drive
Pittsburgh, PA 15238
(412) 963-2400
I own a Delta table saw, shaper and
jointer. What more can I say?

Leigh Industries
P.O. Box 357-A
Port Coquitlam, B.C.
Canada V3C 4K6
(800) 663-8932
Dovetailing jigs.

Milwaukee Electric Tool Corp.
13135 W. Lisbon Rd.
Brookfield, WI 53005
(414) 781-3600
Heavy-duty tools for the professional.

Olsen Saw Co.
Div. of Blackstone Industries
Stony Hill
Bethel, CT 06801
(203) 792-8622
Makers of Olsen sawblades for the
bandsaw, jigsaw and table saw.

Pootatuck Corp.
P.O. Box 24
Windsor, VT 05089
(802) 674-5984
Lion miter trimmer.

Porter-Cable Corp.
P.O. Box 2468
Jackson, TN 38302
(901) 668-8600
Excellent routers, dovetailing jigs, and the
best orbital sander I know of.

Sears, Roebuck and Co.
Sears Tower
Chicago, IL 60684
(312) 875-2500
Dovetailing jigs.

Stanley Hardware
Div. of The Stanley Works
195 Lake St.
New Britain, CT 06050
(203) 225-5111
I can't say what it is about Stanley
that brings me back, but I buy a lot
of their products. I love the black-
handled chisels.

Wetzler Clamp Co., Inc.
P.O. Box 175
43-15 Route 611
Mt. Bethel, PA 18343
(800) 451-1852
Very good quick-action clamps.

Information

American Forest Council
1250 Connecticut Ave., N.W.
Suite 320
Washington, D. C. 20036
(800) 424-2485

American Plywood Association
7011 S. 19th St.
Tacoma, WA 98466
(206) 565-6600

Decorative Laminate Product Assn.
600 S. Federal
Suite 400
Chicago, IL 60605
(312) 922-6222

Forest Products Research Society
2801 Marshall Court
Madison, WI 53705
(608) 231-1361

Hardwood Plywood Manufacturers Assn.
P.O. Box 2789
Reston, VA 22090
(703) 435-2900

National Kitchen and Bath Association
124 Main St.
Hackettstown, NJ 07840
(201) 852-0033
They offer courses about kitchen and
bath design and standards.

National Kitchen Cabinet Association
P.O. Box 6830
Falls Church, VA 22046
(703) 237-7580

Further reading

Cary, Jane Randolph. *How to Create Interiors for the Disabled.* New York: Pantheon Books, 1978.

Clark, Sam. *The Motion-Minded Kitchen.* Boston: Houghton Mifflin Co., 1983.

Conran, Terence. *The Kitchen Book.* New York: Crown Publishers, 1984.

Day, Richard. *The Home Owner Handbook of Plumbing and Heating.* New York: Bounty Books, 1974.

Dovetail a Drawer with Frank Klausz. Video, 60 min. Newtown, Conn.: The Taunton Press, 1985.

Feirer, John L. *Cabinetmaking and Millwork.* 2nd rev. ed. New York: Charles Scribner's Sons, 1983.

Frid, Tage. *Tage Frid Teaches Woodworking: Joinery: Tools and Techniques.* Newtown, Conn.: The Taunton Press, 1979.

Hylton, William H. *Build Your Harvest Kitchen.* Emmaus, Pa.: Rodale Press, 1980.

Johnson, Robert C. *Electrical Wiring.* Englewood Cliffs, N. J.: Prentice-Hall, 1971.

Joyce, Ernest. *The Encyclopedia of Furniture Making.* New York: Sterling, 1979.

Kitchens. Alexandria, Va.: Time-Life Books, 1985.

Lifchez, Raymond, and Barbara Winslow. *Design for Independent Living: The Environment & Physically Disabled People.* Berkeley: University of California Press, 1981.

Link, John D. *Handbook of Simplified Electrical Wiring Design.* Englewood Cliffs, N. J.: Prentice Hall, 1975.

Mueller, Edward J. *Architectural Drawing and Light Construction.* 2nd ed. Englewood Cliffs, N. J.: Prentice-Hall, 1976.

Paradies, Klaus. *The Kitchen Book.* New York: Peter H. Wyden, 1973.

Planning & Remodeling Kitchens. Menlo Park, Calif.: Lane Publishing Co., 1976.

Raschko, Bettyann B. *Housing Interiors for the Disabled & Elderly.* New York: Van Nostrand Reinhold Co., 1982.

Index

Managing editor   Deborah Cannarella
Editors   Paul Bertorelli, Mark Feirer, Scott Landis
Design director   Roger Barnes
Designer/art director   Ben Kann
Illustrator   Lee Hov
Copy/production editor   Ruth Dobsevage
Art assistants   Marty Higham, Cindy Nyitray
Production manager   Peggy Dutton
Production coordinator   Robert Marsala
Composition systems manager Dinah George
Systems operator   Nancy-Lou Knapp
Technician   Margot Knorr
Production assistants   Lisa Carlson, Mark Coleman, Priscilla Rollins, Tom Sparano
Editorial assistant   Maria Angione
Indexer   Harriet Hodges

Typeface   ITC Korinna
Paper   Warrenflo, 70 lb., neutral pH
Printer and binder   Arcata Graphics/Kingsport, Kingsport, Tenn.

Watch Paul Levine on video

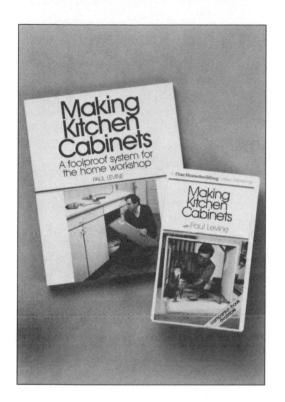

Now you can watch Paul Levine demonstrate firsthand the cabinetmaking procedures that he details in this book. Created by the award-winning Taunton Press video-production team, the tape shows you just how simple it is to build a cabinet in a small basement workshop. You'll be encouraged to go ahead and start your own cabinet project.

The video format brings you up close to see just how Levine makes durable, easy-to-clean doors, drawers and shelves. You'll also see how to install trouble-free slides and hinges that allow drawers to be easily mounted and adjusted. And you'll find page references right on the screen—so you can refer quickly back to the book whenever you want.

Together, the book and video offer a wonderfully complete way to learn Levine's foolproof cabinetmaking system.

Rent Paul Levine's video for only $9.95

Rent Paul Levine's video for 10 days for just $9.95, plus $2.50 postage and handling (CT residents add 8% sales tax). If you decide to keep the tape, just hold onto it and we'll charge your credit card the balance due of $20.00. Just fill out the coupon below and give your credit-card information (credit-card orders only, please).